Gill Edwar author. She runs workshops on conscious medicine. H *Life is a Gift, Wild Love, Stepping into Magic, Pure Bliss* and the bestseller *Living Magically*.

Visit www.livingmagically.co.uk for more information.

s Medicine

'*Conscious Medicine* shows us how medicine *could be* if we applied all that is known now about the body, its energies, and the intelligent force fields that surround us and surge through us. The book is expansive like the consciousness it describes, taking us on a survey of some of the most exciting ideas and healing methods of the past decade . . . I recommend it highly'
Donna Eden, energy healer and author of *Energy Medicine* and *Energy Medicine for Women*

'This is the New Medicine. This is where we are going. This is it – expressed with gentleness and wisdom'
Dr John McGregor, consultant radiologist and shaman

'I join Gill Edwards in heralding conscious medicine as the essential sustainable healthcare reform for our time. Because she speaks from the heart of her own experience she conveys skillfully and precisely each step in this humane revolution. You can feel your cells reorganise as you read her trustworthy words of guidance and inspiration'
Stephanie Mines, Ph.D., neuropsychologist and author of *We Are All In Shock*

'This landmark book deserves to be read by all doctors, therapists, healers and patients alike. We are all in the business of healing – ourselves as well as others! At medical school we learnt a lot about disease of the body, but very little about the science of healing and the healthy mind. *Conscious Medicine* fills the gap . . . A "must-read" for everyone who wants to be truly healthy'
Dr Andrew Tresidder, family doctor and author of *I'm Fine!*

'*Conscious Medicine* highlights and expands a much-needed paradigm shift in healthcare. It blends the latest understanding from quantum physics and the new biology with Gill's vast knowledge of today's complementary therapies, maintaining fluidity and accessibility throughout, which is typical of her wonderful writing style . . . This book will teach you how to take your health and well-being back into your own hands instead of relying on the pharmaceutical industry. Buy

this book to enhance your health, wealth and happiness on so many levels'
Karl Dawson, EFT Master, co-author of *Matrix Reimprinting Using EFT*

'This wonderful book provides a vital roadmap for anyone who has any confusion about how to activate the mind–body connection for healing. You'll be fascinated by the most convincing scientific and medical facts that will dispel any doubts, while clear easy-to-follow examples and exercises pave the way for clear understanding. Just reading this book will uplift you, help you release stress and heal'
Arielle Essex, NLP Master Practitioner and author of *Compassionate Coaching*

'Gill Edwards makes a compelling case for the governing role of consciousness in our physical/mental well-being. This beautifully written book is on my list of highly recommended reading for anyone interested in taking responsibility for their own health and vitality, and anyone who wishes to help others to do the same'
John Bullough, Ph.D., psychotherapist and co-editor of *EFT & Beyond*

'*Conscious Medicine* brings together all the advancements in the new sciences and quantum physics, and couples it with a vast range of cutting-edge information on tools and techniques that transform the bodymind. The book not only explains why spiritual and emotional healing is essential for physical health, it also takes you on a journey of self-exploration that is really accessible. The fact that the book has been inspired by Gill's own healing journey ensures there is heart-felt depth to its contents. She has taken the mystique out of healing, and shows how to access "miracles" in your everyday life. In short, Gill has made an outstanding contribution to new paradigm medicine'
Sasha Allenby, energy therapist and co-author of *Matrix Reimprinting Using EFT*

'*Conscious Medicine* needs to be read, understood and especially *felt* by anybody working in any healthcare position, be it conventional or complementary. My suggestion: read the text and feel the dawning shift in medical approach of which this book is such a clear messenger'
Tjitze de Jong, energy healer and Bodies of Light teacher

'Full of wisdom, insight and practical suggestions, this book is essential reading for everyone interested in health and healing. Buy it for all your friends'
Penelope Quest, Reiki Master and author of *The Reiki Manual* **and the bestselling** *Reiki for Life*

Conscious *Medicine*

CREATING HEALTH AND WELL-BEING IN A CONSCIOUS UNIVERSE

GILL EDWARDS

PIATKUS

First published in Great Britain in 2010 by Piatkus

A CIP catalogue record for this book
is available from the British Library.

ISBN 978-0-7499-4198-7

Text design by Sam Charrington
Typeset in Sabon by Palimpsest Book Production Ltd,
Falkirk, Stirlingshire
Printed and bound in Great Britain by
CPI Mackays, Chatham ME5 8TD

Papers used by Piatkus are natural, renewable and recyclable
products sourced from well-managed forests and certified
in accordance with the rules of the Forest Stewardship Council.

Piatkus
An imprint of
Little, Brown Book Group
100 Victoria Embankment
London EC4Y 0DY

An Hachette UK Company
www.hachette.co.uk

www.piatkus.co.uk

For everyone in the Conscious Medicine Circle
– with love and gratitude

Caution

This book is not intended to be a substitute for healthcare by a qualified health professional. The author and publisher can take no responsibility for the health and well-being of those who read this book, nor for the choices they make with regard to healthcare. If you have any emotional or physical condition, you are advised to seek care and support from a health professional.

Contents

Acknowledgements   ix

Foreword   xiii

Chapter 1   Six Impossible Things Before Breakfast   1

Chapter 2   The Conscious Universe   19

Chapter 3   Bridge to a New Reality   44

Chapter 4   Frozen in the Past   72

Chapter 5   Moving into the Wave Response   104

Chapter 6   Everything is a Friend   125

Chapter 7   Stairway to Happiness   153

Chapter 8   Body Language   182

Chapter 9   Our Conscious Biofield   201

Chapter 10   Finding a Giant Pendulum   230

Chapter 11   Journey to Ithaca   248

Chapter 12   From Cocoon to Butterfly   273

References   289

Recommended Reading   303

Resources for Health and Well-being   325

Index   333

Acknowledgements

Firstly, my grateful acknowledgements to everyone in the Conscious Medicine Circle – Venetia Young, Paul Davies, Angie Jackson, John McGregor, Sue Birkett, Andrea Baqai, Mary Parr, Sarah Crocombe, Peter Thompson and Anne Bennett; and also, now back home in Chile, Gabriela Maass. Our conversations and friendships have enriched my life enormously, and helped me shape and mould the clay that has turned into this book. You are an extraordinary bunch of visionary healer-practitioners, not to mention lovely people. I am so grateful that you are in my life, and that we all came together as a Circle.

My love and thanks to my parents for proofreading the original manuscript with their usual meticulous care, and for their helpful comments – and for being there with love, as always. Much love and a big hug to my son Kieran, for putting up with a mother who has been passionately focused on writing this book; we danced together in delight when it was finished at last! Infinite thanks to my 'team' from the unseen realms who served as collective midwives for this book, and for whispering in my ears day and night – even though I sometimes asked them to buzz off and give me a break!

My love and gratitude to close friends who have supported and sustained me, especially those friends who are doctors, healers and therapists, with whom I've had so many stimulating conversations about health and medicine, and who have reassured me that my 'crazy' ideas do make intuitive and scientific sense. Huge thanks to my office goddess and dear friend, Susie Thomas – an angel of light – for dealing with the Living Magically office with her amazing grace and efficiency so that I could get on with writing. Thanks to my lovely friend Sue Robinson for proofreading the manuscript while cat-and-chicken-sitting for me. Thank you to Andrew Tresidder for the orchid that oversaw my final revisions, and for our conversations about medicine and spirituality. And special love to my dear friend and soul sister Trina Laydon-Walters – for all our long conversations, and for always being there for me.

Thanks to the gifted practitioners who helped me in my journey through cancer – in particular, energy healer Tjitze de Jong, homoeopaths Angie Jackson and David Evans, Darren Weissman of the Lifeline Technique, EFT therapist Kay Gire, EFT/Matrix Reimprinting practitioner Ted Wilmont, and Sara Rowan from Nutri-Energetics. Thanks also to the innovators of energy tools I used during my healing journey: to Gary Craig for EFT, Tapas Fleming for TAT, Rob Williams for Psych-K, Stephanie Mines for the TARA Approach, Donna Eden for energy medicine tools, Barbara Brennan for her energy healing science, Richard Bartlett for Matrix Energetics, Peter Fraser and Harry Massey for the Nutri-Energetics (NES) System, Karl Dawson and Sasha Allenby for Matrix Reimprinting and also to the pioneering Institute of HeartMath.

I would also like to thank the countless authors, doctors and other health practitioners who have influenced and inspired me in the thirty years or so that led up to writing this book. They are too numerous to mention, though the reading list at the end of this book includes many of those whose work I admire and value. Many are also mentioned in the text. My special thanks to Bruce Lipton, for his ground-breaking work in the new biology, for his passion and inspiration, and for his generosity in having conversations with me about the emerging new medicine; also to Stephanie Mines for helpfully clarifying some of my questions. Thank you to Byron Katie and Stephen Mitchell for permission to use Katie's exercise on relationship turnarounds. Thanks to

Abraham (and Esther and Jerry Hicks) for all the wisdom and inspiration and for permission to print my own version of the Emotional Scale. And my thanks to those who have written about their own and others' healing journeys, for spreading the positive message that any disease can be healed.

Thank you to all of my fabulous and fascinating clients and workshop attendees, who have taught me so much about emotional and physical dis-ease – some of whose stories are in this book. (Names and some personal details have been changed to protect their privacy, unless they requested other-wise.) I have known some of you for many years, and I follow your unfolding journeys with interest and love. Thank you so much for sharing with me.

Finally, my thanks to Gill Bailey, Claudia Dyer and everyone at Piatkus Books – and to my favourite external editor, Liz Dean, who helped to refine the book in its final stages. You have been fabulous colleagues, and endlessly helpful, patient and supportive, as always. I am hugely grateful to have had you as my publishers for nearly twenty years.

Foreword

The medical establishment will eventually be dragged, kicking and screaming, into the quantum revolution.

Bruce Lipton[1]

Three years ago, I woke one morning to discover a hard, pea-sized lump in my breast. A chill ran down my spine and I took a deep and shuddering breath, as I sensed that a new journey was beginning. For several days, I did not mention the lump to anyone while I slowly came to terms with what might lie ahead. I had been through a prolonged period of emotional stress and turmoil, which left me with an un-resolved conflict which troubled me deeply on a daily basis. My knowledge of mind–body medicine told me that it was a perfect set-up for breast cancer. Although I tried to remain positive, I knew in my heart that the lump was likely to be malignant.

Two weeks later, the diagnosis of cancer did not come as a surprise. What might seem more surprising to others is that I actually found myself dancing around my kitchen that night. I could see that the tumour would give me 'permission' to resolve the stressful situation that had triggered it – a situation that had driven me half-crazy. And since I was planning to write a book about the emerging new medicine – a book I had wanted to write for thirty years – I knew that a journey through cancer would provide an ideal first-person experience of healing from serious disease. Soon afterwards, when I 'spoke' to the tumour for the first time, it said, 'I came in answer to your prayers.' A new journey had indeed begun.

Now before you begin to think that it sounds downright crazy that anyone might *welcome* a cancer diagnosis – or that I felt little or no fear in response to it – I need to explain a bit more about my background. Once you know where I was coming from, and see how the model of conscious medicine was beginning to unfold through my life's work, you will perhaps understand why I saw cancer as the beginning of an adventure – an adventure which I trusted would lead me towards greater health, happiness and well-being. Once you understand conscious medicine, you will know what it takes to heal from illness and disease; that there is nothing to fear – and that your body is always your friend. Whatever your current state of health, this book is for you, and will help you on your healing journey.

THE JOURNEY BEGINS

Let me go back to twenty-five years before this cancer diagnosis, at a time when I was a young psychology graduate. I had applied to do a Ph.D. in mind-body medicine – but before I could begin, I was invited to apply for a postgraduate training course in clinical psychology. It seemed like a good career move, so I trained and worked for ten years as a clinical psychologist in the National Health Service.

As a psychologist, I saw no essential difference between mental and physical disorders, and recognised that the body mirrored what was happening in our emotional lives. I routinely asked my clients about physical symptoms, knowing this could give me useful information that they might not be consciously aware of. The body seemed to reflect our subconscious beliefs and inner conflicts. One of my special interests was the psychology of cancer. I offered psychotherapy to women with breast cancer, worked with holistic cancer groups and – early in my career – published a pioneering article about the 'cancer personality' (while recognising that I shared many of those characteristics).[2]

When I had pneumonia at the age of twenty-six, I suffered

a bad reaction to antibiotics, which left me seriously ill for many weeks and with multiple allergies. Eventually I saw a homoeopath, who saw that I had never fully recovered from glandular fever in my late teens. After taking a single dose of a homoeopathic remedy, I felt my despair lifting and my life force returning. It felt like a miracle; I was able to return to work within a few days – and the frequent bouts of glandular flu-like symptoms never returned. I have used homoeopathy for health issues ever since.

I had been interested in energy medicine for several years by then, but this was my first experience of dramatic healing – using a method that most doctors and scientists would have dismissed as nonsensical, since not a single molecule of the original substance remained in the homoeopathic remedy I had taken. It contained only an 'energetic signature'. Yet its impact was immediate and undeniable.

Fifteen years later, as the mother of a toddler, I wrenched my back on holiday while lifting my son awkwardly into the back seat of a two-door hatchback. I was in severe pain and unable to walk, and came home in a wheelchair. I immediately called a cranial osteopath who visited me at home. By gently touching my neck and spine with his fingers, he corrected my subtle energy system – the energy field which provides the blueprint for the physical body (see Chapter 9) – comparing it to reconnecting a telephone switchboard. I felt as if I was being knitted back together, and tingling energy flowed down my spine and into my legs. After forty-five minutes, I stood up and walked across the room without my crutches – and without pain. My back was healed.

This was another miracle for energy medicine – and left me in no doubt that the body is an energy system, far more than it is solid flesh and bones. I haven't used conventional medicine or taken any pharmaceutical drugs since that first dramatic healing with homoeopathy. The fact that medicine ignored the invisible realms of energy and consciousness was enough to convince me that it looked at the world while wearing blinkers.

I had been aware of the unseen realms from an early age,

as the house I grew up in was haunted – which made me highly sensitive to energy. I soon became fascinated with what lies beyond physical reality and as a teenager devoured countless books about mysticism and the paranormal. I explored quantum physics and the emerging new science (which connects the seen and unseen realms, and looks remarkably like mysticism). I began meditation and yoga in my teens, and was a Buddhist until my mid-twenties. I also studied Silva Mind Control, which accesses the alpha brain-wave state for intuition and distant healing.

Then I studied the fascinating teachings of Seth, an 'energy personality' channelled by Jane Roberts, who taught that we create our own reality – and that life is a chosen adventure in consciousness. This was a milestone along my spiritual path. I knew intuitively that we are eternal beings, and that we live many lifetimes, and was often puzzled that people rarely talked about the invisible world of spirit, and seemed to pretend it did not exist.

Many years later, at the age of thirty-three, I had a mystical experience that shifted my consciousness for ever.[3] I immediately resigned from the Health Service, since I wanted to fully embrace my spirituality – and a new vision and purpose was calling me. I could no longer fit myself into the tight-fitting shoe of a conventional clinical psychologist, and pretend that the visible world was all that is real. Nor could I see mind and body as separate. I needed to inhabit a more expansive world in which mind, body and spirit were seen as one – and I was fascinated by how we create our reality. I wrote my first book, *Living Magically*, and became a spiritual author and workshop facilitator. I had found my true vocation – and I loved it.

Fast-forward to my mid-forties. When my son was six years old, I fell in love with a dear friend who felt trapped in an unhappy marriage. We both felt a deep soul connection, and my own marriage unravelled as I recognised myself in his mirror. Like him, I longed for a true soulmate in my life, and realised that – under pressure from my biological clock – I had married a close friend whom I did not truly love. I had shrunk myself to fit the relationship (as had my husband), but the marriage was not working for either of us. I had spent too much of my life trying to be good and perfect, and holding back my truth, and I had to be true to myself.

Choosing to leave my marriage was tough, but it was an authentic decision that I never regretted – and my husband soon found his ideal partner, and happily remarried. However, the close and loving relationship with my married friend, though never sexual, became a painful journey of frustrated love and separation. (See my earlier book, *Wild Love,* to read more of this story.) We felt unable to speak to each other for nearly three years – which was tough in a small rural community, with many mutual friends – and I could not find a way to resolve the issue. This prolonged emotional turmoil, along with my passionate yearning for an intimate relationship, are what triggered the cancer.

THE HEALING JOURNEY

Once I was given the cancer diagnosis, I had to decide how to tackle it. Although I had several close friends who were doctors, I had little faith in conventional medicine and knew too much about its risks. I had not even taken a painkiller (or any other drug) for twenty-five years, and consulted a doctor only once during that period. When I gave birth to my son at home – a beautiful and soulful experience – my midwife had only homoeopathic remedies in her bag. It was hard to imagine having a surgical operation, or taking powerful and toxic drugs. Yet I knew that I must take the cancer seriously.

The warm-hearted oncologist who had given me the cancer diagnosis was supportive when I told her of my background in mind-body medicine. She agreed that I needed time to think, saying that it was my body and my decision. I quickly ruled out chemotherapy and radiation on the basis of what I knew, but I hadn't yet ruled out surgery.

Three months later, I saw a surgeon about the possibility of having the tumour removed. I told her that I had not yet made a decision about surgery, but she warned me of the dangers of leaving 'even one cancer cell' in my body, and how the cancer could then metastasise to essential organs and kill me. Since the average person has thousands of cancer cells in their body at any one time, which are destroyed by a healthy immune system, I knew this was simply untrue. She also told me that she would remove several lymph nodes to check for signs of cancer, and that I would then be given chemotherapy and radiation. She would not hear of doing a simple lumpectomy. ('That would be sub-optimal treatment.')

I was aware that some authors suspect that surgery might spread or trigger cancer in itself, quite apart from the stress and trauma it would cause my body at a time when my health was already compromised – and that the research support for chemotherapy was weak and equivocal.[4] Pouring toxins into an already sick body made little sense to me. After twenty minutes, I realised that the surgeon was doing her job in the best way she knew how – given her beliefs and training – but it just did not feel right for me. We lived in different worlds. I said that we were both wasting our time, thanked her for seeing me and walked out.

I skipped away from the hospital with a light heart, having decided not to pursue orthodox medical treatment. I was free to find my own path. I committed myself to a healing journey that would honour my body's needs, and which felt nurturing, stress-free and joyful. (My family doctor, who is also a personal friend, immediately found me another surgeon who *would* have offered a simple lumpectomy – and I kept this aside as a possibility, but did not pursue it.) I wanted to approach the cancer as a friend and teacher, not as an enemy. Yes, I could have done this while *also* having the tumour removed, but I knew that the tumour was an indicator of unresolved emotional issues – and if I simply had it removed, I would lose that helpful indicator.

I am not recommending my unconventional healing path to others. For many people – whatever their diagnosis – surgery and/or drugs would be an appropriate choice, and I have huge respect for the challenging work that doctors do. You can certainly combine conventional medicine with the insights and tools of conscious medicine – this is usually known as 'integrative medicine' – and many people do so. Using conscious medicine alone was simply the right path for *me*, with my background, my beliefs and professional background, and my knowledge of health and healing.

I believe that I was guided to take this approach so that I could be a wayshower for conscious medicine. I knew that I had created this tumour, and that I could un-create it. (And if we can un-create cancer, we can potentially un-create any disease.) I had been teaching and writing about the principles of reality creation for twenty years, and knew that we are responsible for everything that happens in our lives. I had been steeped in alternative approaches to health for thirty years, and had run workshops on health and healing for most of that time. I had worked one-to-one with thousands of clients to heal emotional and physical disease – and trained extensively in shamanic healing, energy psychology and energy medicine. I trusted that I would be guided towards whatever and whoever I needed, and I had no doubt that my body could heal itself of cancer, if only I could resolve the underlying emotional issues, and drop any resistance to healing – in effect, get out of my body's way.

I already had a vast library on alternative health, and now immersed myself in the latest research on health and the new biology, consulted many gifted practitioners, attended conferences and workshops, and trained in umpteen new approaches to healing – including Matrix Energetics, Advanced Psych-K, Reconnective Healing, the Sedona Method, Quantum Touch, Emo-Trance, Meta-Medicine, the Lifeline Technique and Matrix Reimprinting (see Resources for Health and Wellbeing, p. 325) – on top of twenty years' training in metaphysical approaches to health, shamanic healing, energy psychology and energy medicine, plus my background in clinical psychology and family therapy. In the process, I began to understand more and more deeply how we create disease, and its deeper meaning and purpose – and how to create health, happiness and vitality, whatever our starting point.

In *Conscious Medicine*, I will share what I learnt from this whole journey – and how you can apply it in your own life, whether to understand and heal symptoms and disease, to prevent future health problems, or to support others in healing. You will come to see why every symptom or illness needs to be embraced and welcomed – rather than feared or resisted – and why a sick body is always your friend.

If we listen to the whispers, the body does not have to shout at us. Even minor symptoms such as a headache, twisted ankle or itchy finger can be sources of awakening, leading us to heal and release the past, think in new and positive ways, reclaim lost parts of the self, find a new sense of purpose, or remember our dreams and visions. However, even if you have a nasty diagnosis, it is important to trust that everything is unfolding perfectly. It is my firm belief that nothing ever 'goes wrong' within the bigger picture – and that the more serious a diagnosis, the greater the potential it offers for growth and transformation. Through illness and disease, you are being invited to become a new and expanded self.

The cancer led me on a fascinating journey, and I always trusted that it had personal gifts for me. It was an emotional rollercoaster at times, and took two-and-a-half years to resolve the relationship that triggered it, and restore my health and well-being – but in the process, I found more inner peace, freedom, joy and illumination than I could ever have imagined. It has changed me profoundly. My journey also pushed me to clarify a model of health and disease that would integrate the new science with spirituality and energy medicine. Gradually I built a model of what I call 'conscious medicine'.

THE CONSCIOUS MEDICINE CIRCLE

Two years ago, along with one of my doctor friends, I set up a Conscious Medicine Circle – six visionary doctors and six alternative health practitioners who meet each month for several hours to share our ideas, our tools and resources, and our journeys through life. Our Circle broke down the us-and-them barriers that had existed between those inside and outside the National Health Service, or between medics and non-medics. The mutual respect and support in the group was palpable from the start.

Within the Circle, we began to build bridges between conventional medicine and conscious medicine, and slowly reached a consensus about core assumptions that lie at the basis of the emergent new medicine – such as seeing physical symptoms as reflecting emotional issues, and viewing energy-consciousness as the basis of reality. The Circle quickly became a precious support group for us all, and remains so today – and has been a crucible for our personal and professional development. As I write, other health practitioners are in the process of setting up Conscious Medicine Circles elsewhere.

HOW THIS BOOK WILL HELP YOU

In *Conscious Medicine*, I offer an integration of the new physics, new biology, alternative medicine and healing, Chinese medicine, positive psychology, shamanism, energy medicine, metaphysics, the law of attraction and energy psychology, showing how these all express aspects of what I call 'the wave response' and 'the particle response' – that is, the state of our consciousness. I show how our consciousness relates to our mental and physical health – and how you can use this knowledge to heal yourself, or to prevent illness and disease, and to remain healthy and happy.

Whether you have troubling symptoms or a serious diagnosis, or just want to stay healthy, this book will guide you towards finding your own path to health and well-being. If you are a health professional, healer or therapist, it might give you a new framework for what you already do – or illuminate a new way forward. If you are already familiar with quantum physics and the new biology, it might help you to understand how the new science relates to health and healing. And if you are on a spiritual path, and wonder how our health relates to our spirituality, this is the book for you.

For doctors or those steeped in conventional medicine, this book offers some radical ideas about health. Conventional doctors *can* incorporate conscious medicine into their practice, and some already do – but one of the doctors in our Conscious Medicine Circle found it increasingly hard to write a prescription once she began to see illness and disease through the 'new eyes' of conscious medicine. You have been warned! You *can* live with a foot in both worlds, but in my experience, the world of conscious medicine inexorably draws you in – until it feels more and more uncomfortable to step back into the 'old world' of conventional thinking. The new world is so much more fun. It feels like stepping into a parallel universe, a playground of exciting possibilities, and you might not want to come back again!

What Is Conscious Medicine?

Conscious medicine is an approach to healthcare that recognises the primacy of consciousness in health, and sees the bodymind as an integrated energy system that is inseparable from the universal energy field (or zero point energy field, or Divine Matrix, or Infinite Intelligence; our connection to a greater power).

In order to heal symptoms and disease, conscious medicine addresses energy-consciousness – releasing blockages or limitations, shifting negative beliefs, resolving inner conflicts, discharging past traumas, or helping energy flow more freely. The tool used might be acupuncture, homoeopathy, kinesiology, energy psychology, flower essences, shamanism, energy medicine or a host of other psycho-energetic approaches – some of which are introduced in this book – but the underlying assumptions are very similar.

Within conscious medicine, we are psycho-energetic beings in a conscious universe. Our energy flow mirrors our state of consciousness. When we are in harmony with our higher self, our energy flows freely – we are aligned with the universal energy field (or unconditional love) – and the natural outcome is happiness, health and vitality.

Here is a brief summary of the journey into *Conscious Medicine*:

Chapter 1: Six Impossible Things Before Breakfast looks at how the body is designed to heal itself – and suggests it is not our physical body that holds disease, but our *personality*: that is, our characteristic beliefs, attitudes and emotional states. Case studies show that healing can occur in miraculous ways, if we shift our consciousness or release blocked energy – which implies that health and vitality are our natural state of being.

Chapter 2: The Conscious Universe takes us beyond the old scientific model of a solid, material world, and into a magical new world of energy-consciousness: a conscious universe. Instead of seeing the body as solid and material – a physical bundle of flesh, blood and bones – we might see it as a condensed form of energy-consciousness. This is the world of cutting-edge science.

Chapter 3: Bridge to a New Reality outlines the crucial role of the particle (or stress) response in creating disease, and how our thoughts and beliefs become hard-wired into the body. Crucially, it explains why we are not victims of our genes and heredity – and how we can change our health by changing our thoughts and beliefs. Our body mirrors our consciousness.

Chapter 4: Frozen in the Past explains why undischarged trauma – leading to the 'freeze response' – gets stuck in our energy system, and makes us vulnerable to further trauma and disease. It shows how early childhood experiences set up beliefs that can cause chronic stress, leading to emotional and physical disease.

Chapter 5: Moving into the Wave Response explores the qualities of the wave response, which allows healing to occur naturally. It outlines the characteristics of living from the wave response – such as following your bliss, finding a purpose and connecting with nature – and how it is linked with unconditional love.

Chapter 6: Everything is a Friend looks at a major source of stress in our lives: our personal relationships. It shows how the particle response damages relationships, setting up toxic patterns of fear and resistance that threaten our mental and physical health. And it offers some powerful tools for shifting towards unconditional love.

Chapter 7: Stairway to Happiness shows why emotions are central to health and healing – and why you have to *feel* better before you can *get* better. It suggests that health is all vibrational, and that our emotions are an ever-present indicator of our vibrations. It also explains how health relates to the universal law of attraction.

Chapter 8: Body Language reveals how the body 'talks' to us through symptoms and disease – pointing towards the emotional blockages or conflicts that need to be tackled. It helps you understand the language of the body, and offers a 'dream dictionary' of the body's illnesses, suggesting the emotional root of physical problems.

Chapter 9: Our Conscious Biofield explores the energetic structure of the body, and how the body can express symptoms through the language of the meridians and chakras – and how you can balance the meridians and chakras yourself. It also looks at how to activate the 'strange flows', which are crucial to healing.

Chapter 10: Finding a Giant Pendulum looks at the role of health practitioners – and how they can help or hinder the healing process. It explores the risks of diagnosis, and the perhaps unhealthy beliefs of some health professionals. It offers some guidelines for choosing a health practitioner or healing approach.

Chapter 11: Journey to Ithaca notes that healing can be a slow process, and that a rapid healing journey is not necessarily better. It looks at some of the hidden factors that can prevent healing – such as secondary gain, victim mentality and subconscious death wishes.

Chapter 12: From Cocoon to Butterfly outlines a step-by-step approach towards healing any emotional or physical disease using conscious medicine. It suggests that any symptom, illness or disease is a gift – an invitation to expand your consciousness, and become your future self. It can help you evolve into a butterfly.

This book builds upon all of my previous books – in particular, *Pure Bliss*, *Wild Love* and *Life is a Gift* – and has been at least thirty years in the making. Until very recently, it would not have been possible to write it. Although I have been teaching the principles of how health mirrors our consciousness for more than twenty years, the *science* behind conscious medicine is only just emerging. In recent years, the new biology has established the pathways and mechanisms through which our consciousness guides our physiology – and even our genes – as mystics have always known. What used to be seen as flaky metaphysics is now at the cutting edge of scientific knowledge.

For decades now, research in mind-body medicine has shown us that the mind *affects* the body – but conscious medicine takes us into a new era, in which consciousness is seen as the overall manager-controller of the body. One of my greatest joys is to explore pioneering theories from disparate backgrounds, ask searching questions and mould diverse ideas together into a model that is both theoretically sound and practically helpful – and then hopefully communicate all of that in a down-to-earth and accessible way.

Over the past eight years, I have specialised in working with clients with physical disease using energy psychology, as well as running workshops in energy medicine and (more recently) conscious medicine. The primary focus of my life's work has been the cosmic dance between the visible and invisible realms, and how this plays out in our everyday lives. This cosmic dance lies at the heart of conscious medicine.

Whether you are a healer or therapist, or on a healing journey yourself, or simply curious about the cutting edge of healthcare, this book will give you a framework for the new medicine, and many tools which you can use to promote health and well-being. Throughout the book, there are exercises for self-healing and awareness – from energy psychology to inner journeys using visualisation. Making the most of this book will require reading and re-reading it several times, and working your way through the exercises. We tend to learn slowly and through repetition, so you will find similar ideas spiralling their way through the chapters. I suggest that you read slowly, pausing often to reflect on the ideas and stories. If you read it quickly, then place it back on your bookshelf, it will not have served its true purpose.

My belief is that I only teach people what they already know – that I can only confirm your intuitive knowing. However, sometimes our intuition gets buried under a woodpile of conventional assumptions about how reality works. I hope this book will shift how you think about health and the body forever – and perhaps how you think about your relationships with yourself, others and the world. And if it shifts your consciousness, it will also change your life.

Conscious Medicine will open your heart and mind to everyday miracles, and hopefully make you gasp at the beauty, richness and depth of who we are – and at the nature of the universe. It will also help you to feel safer in your physical body, knowing that you can never be a 'helpless victim' of illness and disease. And alongside all that, it will offer many insights into how to find happiness, inner peace and freedom – whatever your situation. Welcome to the wondrous world of conscious medicine.

Chapter One

SIX IMPOSSIBLE THINGS BEFORE BREAKFAST

Future generations, looking back, will regard conventional medicine during the twentieth century as being as limited as five-finger arithmetic. A new medicine is arising – one that embraces spirituality and consciousness as emphatically as conventional medicine has dismissed them.

Larry Dossey[5]

The body is designed to heal itself. A common cold will pass in a matter of days; an upset stomach or headache will soon sort itself out. Even a broken bone, once set in place, will mend. Yet when faced with more serious or chronic disease – such as a malignant tumour, diabetes or recurrent migraines – most of us assume that the body has exceeded its capacity for self-healing. The body is seen as faulty or inadequate, and we trot along to a doctor for drugs or surgery to correct the situation, rather like taking a car to the garage.

But is it really true that the body cannot heal itself of serious disease? Does it make sense to look for healing outside ourselves – as if our bodily malfunction has nothing to do with who we are, how we think and feel, and what is happening in our lives? And are drugs and surgery the most appropriate forms of healthcare? Or could it be our conventional model of healthcare that is faulty and inadequate?

A new model of health and disease is now emerging, which draws upon the remarkable vision of reality offered by quantum physics and the 'new biology'. This model is supported by innovative health practitioners who have found that shifting our consciousness – or removing blockages in our energy field – can heal serious emotional and physical disease. Ancient mysticism and shamanism have long declared a similar message. In the twenty-first century, cutting-edge science, spirituality and psycho-energetic approaches to healing are together pointing towards a radical new paradigm for health: conscious medicine.

This book offers a framework for understanding this exciting revolution in healthcare and medicine, along with many tools and ideas which will help you to shift your own energy-consciousness, and bring mind, body and spirit into harmony – so that you can create lasting health, happiness and vitality.

EVERYTHING IS POSSIBLE

My favourite book as a child was *Alice's Adventures in Wonderland*. I read it countless times, with a sense of wonder and longing – and now see it as a shamanic journey into the Otherworld, a tale of initiation into expanded consciousness, the wisdom of questioning convention or authority and seeing things through different eyes. 'There's no use trying,' says Alice at one point, 'since one can't believe impossible things.' 'I dare say you haven't had much practice,' replies the Queen. 'When I was younger, I always did it for half an hour a day. Why, sometimes I've believed as many as six impossible things before breakfast.'[6]

What an excellent daily practice that would be! So many of us believe that we understand how the world works, and what to expect – so that anything that does not fit into our fixed world view is then ignored, or becomes invisible to us. There are widely held assumptions about reality – such as seeing the world as solid and material, or believing that medical treatment is needed to cure serious illness, or that we are helpless victims of our genes – which are collapsing before our very eyes. But you have to be willing to question your common sense in order to see the world through fresh eyes. To shift towards conscious medicine, you have to be willing to think outside the box of conventional medicine, and to ask some big questions. Like Alice, you have to enter into a strange new land.

Let's take the fascinating example of multiple personality, now known as dissociative identity disorder, or DID. This is where two or more separate personalities (or 'alters') coexist in the same body, taking over as the conscious self at different times. It became well known back in the 1970s through films such as *Sybil* and *The Three Faces of Eve*, and seems to occur when there is such severe emotional trauma in childhood that one or more personalities splits off from reality, leaving another self in charge which seems better able to cope. There might be a handful or even dozens of different personalities – all of which hold different sets of memories.

Crucially, many physiological differences have been found between 'alters' in the same person. One personality *within the same body* might need insulin shots for diabetes, while another personality is not diabetic at all. Some alters might be short-sighted or colour-blind, while others are not. One personality might be severely allergic to citrus fruits, cats or cigarette smoke, while other selves do not react at all. The dissociative personalities in a woman might have differing menstrual cycles, and alters have also been found to have different brainwave patterns. One alter might be epileptic, or suffer from migraines, whereas others do not.[7] One practitioner saw a woman who turned up for treatment for diabetes, which mysteriously disappeared; then she came for treatment of hepatitis, which likewise vanished. Other diseases came and went in the same woman, all backed up by CT scans and test reports – which was baffling until the practitioner twigged that she was a multiple personality.[8]

Such observations should be enough, in themselves, to shake conventional medicine at its very core. They suggest that *it is not the physical body that holds disease*, but rather the mind or personality. Mind and body are not separate, as medicine might have us believe. On the contrary, it is perhaps consciousness that is in charge when we show signs of disease. Might disease *always* be an expression of emotional dis-ease? Is consciousness in charge of the physical body? If so, this would lay the foundation for a radical new approach to healthcare and medicine.

In 2002, a study published in the *New England Journal of Medicine* showed the crucial role that the mind plays in healing.[9] This study of 180 patients with painful osteoarthritis in the knee was designed to find out which method of treatment was more effective: simply flushing out the kneecap, or scraping away torn or loose cartilage beneath it. Normally a control group would receive no treatment, but this study was unusual. The control group was given a sham operation in which they were sedated, and incisions were made in the knee – but no treatment was given. After two years of follow-up, the treatment groups who had had surgical operations were found to have the same success rate – but so did the control group. In other words, a fake operation was as good as the real thing!

When told they were in the control group, some patients in this study protested that there must have been a mistake, since their knee had improved so dramatically.[10] One man who had been hobbling around with a stick before the fake surgery was now playing basketball with his grandchildren! In 2009, a Canadian study likewise found that knee surgery was of no benefit in itself.[11] Despite this, billions of dollars continue to be spent annually on arthroscopic knee surgery. (A classic study of fake angina operations came up with the same result: the fake operation was not only as good as the real thing, but slightly better.[12])

So what is going on here? Presumably many operations

are rather like a shamanic ceremony, in which the impressive ritual of going into hospital, gowns and masks, the operating theatre, being sent to sleep and white-coated doctors who assure you that the operation will be a success all contribute to the expectation of a sudden healing. And so it is. This isn't to say that nothing 'real' happens in a shamanic ceremony, or in a physical operation. But perhaps the primary healing factor is whether the patient expects the ritual to be effective – and whether the healers involved also have a strong intention and expectation of healing. If so, then unless other factors such as unresolved trauma get in the way, as we shall see, the body simply *heals itself*.

Isn't this exactly how Jesus healed? 'Your faith has made you whole,' Jesus told the woman who was healed by touching his robe.[13] In other words, the healing power was coming through her connection to a greater power that we might term God, Holy Spirit, Source energy, the Divine Matrix, the Web, the Universe, the zero point energy field or higher self. Conscious medicine is largely about doing just this: clearing away inner obstacles that block the flow of divine energy, so that the bodymind can do what it does naturally. It heals itself.

HEALING STORIES

Conventional medicine does not sit easily with miracles of healing. It tends to ignore them, dismiss them, call them misdiagnoses or rename them something more comfortable, such as 'spontaneous remission'. What it rarely does is say, 'Wow! How amazing! I wonder how that happened and what we can learn from it?' Which is a pity – because the world is full of miraculous healing stories and amazing research studies on health that turn our common-sense view of reality inside out and upside down, and which call into question our basic assumptions about mind and body, and even the very nature of reality.

Martin Brofman had a spinal cord tumour in 1975. Since

he was told he had only a few weeks to live, he gave up a career that no longer interested him, left an unhappy marriage and began to cruise the oceans of the world. Since he saw himself as dying he did even not bother to eat a healthy diet. However, after a couple of months he noticed that, far from dying, he was feeling much better! So he began to work on himself using meditation, visualisation and affirmations. Medical investigations later confirmed that the tumour had disappeared – and he has been teaching people how to heal themselves ever since.[14]

In 1986, chiropractor Joe Dispenza had a serious cycling accident that led to multiple compressed fractures of the spine. Every medical expert urged him to have an immediate and risky operation, which might have left him paralysed. He refused, trusting in the body's innate healing ability, and instead discharged himself from hospital. Using meditation, self-hypnosis, hands-on healing, affirmations, good nutrition and gentle exercise, his spine completely healed itself. Only ten weeks later, Joe returned to work as a chiropractor.[15]

Donna Eden had a heart attack at the age of twenty-seven, along with multiple sclerosis, asthma and a whole array of severe allergies. Her health was breaking down in every way, and she was told that she would soon be in a wheel-chair, and had between one and five years to live. Since she was the mother of young children, she was not willing to accept this prognosis – so she looked for ways to heal herself using energy and consciousness. Not only did she recover her own vibrant health; she went on to become the well-known clairvoyant healer and author of *Energy Medicine*.[16]

Metaphysical author Richard Moss describes an elderly woman, supposedly dying of cancer, who came to a work-shop he was running. Instead of dancing freely and spontaneously to the music, the woman was hardly moving. When Richard asked her why, she said it was because of her illness. He began to goad her into letting go and moving freely, telling her she was 'not dead yet'. Eventually she became angry with him, and began to dance more vigorously. She danced and danced – and had a huge expansion in awareness, during which she realised she was an indivisible strand of the Oneness of life. The dancer became the dance. The next morning, her tumours had gone.[17]

Richard Bartlett is a naturopathic and chiropractic doctor who has developed the quantum healing system of Matrix Energetics. When I attended a training workshop with him two years ago, Richard spoke about a recent workshop in Canada in which he briefly closed his eyes while dancing on stage, and unknowingly stepped over the edge. He landed on a straight leg, and heard his leg go 'pop'. The white-hot pain was so extreme that he dissociated from his body. He instantly diagnosed a compound fracture – which is not good news while running a workshop for three hundred people! He quickly began to use his own healing system, searching for a 'parallel reality' in which he had two healthy legs. It worked, and within minutes he was back on stage and teaching again. Despite some severe discomfort at first, he did not need medical treatment for his broken leg. Two weeks later, his leg was fine.[18]

In 2002, Sylvia Black was told that she was terminally ill with cancer. Soon after an operation she went to see healer Tjitze de Jong – a healer I saw during my journey through cancer – who could see her life force slipping away during her first healing session. She was indeed at death's door. Nevertheless, he gave her energetic healing sessions (to clear and re-balance the subtle energies of the body) – alongside medical treatment – and she soon began to respond. (Curiously, hospital scans showed a tumour in one of Tjitze's clients disintegrating from the *inside out* – whereas chemotherapy attacks tumours from the outside in.) Over the next few months, Sylvia fully recovered her health. Eight years on, she remains vibrantly healthy.

Healing miracles are not as rare as you might imagine, and if even one person can heal in such unconventional ways, then others can do so. It is simply a case of understanding what is going on, then applying the same principles. Dramatic healings have been reported for almost every disorder you can think of – however 'terminal' or 'incurable' the diagnosis, according to conventional doctors – and more gradual forms of healing are commonplace.

Just as Alice fell down the rabbit hole into Wonderland, we simply need to let go of our familiar beliefs and step into a new world. Conscious medicine takes us into a new reality in which the rules are different, and reality is more fluid. As Richard Bartlett says, 'Miracles fall outside of the realm of linear physics, but quantum physics actually predicts miracles.'[19] Quantum physics allows for sudden transformation, for instantaneous healing – and for consciousness impacting upon physical reality.

ENERGY AND CONSCIOUSNESS

Early in the twentieth century, quantum physics revealed that everything is energy – and that the material world is, in a sense, just an illusion. We will look more at how science is transforming our view of reality in the next chapter, but for now, let's just hang on to the idea that *everything is energy*. This means that a chair or a candle is just energy. Your body is just energy. And a thought or emotion is just energy. There are *visible* forms of energy you can see and perhaps touch. Then there are *invisible* forms of energy, such as sound waves, microwaves, electromagnetism – and (crucially) consciousness. When you feel the crackling tension in the air before a thunderstorm, or the sense of peace in a cathedral, you are picking up invisible energy.

In a quantum universe, energy and consciousness are inseparable. Consciousness interacts with and moulds energy in such a way that it makes sense to talk of 'energy-consciousness' – rather than 'solid stuff' – as the basic building block of the universe. An exciting picture is now emerging of a psycho-energetic universe – a picture with huge implications for medicine and healthcare. The latest approaches to healing (along with many older approaches which pre-date modern medicine) all focus on energy and consciousness – two concepts that are pretty much ignored by conventional medicine.

The human body can be seen as a visible and structured energy system, which interacts with structured 'invisible energies' such as thoughts and emotions, as well as with the universal energy field. *Understanding this cosmic dance between the visible and invisible realms is the foundation of conscious medicine.* Bringing energy and consciousness into our model of health, and seeing how energy–consciousness gets 'downloaded' into the physical body, has been our central focus within the Conscious Medicine Circle (see the Foreword, page xx) – and I see this as the central difference between conventional and conscious medicine.

ENERGY PSYCHOLOGY

One practical approach within conscious medicine is the relatively new field of energy psychology, which offers thousands of anecdotal reports of healing. The most widely used form of energy psychology is EFT (Emotional Freedom Technique). This became popularised as the 'five-minute cure for phobias', which made me sceptical about it for years. It was only when I saw a woman being cured of chronic asthma in less than a minute that I knew I must train in this strange-looking technique! That was back in 2001. Since then, I've used EFT in many hundreds of sessions with my clients, and taught it extensively to others.

EFT involves tapping gently on specific points on your body while focusing on emotional or physical issues. (There is a practical guide to EFT in Chapter 9.) Biofeedback experts Donna Bach and Gary Groesbeck found that when EFT is applied, our brainwaves show rapid and significant changes. The brain patterns linked with stress, anxiety and emotional intensity are greatly reduced, both hemispheres come into balance, and there is general movement towards the optimal brain functioning associated with health and well-being.[20]

A businessman who had severe neck pain for fifteen years saw an EFT therapist. In twenty minutes, he released childhood beliefs that 'Life is hard', and that he had to work hard and carry so much responsibility. His neck pain reduced to zero. A month later, he reported that the pain had not returned, and that he could now sleep soundly.

Sue Sawyer was asthmatic for thirty-four years, and had used drugs daily since childhood. Initially sceptical that EFT could help with a 'physical' problem such as asthma, she had a breakthrough when she began tapping for loving and forgiving herself and others for anything that might have contributed to the asthma. A flood of memories came through, which she healed and released using EFT – and she felt a massive change in her breathing. The next day, she reduced her medication by half. After three weeks, she put her drugs aside – and she is now free from asthma. (For more EFT success stories, see Chapter 9, page 205.)

EFT has had impressive results with almost every kind of emotional and physical disorder, and energy psychology is now often used to help victims of war, genocide and natural disasters to recover rapidly from the trauma. Although healing can take hours, weeks or even months rather than minutes – depending on the complexity of the problem – EFT almost always has a positive impact, and can be mind-boggling in its speed and effectiveness.

Like Chinese medicine and acupuncture, EFT is based upon the idea that emotional and physical symptoms arise when our energy system has been disrupted. This is consistent with many other healing approaches, including the wisdom of ancient indigenous cultures – and it fits with what the new physics and new biology are revealing about the nature of physical reality, and the links between mind, body and the universal energy field.

Other forms of energy psychology, such as TAT (Tapas Acupressure Technique) and Psych-K, which I've also used with clients for nearly ten years, have likewise found dramatic success in treating a huge range of disorders.[21] TAT uses intention and touch to shift energy patterns and beliefs; Psych-K is based upon muscle-testing and installing positive beliefs in the subconscious mind, using simple processes that you will learn in Chapter 4.

One striking example of TAT involves a woman who had chronic shoulder pain after a skiing accident. (From the perspective of conscious medicine, there are no 'accidents'. Everything is meaningful and significant. We only have accidents when our energy is out of alignment, because something is bothering us.) Through talking about the accident, the woman soon uncovered issues around unworthiness, forgiveness and letting people down, which she released using energy psychology. A single session of TAT left her face glowing with peace, and her posture was transformed. She could now move her shoulder normally, and was totally free of pain.[22]

Paul had been severely allergic to beans for forty years – and had almost given up on healing the problem, when he came across TAT. He recalled an incident from childhood in which his parents had forced him to eat against his will, and he was screaming and crying, so he used TAT on himself to release it. After two brief sessions of TAT, he found he was no longer reviled by the sight of beans. He tried some chilli and was amazed to find he had no reaction. After this, he could eat beans without any problem.[23]

Johnnia had a ninety-minute session of Psych-K for her diabetes. Her blood sugar returned to normal, and she came off all medication for diabetes. Three years on, she could eat whatever she wanted, her blood sugar remained normal and she had also lost a lot of excess weight.[24]

It is easy to believe six impossible things before breakfast if you go looking for them. Such stories show that shifts in consciousness, or helping energy to flow, can heal serious and chronic disease – sometimes within hours or even minutes. So why do we rarely hear such stories? Because they challenge our current view of physical reality, and our touching faith in conventional medicine. And because natural approaches and energy healing do not rake in the massive profits of the pharmaceutical industry, funds for scientific research are very limited – which often leads to the accusation that such claims are 'merely anecdotal' or unproven.

Scientists and doctors have become the priests of our day, offering a scientific dogma – a way of seeing reality – which most people blindly believe, just as we once believed in a raging God who threw down thunderbolts from the sky, or that the earth is flat. Science and medicine have become our new religion, and having to dismantle our belief system is challenging! As the economist John Kenneth Galbraith put it, 'Faced with having to change our views or prove that there is no need to do so, most of us get busy on the proof.'[25]

It is much easier to hold on to familiar old beliefs – such as the belief in a solid material world, and the belief that we need *physical* interventions such as drugs and surgery to heal the body – but we do pay a price for clinging to these old beliefs. It closes our mind to other possibilities, disempowers us, blocks us from seeing the bigger picture and makes us over-gullible when it comes to conventional medicine – which could be surprisingly dangerous.

PROBLEMS WITH CONVENTIONAL MEDICINE

Since you are reading this book, you are probably more sceptical about conventional medicine than the average person, or at least open-minded about alternative approaches to health. Most people turn to conventional medicine when they are ill, then assume *it* made them better if they heal – or that they have just been 'unlucky' if it fails to work, or even makes them worse. As a society, we often assume that Western medicine is mostly helpful and effective, and based on sound scientific research. It is time for a reality check on this.

Physician Norm Shealy reports on a review of the research which suggests that 80 per cent of medical conditions are either self-limiting – that is, the body simply heals itself in time – or cannot be helped by modern medicine. In just over 10 per cent of cases, medical treatment can help. However, in 9 per cent of cases, the patient is left with iatrogenic (or treatment-caused) disease. Shealy points out that this leaves an overall effectiveness for conventional medicine of only 1 per cent![26]

Despite its very low effectiveness, conventional medicine is cripplingly expensive. In the UK, the National Health Service cost £110 billion in 2009. In the USA, healthcare costs more than $2.4 trillion each year. This is clearly not a sustainable approach to healthcare in the long term. Modern medicine can also be highly dangerous. According to official US government statistics in 2001, 784,000 deaths per year are caused by medical treatment in the USA – far more deaths than from heart disease or cancer. And these are only the *official* statistics! This makes medical treatment the most common cause of death and injury in the USA. What is more, despite all the talk of 'evidence-based medicine', *New Scientist* notes that 80 per cent of medical procedures have never been properly tested – and even when studies show a treatment to be ineffective or even dangerous, the results are often ignored.[27]

Not surprisingly, many experts suspect it is the vast profits of the pharmaceutical and medical industries that are responsible for this bewildering state of affairs, in which our primary 'healthcare' approach is not only hugely costly and pretty ineffective, but is also directly responsible for a huge number of deaths. Yet rather like the Emperor's new clothes, no one appears to notice. Modern medicine is big business.[28]

More than 90 per cent of drug trials are funded by drug companies, and the vast cost of launching new drugs means that research findings are often twisted to fit, while whistleblowers can be silenced and even threatened. Independent research often shows that drugs are not only ineffective but dangerous, with side effects that can be worse than the condition they are meant to treat. Most clinical trials show that placebos (dummy pills) are just as effective as drugs.[29] Yet we hang on to the comforting myth of the 'magic bullet' – the concept of a drug that can cure disease without any unwanted side effects – despite the constant flood of news reports which reveal the latest horror stories about the dangers of prescription drugs, and (as I write) the pharmaceutical industry's massive profit from the panic over swine flu.

The US Congress has stated that 85 per cent of drugs in

use do not have any satisfactory research basis. A senior executive in one of Britain's biggest drug companies, Glaxo, has admitted that most prescription drugs do not work for most people.[30] Although doctors tend to deny that they are influenced by commercial pressures and fringe benefits, research repeatedly shows that medical practice is hugely shaped by such factors. (For example, doctors widely prescribe statins to control cholesterol even though moderate exercise and a healthy diet – or simply taking afternoon naps – is known to be far more effective and much safer.[31]) Many people are also taking cocktails of prescribed drugs, the combined effects of which are unknown and untested.

Drugs are like clumsy blunderbusses that can wreak havoc in the body, leading to further imbalances and toxicity – which are often addressed with yet more drugs that create further problems. In any case, a prescription drug can only work if there are already receptors for that chemical in the brain – which means that the brain is quite capable of producing that drug in a natural form, and without any side effects. (Endorphins are a natural form of morphine, for example, and can be stimulated in a host of natural ways.) And as homoeopaths know all too well, suppressing symptoms with drugs can drive disease deeper into the body, resulting in more serious and chronic illness in the long term.

What about infectious diseases? Modern medicine might have a poor record with chronic and degenerative disease, but hasn't it had amazing success in wiping out deathly epidemics of cholera, dysentery, smallpox and other diseases – thanks to mass vaccinations and the wonder of antibiotics? Not according to medical historians, who have repeatedly noted that the control of infectious diseases was mostly due to improvements in sanitation, water quality, diet and hygiene. Vaccination is not considered to be a major factor.

There is little evidence that vaccination works at all – but it *is* hugely profitable for the medical industry. Smallpox, measles and other epidemics have occurred in areas where

95 or even 100 per cent of people have been vaccinated. Flu vaccines have been acknowledged to be worthless. And in many cases, deaths from a disease have *increased* after vaccination was introduced. Large-scale studies have failed to show any significant benefit from vaccination.

And what about the highly dubious *safety* of vaccinations? As early as 1856, the first of many books[32] warned of the danger of vaccinations, which still contain horrific chemical cocktails, including heavy metals and toxins such as mercury, aluminium and formaldehyde – and even macerated cancer cells. Many doctors and health experts have warned that vaccination is not only ineffective, but far more hazardous than the diseases it is intended to prevent, and that immunisation of children might be a major health risk.[33]

Today – despite constant reassurances from the drug industry – mass vaccinations have been linked with huge increases in autoimmune and neurological diseases, including cancer, leukaemia, AIDS, rheumatoid arthritis, multiple sclerosis, heart disease, encephalitis, dementia, cot deaths and childhood autism. Likewise, the overuse of antibiotics has been linked with a general weakening of our immune systems, as well as the development of dangerous antibiotic-resistant 'superbugs'. Hospitals are hugely risky places to be.

Yes, there are occasions on which technological medicine can be helpful, amazing and even life-saving – but many of the apparent successes of conventional medicine are illusory, or have come at a huge price. It is little wonder that more and more people in Western society are turning to complementary and alternative medicine.[34] It is time for a radical change in our approach to health and disease.

THE FUTURE OF HEALTHCARE

Countless books have been written about the problems with conventional medicine, and I have no interest in doctor-bashing. Many of my closest friends are doctors, and I have enormous respect for them. They perform a stressful, almost impossible job in a highly dysfunctional system, and offer a high level of caring, compassion and commitment. Given their training and background, and the often fixed expectations of their patients, they are doing the very best job they can. But there are good reasons why we need a new approach to health – and many doctors agree with me, and are working actively to transform their own practice and the healthcare system.

Conventional medicine does have its place. Some believe that while it is good at diagnosis, it is generally poor at treatment – except in emergencies. (We look at the pros and cons of diagnosis in Chapter 10.) If you have a heart attack or get mangled in a car accident, going to hospital is an excellent option. However, physicist Amit Goswami,[35] author of *The Quantum Doctor*, suggests that medical treatment should be pretty much reserved for emergencies – and that in most other cases, it is more of a liability than a help. Once the emergency is over, we should turn to non-conventional approaches that address energy and consciousness, and ask bigger questions about what is going on.

Rudolph Ballentine, a holistic physician, likewise says that drugs can sometimes be used to 'buy time' while one plans a course in healing that will address the deeper issues which are causing dis-ease – but that drugs must not be seen as resolving the problem. As he says, 'Resorting to a drug to correct a human problem is analogous to dealing with a computer glitch by grabbing a screwdriver or a pair of pliers and trying to rewire its circuits.'[36]

For the time being, conventional medicine has a place for those who are steeped in materialist thinking, with little interest in exploring emotional issues or taking responsibility for their health. In the face of emergency, it is often a wise choice. And sometimes people feel desperate and want to hand themselves over to an 'expert' for a while, or take drugs or have surgery while they move through a crisis. There is no right or wrong approach. However, we need to have a whole smorgasbord of approaches available, so that people have genuine choices in healthcare.

Conventional medicine does need to get off its podium and acknowledge that it does not have all the answers. It needs to wake up to its own shortcomings, and recognise that drugs and surgery address only the symptoms, and not the causes of dis-ease. The time has come for new approaches which treat the *whole* person – body, mind and spirit – and which recognise the central role of consciousness in health.

Having briefly outlined the problems with conventional medicine, my main aim is to offer a positive vision for the future – a model for healthcare that is safe, gentle, low-cost and empowering, which honours our wholeness as embodied souls and acknowledges that we live in a conscious universe. This is a model that restores hope and optimism, gives us back our power and responsibility and shows that a world of magic and miracles is not a childlike fantasy. You can combine this new approach with conventional medicine if you wish. And excitingly, it is a model that is grounded in cutting-edge science.

The sun is now rising on a remarkable new era within healthcare: the era of conscious medicine. More and more people are now turning to psycho-energetic approaches to healing which honour our consciousness and spirituality, the innate wisdom of the body and the hidden gifts of disease. More and more people are refusing to accept a poor prognosis, turning their minds in a more positive direction, and opening their hearts to new possibilities. And what now might seem strange, unconventional or even miraculous will slowly become normal and 'common sense'.

It is no coincidence that the current shift towards a new medicine also marks a huge cultural shift in our consciousness. Many have called this the Age of Awakening, or the Age of Consciousness, and ancient prophecies have pointed to this era as a time of transformation. More and more people are going through spiritual awakening, and searching for greater meaning or purpose in their lives. Quite often this comes in response to a serious diagnosis or other life crisis.[37] Some visionaries have even suggested that we are becoming a new species: *homo spiritus* or *homo luminus*. And this expansion in awareness is mirrored in the emergent new medicine.

In the next chapter, I will walk beside you as we step into the conscious universe. I will show that many different disciplines and theories are converging to bring us a stunning new view of reality, which has huge implications for healthcare and medicine. As we come to inhabit this new world – as we shift towards a higher level of consciousness and release the limiting beliefs and traumas of the past – healing from *any* disease becomes not only possible, but more and more probable. It might take time to heal, but it is almost always possible. In later chapters, we will see that illness or disease is not necessarily a problem, but is better seen as a meaningful message – and even a precious gift.

Chapter Two

THE CONSCIOUS UNIVERSE

> ... research is screaming at us with the urgent message that consciousness can harness the powerful healing forces of a quantum universe, forces far more potent than pills in a bottle.
>
> **Norman Shealy and Dawson Church**[38]

Imagine a company that makes wooden garden furniture, all of which is painted green. The company is highly successful, and all goes well – until some of the furniture begins to emerge from the factory in bright pink. No one wants to buy it, and the pink furniture begins to pile up outside the gates, causing a blockage for wood and paint supplies coming in, and for green furniture going out. Eventually a consultant is called in, who suggests a solution: take on more painting staff and buy in extra green paint, and repaint the pink furniture as it emerges from the factory. However, the repainted green furniture doesn't look as good as the originals, and has to be sold at a lower price. Even worse, more and more of the furniture is now coming out pink, so the problems are growing. So the consultant suggests taking on even more staff, and buying even more green paint.

Now the factory has some new problems: the additional staff are blocking the gates, and profits are reduced by the extra costs and lower selling prices. The company is running into financial difficulties. So the consultant suggests they borrow money from the bank, and take on extra staff in the accounts department. By now, almost all the furniture is coming out pink – and the company has a bank loan to repay each month, and even more staff to pay. They are now heading towards bankruptcy. The consultant's advice covered up the initial problem, but created a whole set of new problems. And still no one has asked *why* the garden furniture is being painted pink, and *who* gave those new instructions . . .

This is pretty much how conventional medicine operates. If your pancreas isn't producing enough insulin, doctors call it (type 1) diabetes, and prescribe extra insulin on a daily basis. If your blood pressure is too high, you are given drugs that aim to lower it (though these are fairly ineffective and carry considerable health risks).[39] If you have heavy periods or problematic fibroids, you might have a hysterectomy to 'solve' the problem. If you feel depressed, you are prescribed the latest round of (almost useless) anti-depressants. If you have pain in your knee, a doctor might prescribe painkillers or anti-inflammatories, or a surgeon might scrape out the area beneath your knee.

Once the problem is given a name – such as diabetes, fibroids, hypertension, depression or osteoarthritis – the diagnostic label is often seen as the 'explanation' for the problem. You 'have' arthritis, or you 'have' depression, which is rather like calling it Pink Paint Syndrome. Then drugs or surgery are prescribed in an attempt to cover up the pink paint.

From a conscious medicine perspective, if you focus on the physical level and try to solve problems *at that level*, you are not seeing the bigger picture. Any organisational consultant worth his or her salt would go straight to the CEO or top management team, and find out what was *causing* the pink paint problem. Is there a lack of communication? Is there conflict between the managers? Is there a supply problem? Is someone trying to sabotage the company's success? Is there a new vision for the company? What is really going on? Through conflict resolution, healthy communication and clarifying the company's vision, the consultant will not only iron out the problem, but also create a stronger and healthier company for the future. And this is exactly what conscious medicine aims to do.

THE GHOST IN THE MACHINE

It sounds pretty obvious to look for the cause of problems rather than painting over the symptoms – so why doesn't it happen within conventional medicine? Because its model of reality starts and stops at the physical level. It is often blind to the very existence of the CEO and management team. It sees the factory workers as automatons that can develop faults, and need to be corrected. It sees the body as a machine that can wear out, go wrong or have faulty parts. The body is merely a bag of biochemistry and genes, which is somehow disconnected from the *person*.

How did this mysterious state of affairs come about? Well, let's take a brief excursion into history. During the Reformation, when the rational, masculine world of Protestantism suppressed the more feminine world of Catholicism and the Holy Mother, a new science was also born. In the seventeenth century, Newton developed the idea of a 'clockwork universe' that had been set into motion by God, then left to its own devices; Descartes split mind from body, and saw the person as a mere 'ghost in the machine'; and scientists came to an arrangement with the Church whereby science would deal with the visible world (including nature and the body), while religion would address the unseen realms (including the mind and morality). By the end of the seventeenth century, in the eyes of science, nature was no longer seen as sacred, or even as alive. It had become 'inanimate matter in motion'.[40] And God was becoming increasingly irrelevant. The Cartesian–Newtonian model of the universe was born.

It was another three hundred years before we began to see the problems created by such a mechanistic and fragmented view of reality – a view that not only informs how we currently see reality, but which also became the basis of conventional medicine. Whenever you pop a pill because you have a headache or see a doctor over recurrent sore throats, who then peers down your throat to see 'what is wrong', you might not be aware that you are seeing the world through the eyes of Newton and Descartes – but you are. The question of *who* is occupying the sick body is seen as irrelevant. You have become a mere ghost in the machine.

As naturopath William Mitchell pointed out, 'A headache is not caused by a deficiency of aspirin'[41] – so why do we imagine that taking pills has somehow resolved the problem? For tribal peoples who use traditional methods of healing, the idea of suppressing symptoms with drugs, or looking more closely at the body to find out what the problem is, would be seen as patently absurd. It would be taken for granted that something is out of whack with you, the person – with your current relationships with self, others, life or the spirit world – and the focus would be on restoring 'good relations', so that your energy could flow in healthy ways. Traditional healers or shamans might also use herbs or other natural equivalents of modern drugs, but they see symptoms or illness within a bigger picture. They look at the whole person, their context and their environment. They seek to address the cause, not the symptom – and always see disease as an expression of *dis*-ease within the self.

I am not advocating a return to the past. Nor do I wish to romanticise a shamanic approach to healthcare, which can have its own shortcomings (such as giving too much power and responsibility to the shaman). However, we can learn a great deal from cultures that have kept a close connection to spirituality and to nature – which recognise the intimate connection between body, mind and spirit, and honour the body's natural ability to heal itself once we get out of our own way – that is, when we resolve whatever issues are causing our dis-ease.

One Native American shaman, when asked by a Western doctor how he would treat arthritis, replied, 'I don't know

– bring her to me and I'll show you.'[42] He did not treat diseases; he only treated people.

Lewis Mchl–Madrona is one doctor who began to explore his Native American roots while still training in Western medicine. After being horrified by the damage that conventional medicine could do, and the ways in which it often de-humanised people, he witnessed some astonishing healing by traditional shamans – then spent many years training in shamanism himself, alongside extensive medical training. He now devotes his time to building bridges between conventional medicine and ancient healing wisdom, and urges doctors to hear the 'story' behind someone's illness, rather than simply rushing to a diagnosis and dispensing treatment mechanically.

Once you understand the whole story, there is an opportunity for true *healing* – rather than temporary relief of symptoms. Good doctors still know this. The reassuring bedside manner of the old-fashioned family doctor was far closer to the traditional shaman than to the modern techno-medic who dispenses pills, anxiously arranges batteries of tests, or refers you to a 'specialist' who has studied a single part of your body in detail (and therefore has an even more fragmented view than a family doctor).

Widely satirised for their fragmentary approach to the body, doctors have been accused of being heavily influenced by the pharmaceutical industry and seeing patients as 'the appendix in bed 3'. Yet every doctor I know has a strong intention to be a healer, is well aware of the limitations of modern medicine and is hungry for change. On returning to his frantic health centre after a workshop on energy medicine, one of the doctors in our Conscious Medicine Circle said that the need for change in conventional healthcare has become a real emergency.

THE MATERIAL UNIVERSE

It is easy to forget that science simply offers a *story* about reality, rather than the objective truth. Just as religion was once taken to be the whole truth, scientists and doctors have become the new priests of our age, whose opinions are often taken to be factual and accurate. But our ever-changing science is just a story – and stories are not true or false. They are just more or less helpful and enlightening. And it seems that a new story is now unfolding.

The Cartesian–Newtonian world view is based upon materialism. That is, it sees the world as real and solid, and assumes that the physical world is all there is. In this clockwork universe, everything is made up of separate objects that can bump up against each other like billiard balls, but which have no real connection. What really matters in this world view is the solid stuff – the 'matter' – and everything else can be explained at that level.

To the materialist, the body is a machine – and consciousness is a mere epiphenomenon, an after-effect. Mind somehow emerged from the primordial broth and random genetic mutations, presumably because it had some advantage in survival terms as animals slowly evolved from the plant kingdom. But since mind is not 'solid stuff', it is not really important.

Despite overwhelming evidence to the contrary,[43] the materialist assumes that mind cannot affect matter, that consciousness cannot affect anything at a distance, and that mind and matter are fundamentally different 'stuff'. If you see through these blinkered eyes, then drugs and surgery do make sense as an approach to healthcare. If the body is sick, you correct it at the physical level, since the physical level is all there is. You ignore the mind because it is pretty much irrelevant to the physical body. Isaac Newton himself was deeply religious – but a die-hard materialist would now reject the very notion of God or any spirituality. To a materialist, if you cannot see and touch it, it isn't real!

Is materialism even a *scientific* basis for healthcare – let alone a helpful approach? Well, it depends upon which century your 'science' comes from. In recent decades, a new model of the universe has been emerging from the cutting edge of science – a model that turns our common-sense reality upside down and inside out. Countless scientists and visionaries are saying that our way of seeing reality is in the midst of a stunning transformation. This new world view might hold the key to healthcare and other global challenges, and we can no longer afford to ignore it.

If you don't have any background in science, don't worry. I will keep this part as simple as possible. However, to understand the theoretical framework for conscious medicine, you have to grasp that we are collectively shifting from a belief in a material universe – a world of solid stuff – towards an awareness of everything as energy-consciousness.

It might seem like a no-brainer that the world is solid and material. After all, I can see and touch this laptop, cup my hands around this hot mug and taste my peppermint tea. But that is only because we are so good at interpreting complex vibrational frequencies through our senses, and converting them into experiences. The world is not as it appears to be. *Everything is energy, and energy is inseparable from consciousness.*

This is a shift in awareness that is far more profound and significant to our everyday lives than realising that the earth is round rather than flat. It is a mind-blowing shift that shatters our old assumptions about how the world works. When you fully absorb what it means, it changes *everything*. And healthcare can never be the same again.

THE PARADIGM SHIFT

As a teenager, I was fascinated by research in parapsychology, which had produced staggering statistics – studies of telepathy, psychokinesis, remote viewing and other psychic phenomena, which have shown that minds can pick up information in non-physical ways, and that mind can affect matter at a distance, with odds of millions or even billions to one against chance. Extensive studies have shown that the mind can affect a random number generator, for example, with odds against chance of more than a *trillion* to one.[44] (To get this into perspective, results are seen as statistically significant in science – for example, a new drug can scrape through a drug trial and be marketed as effective – if the odds against chance are just *twenty* to one!)

I was even more fascinated, as a budding psychologist, as to why scientists would pooh-pooh the implications of such research, and how people could say that they did not 'believe' in telepathy or clairvoyance. It wasn't a scientific viewpoint – it was merely prejudice. It seemed to me like saying they did not believe in Australia, simply because they had not visited it themselves.

The British healer and psychic Matthew Manning was eager, as a young man, to have his extraordinary abilities confirmed by science. He took part in scientific trials for several years, and proved over and over again that he could inhibit the growth of cancer cells, and influence blood cells and the growth rate of seeds in a laboratory setting. However, he was still met with scepticism or even accusations of being a fraud, and the 'need for further trials'. What he did was simply impossible within the old materialist world view – and he eventually realised that no amount of 'proof' would satisfy the sceptics. He became disillusioned with science, and decided to devote his life to the more productive and satisfying work of healing.[45]

Soon after Matthew Manning became famous as a teenage psychic, on my undergraduate reading list I came across Thomas Kuhn's classic book about paradigm shifts, *The Structure of Scientific Revolutions* – and began to understand why scientists could be so unscientific.[46] I learnt that there is always huge resistance to seeing the world in a whole new way. This resistance usually begins with patronising denial, as the new ideas are denounced as 'stuff and nonsense'. Later on, as the new movement gains ground, the 'old guard' moves into aggressive resistance.

Thank heavens people are no longer burnt at the stake for having heretical views – but they can still be thrown out of their jobs, ridiculed, threatened or lose their status. Heretics are not always popular, and many learn to keep their mouths shut. (I lived for a while with a theoretical physicist who would never have dared to air his mystical views at work. Back in 1543, Copernicus wisely left his theory to be published posthumously, thirty years after he realised that the Earth is *not* at the centre of the solar system.)

Eventually, so much evidence accumulates for a new model that the old paradigm becomes untenable. The Earth really *is* round. The Earth *does* revolve around the sun! Telepathy really *does* happen! People *can* heal others with focused intention! We really *do* create our own reality! It becomes more and more obvious, and those who were clinging to the old view retire or die, or simply declare they had known it all along. It is as if the whole world puts on a new pair of spectacles, and now sees reality differently. The new world view seeps into the collective consciousness, and now begins to be considered normal and common sense – yet society has made a massive change in how the everyday world is seen. A cultural renaissance has occurred, and consciousness has evolved towards seeing a bigger picture.

As I read more and more about the new physics, I came to realise that we were heading towards a paradigm shift – and that instead of matter being seen as primary, we were moving towards seeing consciousness as primary. Having read so much about mysticism as a teenager, this sounded very familiar. As physicist Sir James Jeans put it, 'The universe begins to look more like a great thought than like a great machine.'[47] As we shall see, if we apply this to healthcare and medicine, the *body* begins to look more 'like a great thought than like a great machine'. And so it does!

THE CONSCIOUS UNIVERSE

Back in the 1920s, quantum physics began to reveal a very different world from that inhabited by the materialist: a world in which mystics, ghosts, telepathy and distant healing could come to coexist happily alongside computers, jet planes and MRI scans. In the bizarre world of quantum physics, we can move backwards or forwards in time, communication can occur instantaneously across vast distances between 'entangled' particles and light can be a wave or a particle, depending on who is observing it.

What is more, as physicists looked at tinier and tinier particles of what makes up our physical reality, they concluded that there simply isn't any solid stuff. There is only energy, or in quantum physics terms, 'waves of probability'. And what is it that *decides* which of many probable realities comes into existence, so that it appears to be real and solid? Consciousness. The new physics tells us that *consciousness* determines whether light behaves as a wave or a particle, or whether this event or that event occurs. If we take this further, it is consciousness that decides whether this knee is painfully swollen or healthy, or whether this tumour is 'here or not here'.

For example, in my Conscious Medicine workshops, I often show a video from China in which a woman with bladder cancer is treated at the Hospital With No Medicine near Beijing.[48] The woman lies down, and a large tumour is clearly visible on an ultrasound screen. Three experienced practitioners of Qi Gong (movement and breathing techniques that help circulate subtle energy) then send chi towards the tumour. (Chi is universal energy – also known as *qi, ki, prana, mana,* vital force, Source energy or the Holy Spirit.) In just over a minute, the tumour becomes transparent and reduces by half, then it suddenly vanishes as if it were merely a wisp of smoke. The healers decided that the tumour was 'not here', while holding a high state of consciousness – and the tumour promptly obliged by shifting into another probable reality. The healers briefly applaud their own success – but it is clear that it is all in a day's work for them. (A German film crew captured a tumour dissolving in eleven seconds at the same hospital.)

Crucially these 'operations' in China are only performed after training the person in Qi Gong for several weeks, so that they are inducted into an energetic world view, and have an effective tool for maintaining their own energy flow. Without this shift, it is understood that a tumour would simply grow again. At the Hospital With No Medicine, practitioners are aware that the world is made of energy-consciousness – and that a tumour is simply a bundle of condensed energy that can respond to focused intention.

The new physics tells us that energy-consciousness, rather than 'solid stuff', is the basic building block of physical reality. In other words, this is a psycho-energetic universe. Far from being the misty irrelevancy that materialists would have us believe, consciousness is at the heart of the emerging new science. It is not a mere ghost in the machine, but the creative source of everything.

Mystics have always said that consciousness is the ground of all being, the fountainhead from which everything flows – and some physicists, such as Amit Goswami, have concluded that quantum physics only makes sense if we assume that consciousness not only moulds but also *creates* physical reality.[49] This fits with everything I have taught about reality creation and the power of the mind for the past twenty years. We create everything that happens in our lives – including our state of health and well-being.

The well-known physicist David Bohm offered a model of the universe that was starkly different from Newton's lonely clockwork universe. Bohm viewed the universe as an un-divided wholeness, like a hologram that is forever in flowing motion – a remarkably similar vision to that of Hinduism, Buddhism or shamanism. In his view, everything in the universe was interconnected. He wrote about the 'implicate order' – the unseen dimensions of reality – and how this unfolds into the physical universe.[50]

God is probably another name for the implicate order – the unseen realms from which everything unfolds – though as the term 'God' can have negative connotations, I prefer those such as Source, Source energy, All That Is or the Universe.[51] (I simply cannot push away those childhood images of a bearded, judgemental father figure in the sky!) Other popular terms for the Source are the zero point energy field, the Field or the Divine Matrix. Mystics have also called it the akashic records, or Divine Intelligence. Regardless of what you choose to call it, the point is that the 'solid stuff' of physical reality emerges from these invisible realms of energy-consciousness.

This idea turns the materialist paradigm on its head – yet it is found in most ancient philosophies. It has been popularised in the idea that 'we create our own reality', awareness of which is now spreading to millions of people through best-selling books about the law of attraction, and popular DVDs such as *The Secret* and *What the Bleep Do We Know*.[52] Taking full responsibility for what we experience – knowing that our lives are created from the inside out, that we are not victims but creators of what happens to us – is an inevitable consequence of living in a conscious universe. And it has profound implications for healthcare.

The new paradigm provides a scientific model for such phenomena as distant healing, as well as 'spontaneous remission'. Newtonian physics only allows for objects to affect each other via known physical forces, and within the limitations of space and time – like billiard balls that hit each other. The new physics allows for information to travel beyond the speed of light, and to be directed by consciousness.

The new science also shows that, at a deeper level of reality, all energy and consciousness is interconnected. This means we can heal ourselves and heal each other, as well as making our dreams come true, by aligning our energy-consciousness with that probable reality. We can also tap into any information from anywhere, beyond space and time. The universe is a unified field of consciousness. This opens up whole new frontiers of creative potential – and it makes sense of 'miraculous healing'.

PARTICLES AND WAVES

Physicist Amit Goswami suggests that quantum physics is rather like poetry, which is why materialists have such a hard time understanding it. It is full of paradox, uncertainty and ambiguity. It swirls around in a ghost-like way, and cannot be pinned down. It also brings something as messy and nebulous as consciousness into physics, and dissolves the old distinction between subject and object. In the new physics, we cannot be impartial observers of reality; we are always active participants.

According to the new physics, reality can behave like a solid particle *or* like an energetic wave – depending on how you observe it, and what your intentions are. This seems to be mirrored in our state of consciousness. We can behave in a particle-like way when we listen to our ego – since ego-consciousness is fixed, constrictive, limited and isolated. Or we can behave like an energetic wave by shifting into the wave-like consciousness of our higher self, which is more free-flowing, expansive and connected to others. *These two states of consciousness are central to conscious medicine.*

Consciousness can be like a wave or like a particle. I feel like a separate individual with my own sense of identity, yet like many people I've also had mystical experiences in which all boundaries dissolved and 'I' became part of the Oneness. At these times, my wave self seemed to *encompass* my particle self, rather like a Russian doll that holds many smaller selves within it. My consciousness expanded beyond my ego while also holding an awareness of it, and I felt a loving sense of connectedness to All That Is. I've also had countless intuitive experiences in which I suddenly 'know' something that my rational mind could not have known – in which I have felt connected to the Source, or Divine Intelligence, which knows everything.

This flowing wave-like consciousness supports our health, happiness and well-being as well as our creativity and intuition. Some scientists have dubbed it our 'quantum self', since it seems more aligned with the fluid, limitless and expansive states of consciousness that are mirrored by the world of quantum physics.

Medical intuitives such as Caroline Myss can tap into this wave-like level of awareness (and almost anyone can learn to do this). Myss was found to be 93 per cent accurate in her medical diagnoses – without any medical training – when she was simply given the name and birthdate of a patient. Much of the time, she diagnosed over the phone to physician Norman Shealy, from 1200 miles away, without seeing or speaking to the patient. Her diagnosis might be, for example, 'migraine with myofascial pain' – and his diagnosis would be identical. Norman Shealy said he had never come across anyone so accurate, not even the best doctors.[53]

The particle self – which feels separate and cannot tap into Divine Intelligence – could not make any sense of a medical intuitive. The more condensed, limited, fixed and separate particle state – often known as our ego – is also linked with the stress response. Stress shrinks our awareness, and recent research has shown that it can even physically shrink our brain or create brain lesions if it becomes chronic.[54] It also damages our physiology and biochemistry throughout the body. We are designed to be in a wave-like state most of the time – aware of our particle nature, yet also aware of our connectedness to All That Is. As we shall see, being in a particle state for too long is a serious risk to our mental and physical health.

LIVING FROM THE HEART

One way of grasping the disparity between the old and new paradigms – or particle versus wave states – is to consider the two hemispheres of the brain. The left hemisphere is the more logical, sequential, verbal, analytical half of the brain, which sees distinctions and makes comparisons. It sees itself as objective, and is traditionally linked with masculine energy. It tends to look for differences and separateness, and prefers either-or thinking. It might be compared with the ego self – and is the half of the brain that is identified with old paradigm thinking. The right hemisphere is more intuitive, relational, subjective and holistic. Its knowing is direct and immediate, rather than verbal. It sees the bigger picture, and tends to perceive wholes and connectedness. It is more inclined towards inclusiveness, or 'both-and' thinking. It is also more tuned into emotions, sensuality and bodily awareness.

The right brain is linked with our authentic self, higher self or quantum self (wave consciousness). It has a deep connection to our spirituality, and understands quantum physics intuitively, even if it could not verbalise it. Western society tends to overuse the left brain at the expense of the right hemisphere, and much of our emotional and physical dis-ease – as well as our leanings towards materialism and the ego – might be traced back to this imbalance.

Jill Bolte-Taylor is a neuroscientist who, at the age of thirty-seven, had the amazing experience of observing herself having a stroke after a blood vessel burst in the left hemisphere of her brain. Over four hours, she watched her brain deteriorate in its ability to process information, until she could not speak, walk, read or write, and could recall next to nothing of her previous life or identity – and it took her many years to fully recover.

What is perhaps most fascinating in her riveting account of the stroke is that the loss of her left hemisphere gave her some unexpected advantages. All of the emotional baggage from her past simply dropped away, as did the constant drive to be busy and to accomplish tasks. Instead she found herself in a state of right-hemisphere bliss. 'I morphed from feeling small and isolated to feeling enormous and expansive. . . All I could perceive was right here right now, and it was beautiful.' Instead of seeing herself as solid, Jill experienced herself as a fluid for a long time: 'My soul was as big as the universe and frolicked with glee in a boundless sea.'[55]

This experience has remarkable parallels with mystical experience, and does suggest that – as experienced meditators know – if only we can shut down the constant, superficial ego-chatter of the left brain, we can gain access to blissful and expansive states of awareness. As she healed from the stroke, Jill became more emotionally centred. She noticed how emotions felt in her body, and learnt how to hold on to feelings of joy and peace by directing her thoughts away from judgement and obsessive analysis, and towards loving kindness and acceptance. (In Chapter 7, we will see why emotions play a crucial role in our health.)

The left brain is our normal conscious mind (or limited ego self), while the right brain has access to a far wider spectrum of consciousness. The left brain is designed for focusing, and when it is in balance with the right brain, it focuses helpfully on the positive, and on our goals and desires. But when it is out of balance, the left brain can stress and torture itself with anxiety, blame, guilt, negativity, worry, self-doubt, judgement, pretence, defensiveness and hurry-sickness – whereas our right hemisphere seems to be a doorway to states of inner peace, love, joy, compassion and authenticity. While the left brain is head-centred, our right brain is heart-centred. When the chattering mind becomes silent, we can listen to the heart.

At the Institute of HeartMath in Colorado[56] (an internationally recognised centre for the study of heart intelligence and stress management) research has shown that negative emotions such as anxiety, blame, guilt and insecurity throw our heart rhythms into a state of jagged incoherence and disorder. When you shift your focus to your heart, then activate heart-based feelings such as love, caring and appreciation, this induces a state of 'heart coherence', which has innumerable health benefits, affecting almost every organ and system in the body.

Heart coherence reduces the level of stress hormones, makes us more resistant to infection and disease, lowers blood pressure, boosts anti-ageing hormones, and has been linked with improvement or recovery from a host of physical and emotional disorders, from arrhythmia and auto-immune disorders to fatigue and insomnia. It also helps us see things differently, so that stress-free solutions can be found to problems. In short, being heart-centred is good for our mental and physical health.

When we love and care for others – without *over-caring*, a negative state that is signalled by worry, anxiety and insecurity, along with a burdensome sense of responsibility – it also boosts our immune system. Over-caring or self-sacrifice, by contrast, is linked with lowered immune response, unbalanced hormones and poor decision-making. Caring for others at our own expense, which is characteristic of co-dependency and over-parenting, is *not* good for our health. The heart naturally radiates love towards self as well as others. (The golden rule is to love our neighbours *as* ourselves, not *instead* of ourselves.) When we are heart-centred, our love and care for others is balanced by self-love and self-nurturing.

In traditional Chinese medicine, the heart is seen as the connecting point between body, mind and spirit. A whole bundle of scientific research has shown that the heart has its own 'brain' and nervous system for processing information, which has come to be known as emotional intelligence.[57] When we are in a state of heart coherence – when the so-called 'heart-brain' is functioning well – this seems to coordinate all the systems in our physical body and energy field, so that our physical health is supported along with our happiness and spiritual growth.

A core process that has emerged from the Institute of HeartMath is shifting into heart coherence, which I have taught for many years on my workshops. It seems simple, but it emerged from many years of research into how to shift out of stressful states and reconnect with our true self. It shifts you towards the blissful, right-brain state that Jill Bolte-Taylor experienced after her stroke – *without* having to be seriously ill, speechless and semi-paralysed as she was. Whenever you find yourself reacting badly to a situation, or your thoughts are turning in endless circles, coming into heart coherence will help you to shift into an expanded state of awareness, and move back into your heart's intelligence. From there, you might see the situation differently, or have fresh insights about it, or come up with new solutions – and you will simply *feel better* about it. And learning how to *feel better*, whatever the circumstances, is a key to remaining healthy or healing from any disease.

Exercise
QUICK COHERENCE

This is a rapid method of coming into heart coherence – or connecting with your wave self – that I learnt from the Institute of HeartMath. You can practise this three or four times a day, or as you wake and before you sleep, before making a decision, or whenever you are facing any challenge. If you practise this regularly, it becomes easier to remain coherent in situations that would normally trigger you into stress. It gradually entrains you to live from your higher self. If you are a health practitioner, you can use it before seeing clients or patients. The heart radiates an electromagnetic field that affects everyone around us, so feeling good helps those around you to feel good. This only takes a minute or two, and will quickly bring you into balance:

1. **Heart focus** – Shift your attention to the area of your heart. It might help to place your hand on your heart and/or close your eyes.

2. **Heart breathing** – Imagine that you are breathing in and out through your heart area. Breathe a little more deeply than usual, but let it be easy. Find your natural rhythm, allowing your breath to become smooth, calm and balanced.

3. **Heart feeling** – Carry on breathing through your heart while you bring up a positive heart-centred emotion – such as a time when you felt love and appreciation for a loved one, pet or nature, or doing something that you love. Or focus on something positive that happened today. Or just feel love, caring or appreciation in your heart area.[58]

With a conscious universe, the human body – rather than being controlled by genes and biochemistry – is dancing to the tune of consciousness and subtle energy. This is then *mirrored* in changes in our biochemistry, neurology, organs, muscles and physical structure, and even in how genes are expressed. In other words, what happens at a physical level is merely a symptom of what is occurring at higher levels of organisation – just as we can begin to affect our physical health in moments by connecting with our higher self. Within this new model, changes in the body 'unfold' into physical reality from the invisible realms of energy-consciousness – which, as we shall see, is exactly what cutting-edge research in biology is demonstrating.

In 1847, a highly respected doctor proposed that washing hands and cleaning surgical instruments before operations would reduce the mortality rate. He was ridiculed by the medical authorities for suggesting that something unknown and invisible could affect our health – and as a result, he eventually lost his medical practice. There was no scientific evidence for the invisible world of bacteria until twenty years later.

Today, we are facing an even bigger shift in perspective. Countless authors, scientists and health practitioners are suggesting that invisible forces such as thoughts and energy are critical to our physical health – which threatens the old materialist paradigm in science. Those who cling to the old world view are trying to minimise or ridicule such claims. Yet it is becoming like a dam bursting. At first, there was a mere trickle of dissenters – yet it is now an ever-increasing torrent, which marks the shift to a new paradigm.

Claire Sylvia is a dancer who had a heart-lung transplant in her mid-forties. After the operation, she had a strange sensation that there was another presence within her. She began to crave foods that were unusual for her, such as chicken nuggets, and was drawn towards cooler colours in clothes instead of her usual vibrant oranges and reds. She began to walk differently – more like a man – and was more aggressive and impulsive, and had new desires that she could not explain. Five months after the operation, she had a vivid dream about a young man called Tim, and intuitively knew he was her donor. The hospital had a policy of confidentiality about donors, and would give her no information – but her dream slowly led her to find the family which had lost their eighteen-year-old son, Tim, in a motorbike accident. He loved chicken nuggets, and showed all the qualities and desires that Claire had expressed since the transplant.[59]

Many other transplant patients have reported similar experiences (that gradually fade as the transplanted organs adjust to their new owner). A materialist viewpoint suggests the heart and lungs are merely a pump and breathing apparatus. The new paradigm recognises that cells are imbued with *consciousness*, and that a transplant – or even a blood transfusion – is bound to transfer some of the energy-consciousness of its former owner. We cannot carry on pretending that the physical world is all that is real.

If we do indeed live in a conscious universe, then healthcare that focuses on the physical body is missing the point. It is remedial medicine at best. It is ignoring the CEO of the body – which is consciousness – and instead devoting its attention to workers on the factory floor. Conventional medicine uses a reductionist model of reality that is appropriate for building a house or repairing a clock, but is inadequate and misleading for understanding people and health. We cannot keep peering down microscopes at cells to unravel the mysteries of health and disease. We have to pan back. Instead of meddling with cellular biology, we need to understand the psycho-energetic nature of the universe.

DIAGNOSIS AS A VERB

On his deathbed in 1895, Louis Pasteur reputedly said, '*Le terrain est tout*': that is, the host or environment is everything. Despite the apparent success of penicillin, he recognised that the true *cause* of disease was not the bacteria. That would be like saying that pink paint was 'causing' the problem in the furniture factory. The real question was how the pink paint came to be in the factory, and how it made itself at home there. When we see ourselves as 'having' a disease, it can sound as if the disease is the problem. *It* is causing our symptoms. It has somehow invaded our boundaries and taken up residence in our body. We are forgetting that '*le terrain est tout*' – and mistaking a descriptive label (diagnosis) for a causal explanation.

When we blame a germ or disease, we see ourselves as a victim of outside forces and fail to ask more searching questions about what is going on. After all, not everyone who is exposed to a cold or flu virus becomes ill. In the nineteenth century, a doctor swallowed a whole flask of cholera bacilli to make this point[60] – that we are only vulnerable to cholera (or any disease) when our immune system is already compromised. Cecil Helman, a family doctor and medical anthropologist, points out that the Western notion of being invaded by bacteria or viruses is similar to the indigenous idea of spirit possession – and it shifts responsibility outside the self.[61]

A research study back in the 1970s found that students who were under stress from examinations were more likely to catch a cold when exposed to the common cold virus. That is, the virus is a necessary but not sufficient condition for having a cold. This might seem blindingly obvious – yet the field of psychoneuroimmunology (PNI) – which studies the links between the mind, stress and our nervous and immune systems – only dates back thirty years. Medicine still tends to see disease as somehow invading a person, as if the person is irrelevant to the disease process – hence the 'war on cancer', 'war against AIDS', and so on.

Thirty years ago, I read about a holistic doctor who saw a little boy with measles and told his mother that her child was 'measling'. This turn of phrase always stuck in my mind, and I have heard any diagnosis as a verb ever since. When I was given a cancer diagnosis, I translated this into 'cancering', and began to ask myself how I was cancering, and what I needed to do in order to stop cancering and become healthy again.

As soon as you convert a diagnosis into a verb, it ceases to be a thing with an independent existence, and instead becomes part of what you are *being* and *doing:* how you are thinking and feeling and behaving. You switch from a materialist paradigm – a world full of objects – into consciousness thinking, with a world inhabited by actively participating subjects. If you are being and doing it, you can explore it and understand it, find meaning and purpose in it, and perhaps choose to 'be' or 'do' something different.

When I've spoken with Native Americans, they have commented that translating their mother-tongue into English is tricky, because we have a noun-based language, whereas their language is verb-based. From a materialist view of reality, we see objects and things and fixedness, whereas their holistic viewpoint – seeing themselves as an interconnected part of the web of life – means that they see patterns, relationships and movement. Energy medicine often helps us make this shift from solidity and stuckness towards fluidity and movement – from an objective reality that seems beyond our control to a subjective world of ever-flowing energy which responds to our consciousness: a world in which we are creators and innovators.

FROM MATTER TO ENERGY

Emo-Trance[62] is a form of energy psychology like EFT (see Chapters 7 and 9) that turns a seemingly fixed object into a moving pattern of energy, and often triggers new insights and connections. I was working recently with a woman with infertility – that is, a woman who was blocked from conceiving – and asked her to sense where this blockage was in her body. Looking within, she said there was a rock-hard shape in her abdomen, built of grey bricks and shaped like a chapel. I asked her to focus on this shape and, knowing that everything is just energy, ask it to soften and flow – and then to leave her body. The shape turned into a slimy mass that began to ooze slowly out of her throat and belly button. She realised that it represented the harsh biblical teachings she had grown up with, which told her that sexuality was bad and wrong and that being a woman was something to be ashamed of. As the shape oozed out of her, a lot of shame and guilt disappeared with it. We then transformed some of her early childhood memories, using another energy tool, and re-integrated the womanly parts of herself that she had suppressed as a child.

Almost every woman I have seen with infertility has been struggling with issues around shame, guilt and lack of deserving, along with ambivalence about her body and being a woman. Many have also been through childhood abuse, which they are afraid of passing on to a child. Some are unsure about their primary relationship. Others have simply made motherhood too big an issue, and their desperation to have a child is creating a stressful environment that makes conception unlikely. However, these emotional issues can all be cleared – and I have seen many of these women success-fully become mothers. Why don't infertility clinics do this kind of work? Because they do not live in a conscious universe, and therefore do not practise conscious medicine. They believe that the 'cause' of infertility lies in the physical body – that the fault lies on the factory floor, with the workers – rather than seeing the body as a mirror of consciousness.

Within the old paradigm, the problem lies at the phys-ical level, and needs to be corrected at that level. Within the new paradigm, the physical level is effect rather than cause. Since health lies at the interface between mind and matter, conscious medicine offers a crucial stepping stone out of materialism and duality, and into the new paradigm based upon energy-consciousness – in which mind moulds or translates itself into matter.

As we explore the implications of the new physics, the latest research in biology, and case studies emerging from the new medicine and energy healing, we begin to see that creating health and well-being comes from shifting our state of energy-consciousness. Then we step into the world of conscious medicine.

BUILDING BRIDGES

Several months ago, I was walking with a doctor friend who was concerned about his mother's gallstones. She was going into hospital that week to have them surgically removed. He asked how I would approach gallstones, so I spoke about the gall bladder meridian (see Chapter 9) along with emotional factors that might underlie gallstones, questions I would ask and energy tools I might use. He looked pensive for a minute, then said, 'But what if there are adhesions between the gallstones and the wall of the gall bladder?' I couldn't grasp his question for a while, then a light suddenly came on. 'Oh, I see – you think gallstones are *real*!', I exclaimed. We both laughed, because – even though we largely understood each other's worlds – we had fallen into the chasm between the biomedical model in which he trained and my psycho-energetic view of the universe. For me, gallstones were just condensed energy patterns that had been moulded by consciousness – rather like habitual thoughts – whereas from his world view they were real and solid.

I have learnt from experience that if you mention the word 'energy' to most medical doctors, their eyes tend to glaze over. The word simply doesn't compute. It is like talking about mountaineering to a goldfish. So I have slowly learnt how to build bridges between their world and mine, so that we can begin to understand each other. Talking about the body as an energy system makes no sense to someone whose left brain has been thoroughly trained to name, probe and even dissect innumerable 'separate parts' of the human body.

Energy is a right-brain concept. It does not have fixed boundaries; it is mutable and flexible, and can make quantum leaps. The more left-brained someone is, the less they understand energy – or appreciate poetry. (This isn't to say that all the doctors I know are left-brained, or indifferent to poetry – but most have had to struggle to recover their right brain!) To step fully into the new paradigm, we have to expand beyond the stressed, limited, either-or and separatist thinking of the ego, and align with our authentic or higher self – which intuitively understands everything in this book – and this is rarely a process that happens overnight.

Perhaps the easiest way to bridge between conventional medicine and conscious medicine is via mind–body medicine:

the scientific research that illuminates how the mind affects the body, and how to promote healing. This isn't (yet) conscious medicine. We're not yet talking about how energy-consciousness converts into matter, about waves and particles, or how mind and matter are fundamentally the same stuff. Nor are we yet talking about the body as a conscious biofield, or how the law of attraction works. Nevertheless, we are moving towards the new paradigm. Happily, the new biology has built an easy bridge for us to stroll across – so that is where our story leads us next.

Chapter Three

BRIDGE TO A NEW REALITY

Every thought you think is echoing through your connective tissue communication system, turning genes on and off, producing either stress responses or healing responses. This understanding opens up a vast new panorama of potential self-healing.

Dawson Church[63]

Imagine you are sitting beside a straw-topped beach hut, on a long strand of tropical white sand that seems to stretch on forever. The sea is calm and turquoise, and sparkles in the sun. The gentle lapping waves are rhythmical and soothing. A long ice-cold drink and a basket brimming with exotic fruit rest on a low wooden table at your side. You fill your lungs with fresh salty air, breathing easily and deeply. Maybe you will stroll along the beach in a little while, or take a swim in the warm waters. Or perhaps you will take a nap.

Sitting here on this beach, anything seems possible. You have an expansive sense of timelessness, and a dawning sense of potential. You begin to imagine, to dream, to conjure up new possibilities for the future. Your everyday life of busy routines, tight deadlines, stressed relationships and over-packed diary seems like another lifetime. No computer, no phone, no demands. That nagging tension in your neck and shoulders has vanished. Your toes curl with pleasure and delight. Your mind is strangely still and quiet. You feel relaxed, centred and confident – and there is something else, something almost forgotten? Oh yes, a deep feeling of happiness!

On returning home, you promise yourself that life will be different now. Dreams and desires have bubbled up to the surface. You have fresh plans, and a new sense of priorities. You will take more time out to relax. You will sign up for a yoga class, have more fun, spend more time in nature, keep a journal, devote more time to friends, read more novels – and spend less time watching TV, on the internet, or with people who are energy vampires. Maybe you will even change your job, or move to the country.

A few months later, you wake up to realise that you have slipped back into your packed routine and the same old habits and patterns. Nothing has changed. The happiness and peace of mind of that tropical beach now seem like a mere fantasy. You tell yourself that others are worse off and you should be grateful, that life isn't so bad, that you should grit your teeth and get on with it. You resign yourself to letting go of your dreams, and living with that constant tension in the pit of your stomach. Ah well, retirement is only twenty years away . . .

Sooner or later, your body comes up with worrying symptoms, or you start having panic attacks or get depressed, so you visit your doctor – hoping for a prescription to take the pain away. Yet the solution to your symptoms will not be found in a prescription pad. Nor does it lie a thousand miles away on that tropical beach. All it takes is a shift in your consciousness.

If you recognise these two states in yourself – feeling blissed-out and relaxed, or feeling tense, stressed and over-whelmed – you are on your way to understanding conscious medicine. Ten years ago, in my book *Pure Bliss*, I called these two states living in Hard Time or Soft Time. More recently, in *Wild Love*, I wrote about tame and wild love – or conditional and unconditional love – which also refers to these two states of awareness. I've been studying these two states for a long time, though I only realised in recent years how central they are to our health.

WAVES AND PARTICLES

The new science tells us that there are two ways of looking at reality – both of which are valid in their own way. There is surface reality, in which everything *appears* to be solid and material, and you *appear* to be separate from me, just as a chair seems to be separate from a candle. At this level, reality is made up of separate particles. What is 'real' is limited to the world that we can see, hear, smell, taste and touch with our five senses. Then there is the level of deep reality, or the implicate order, or the Divine Matrix, in which everything is interconnected. The deeper substrate of this reality is energy-consciousness, or the invisible realms.

Surface reality is particle-like – objects seem to be separate, and reality appears to be fixed and solid. It seems to be, well, *real*. Deep reality, on the other hand, is more wave-like – everything is more fluid and connected, more subjective than objective, and there is probability rather than certainty. And when we limit our awareness to surface reality, we get stressed and anxious.

According to the new biology, every cell in your body has two modes it can switch between – and these two modes correspond to these two states of consciousness:

✧ The first mode is a state of relaxed, happy and easy alertness in which healing and growth take place naturally. This is known as the relaxation response, the healing response, the love response, growth mode or 'being in the flow'. It is how you felt on that tropical beach when nothing was bothering you, and every cell in your body switched into relaxation. I call this the *wave response*.

✧ The second state is designed to keep you safe and alive during those rare times when you are in physical danger. This mode has been called the fear response, being 'out of the flow', in protection mode or (most commonly) the stress response. It is what I call *the particle response.*

When you are looking through the eyes of the old paradigm – through the eyes of the ego – you see yourself as a particle. You are focused on surface reality, and see yourself as separate from other people and the world, and even from your own body. You forget that you are a child of the universe, no less than the trees and the stars. You feel small, insignificant, lonely and disconnected. You are often worried and anxious, never knowing what might happen next, and wanting to stay in control. Time seems to press in on you; there is never enough time – or it drags on when you want it to pass. You focus on tasks and lists, rarely living in the moment. You are easily threatened or blaming, and might focus on what others are 'doing wrong', or what bad things might happen. In other words, thinking like a particle throws you into the stress response.

When you see through the eyes of the new paradigm – through the eyes of your heart or soul – you shift into the bigger perspective of quantum reality. You feel more like a wave than a particle. Time feels more flowing and expansive. You feel connected to everything. It isn't that you lose your sense of self, but rather that you expand around it. Being a wave *encompasses* being a particle – just as a wave is part of the sea, yet is still a wave with its own position in space-time. You are fearless in the wave response. There are no enemies, only friends. You feel relaxed, loving, appreciative, joyful and creative. Life seems effortless. There are no problems, only solutions. There is no fault or blame. Even the concept of 'healing' makes no sense from here; you are already healed and whole, and you know it. You are also deeply intuitive, knowing things far beyond the limitations of your five senses.

When your consciousness is fully coherent in the wave response, free from any fear or inner conflict, it feels wonderful. Boundaries and limitations dissolve. You become One with something greater than yourself. This is the state of an artist who is creating a masterpiece in oils, a sculptor who has become one with the clay, a top athlete who is breaking records, a scientist lost in exciting research, an inspirational public speaker through whom words are flowing, a mother cuddling her newborn baby, a toddler splashing happily in the mud, or two lovers who merge in ecstasy as they make love. You are in the flow.

Being in the particle response or the wave response is not an all-or-nothing state. It is a continuum. You might be 80 per cent particle and 20 per cent wave in this moment, or 40 per cent particle and 60 per cent wave. However, most people have a characteristic range – and your emotional and physical health will be mirrored in how separate you habitually feel from your heart and soul, or how connected you are. The closer you are to particle-like consciousness, the more fearful, guilt-ridden, mistrustful, disappointed, frustrated, angry or despairing you feel. The closer you are to being a wave, the more loving, relaxed and joyful you will be. In the particle response, you feel like a lonely and isolated drop in a hostile universe, rather than a wave in a loving ocean.

Why is this relevant to conscious medicine? *Because your emotional and physical health rest not upon your genetic inheritance, but on whether you are habitually in the stress response or the relaxation response.* The more you slip into particle awareness, the more vulnerable you become to disease. If you maintain a wave-like state of consciousness, you will have radiant health and vitality.

Let's look at these two states from a purely biological point of view. Understanding the stress response offers us an easy stepping stone away from conventional medicine, and towards conscious medicine.

THE PARTICLE RESPONSE

Whenever you feel under threat of any kind the amygdala in your mid-brain fires off danger signals. This triggers the body into a cascade of neurochemical events which are designed to deal with an emergency. The HPA axis (the hypothalamus, pituitary and adrenal glands) is instantly primed to prepare your body for action.

Adrenalin, cortisol and other stress hormones now flood your system, preparing you for fight or flight, making you feel hyper-alert. Your heart rate and blood pressure increase. Blood drains away from the visceral organs and towards your arms and legs, so that you are ready to run. Your digestive system shuts down. There is no point in digesting a meal if you're about to be eaten! Your immune system switches off. While that tiger is looking for a meal, there is no point fighting off a virus, or even healing a wound! Growth and maintenance processes in your body come to a near-standstill. This is a biological survival mode — which is perfect when you are facing a hungry tiger, since nothing else matters in that moment. Your life might depend on it.

The stress response also affects how your brain functions. Blood drains away from the frontal lobes — your higher thinking — and moves to the more primitive parts of the brain. The conscious brain cannot react quickly in a crisis. It is designed to focus, and can only process a maximum of twenty bits of information at a time. The subconscious mind, by contrast, can process up to twenty *million* bits of information per second. So under stress, the subconscious mind takes over. We go on autopilot, and launch into habitual reactions based upon the fight-or-flight response.

This is why time appears to slow down or stop if you are about to have a car accident. Everything goes into slow motion, and you seem to have endless time to react to what is happening. Your subconscious, which lives beyond the limitations of space-time, has taken over. Stress puts you into a semi-conscious, trance-like state. You become like an automaton — sleepwalking through life.

Wild animals are rarely in the stress response for long. A lioness strolls towards a herd of grazing impala, and the herd goes into amber alert. Is the lion looking for a meal? If she crouches in readiness or begins to run, the herd's stress response goes into red alert, and they take flight. They bound away at full speed until they are a safe distance from the predator, then return to grazing. All of their physiology reverts to normal, and the crisis is over. Wild animals live in the present moment, and once a threat has passed, they quickly return to a relaxed state.

People are different from wild animals. We have those pesky things called *thoughts* – and it is our thoughts, rather than external stressors, which create chronic stress. The stress response was designed for those rare emergencies in which we can take immediate action to protect ourselves from a threat. A hungry tiger. A runaway vehicle. A madman with an axe. Thin ice collapsing beneath our feet. Real physical dangers in the here-and-now.

However, most of our stress comes from situations in which fight or flight is not possible, or is inappropriate – and in which you are not in any real danger. You just *feel* as if you are under threat, because of stressful thoughts. A computer crashes. Your child becomes sick. A deadline looms. You face a long supermarket queue or a traffic jam. An elderly parent goes into hospital. Dozens of emails scream to be answered. The roof starts leaking. You get a batch of final demands on the same day. The car is making strange noises. Your partner comes home late from work, and seems distant and distracted. The boss makes a critical comment or talks about down-sizing the company, and you wonder whether your job is safe. You feel threatened, overwhelmed, burdened, helpless or disempowered – and your stress response is turned on.

The threat is not physical. It is psychological. You feel at risk of being disapproved of, or criticised, or abandoned, or emotionally hurt, or not being able to meet others' demands, or you feel frustrated because you are 'wasting precious time'. You feel worried about loved ones, or concerned that money will run out, or anxious about losing control of a situation. Or you tell yourself you have too much to do in too little time, and if you don't get it all done . . . What? It is unlikely that the world will stop spinning, yet from the particle response you cannot think clearly. You rarely face your fears head-on, and ask whether they are realistic. You feel like a hamster on a treadmill. You are running on autopilot – too fast and too hard. And not very smart.

The threat does not even have to be a current psychological threat. We human beings are so clever that we can stress ourselves out over what happened last month, or even twenty years ago – and over events that haven't happened yet, and might never happen! ('But what if. . .?!') One reason why so many spiritual disciplines urge you to 'live in the moment' is that stress is rarely in the here-and-now. It is mostly in our heads. Negative thoughts can go round in our heads obsessively, releasing stress chemicals into the body that are not needed for fighting or running away, and which only do us harm.

Here are the most common physical signs of the particle response:

✧ Feeling tense

✧ Rapid heartbeat

✧ Raised blood pressure

✧ Breathing faster and into your upper chest (rather than abdomen)

✧ Shallow breathing, or holding your breath

✧ Tension in your neck, shoulders or lower back

✧ Constipation and /or diarrhoea

✧ Abdominal cramps or bloating; poor digestion; nausea

✧ Aches and pains

✧ Inflammation

✧ Cold hands and feet

✧ Dizziness

✧ Chest pains

✧ Sleeping too much or not enough; disturbed sleep

✧ Eating too much or undereating

✧ Craving sugar, caffeine and junk foods

✧ Storing fat around your waist and hips; being overweight

✧ Smoking, drinking or using drugs

Then there are the common psychological signs of stress:

✧ Worry, tension and anxiety

✧ Feeling overwhelmed by demands

✧ Constantly watching the clock

✧ Inability to relax

✧ Memory loss and poor concentration

✧ Depression

✧ Moodiness, irritability and anger

✧ Feeling agitated

✧ Social withdrawal

✧ Feeling lonely or isolated

✧ Procrastination

✧ Finding it hard to cope with daily life

✧ Nervous habits such as pacing, nail-biting or compulsive talking

✧ 'Getting through the days'; focusing on survival

✧ Feeling unable to make positive plans for the future

✧ Addictions and codependency

✧ Disturbed relationships

✧ Negative emotions such as fear, guilt, anger, frustration, worry and despair

As we shall see, the stress response is always signalled by negative emotion. Everyone experiences stress, but in a healthy state, we balance times of stress with generous periods of relaxation and self-nurturing, and learn how to calm and soothe our own emotions. Unfortunately people can grow used to being in stress, and even become 'addicted' to it – especially if they grew up with chronic stress and tension – so that it seems normal to feel tense, anxious, guilt-ridden, resentful or overwhelmed. That is when you are in trouble. *When the stress response is chronically activated, it is highly likely that you are heading towards disease.*

HEALTH AND THE PARTICLE RESPONSE

Within the new paradigm of conscious medicine, disease begins with dis-ease – which means it begins with stress and negative thinking. Over the past thirty years, research in psychoneuroimmunology[64] has firmly established links between stress and almost every major disease – including heart disease, strokes, diabetes, allergies, hypertension, gastro-intestinal disorders such as peptic ulcers and irritable bowel syndrome, autoimmune disorders, arthritis, cancer, infertility, sexual dysfunction, muscle tension and pain, and a weakened immune system.

Crucially, the body cannot heal itself while you are in a stress response; nor will it fight off bacteria and viruses effectively. There is no point in repairing a wound, fighting off a flu virus or even scavenging for cancer cells when you are facing a hungry tiger! The immune system uses up a lot of energy – so whenever you have stressful thoughts as if you were facing an emergency, your body puts your immune system on the back burner. This not only makes you vulnerable to chronic disease, but also means that healing slows down or even becomes impossible.

A study at Ohio State University College of Medicine, conducted by Ronald Glaser and Janice Kiecolt-Glaser, on the physiological and psychological effects of compassion and anger found that the healing of wounds is slowed down by marital tension.[65] Married couples were given small wounds on their skin, then asked to discuss a neutral topic for half an hour. Their wound-healing was monitored over three weeks. Then the study was repeated, but this time they were asked to discuss a topic on which they disagreed. After having a disagreement, the couples showed slower wound-healing. Among couples who had serious arguments – with sarcasm, criticism and put-downs – their wound-healing was 40 per cent slower. This was after just half an hour of restrained discussion in the presence of research staff! Imagine the knock-on effects on our physiology of frequent marital tension in the home, which would activate the stress response over long periods.

At the Institute of HeartMath, one research study by Rollin McCraty looked at the impact of positive or negative thoughts on our immune system.[66] Volunteers spent five minutes every morning focusing on positive thoughts that (crucially) made them *feel* loving, caring and compassionate. This resulted in a spiking of their IgA, an immune factor that is crucial in the body's defence system against viruses and bacteria. Perhaps more surprisingly, this impact lasted for several hours. Another group of subjects replayed an episode in their mind that brought up anger or frustration for five minutes each morning. These angry, blaming, critical thoughts were linked with an immediate decrease in IgA, and their immune system functioning was significantly depressed for several hours. This shows the physiological impact of just *five minutes* of choosing to feel positive or negative each day.

Japanese doctor and scientist Masaru Emoto has done some remarkable research on water.[67] He found a way of photographing water at the moment of crystallisation into ice – and discovered that water from polluted sources would form misshapen crystals, or refuse to crystallise at all, whereas water from pure sources formed lovely symmetrical crystals. Then he investigated the impact of music, photographs and prayer on the formation of crystals, or taping positive words such as 'Thank you' and 'Unconditional love' or 'I'll kill you' and 'Despair' to water. Again and again, the most beautiful crystals were formed from expressions of love and gratitude – while crystals were distorted, ugly or failed to form when exposed to negativity – whether the words were written down or sent towards the water as thought-forms.

Since the mature human body is 70–75 per cent water, imagine the constant impact on your body of thoughts going through your mind. If your thoughts are loving and positive, all well and good. But if you are in the stress response, and harbour negative thoughts of criticism or fear or guilt or despair, what is that doing to your body?

THE HEALING POWER OF MEDITATION

Countless research studies have found that meditation can extend your life, slow down the ageing process, boost your immune system, lower blood pressure, help insomnia and reduce pain – as well as creating more happiness, inner peace and mental clarity, and resolving emotional issues such as anxiety, depression and substance abuse.[68] (For an introduction to meditation, see *Meditation for Beginners* by Jack Kornfield, or *Getting in the Gap* by Wayne Dyer,[69] both of which include a training CD, or try the simple method overleaf.)

When I became anorexic at the age of nineteen, twice-daily meditation became the single most important factor in my recovery. At that time, little was known about eating disorders, but meditation helped me step aside from obsessive thoughts about food, which ran round my head in endless tape-loops, and find inner peace and new perspectives. It also helped me to reconnect with my body, instead of seeing it as an enemy.

Meditation helps to bypass your left brain's constant busy chatter, and slip into that timeless and dream-like space of the right brain. It helps both hemispheres to synchronise and work in harmony. It allows you to switch from being a fearful particle into a loving wave. Regular meditation – or any technique that focuses on breathing – is one of the best steps you can take to promote your health and well-being.

According to hatha yoga, healthy breathing means a healthy body and mind. The particle response disrupts our breathing, often leading to rapid, shallow or uneven breaths, breathing into the upper chest or even holding your breath. One way of training your bodymind to stay out of the stress response is to focus on your breathing. If you deliberately breathe *as if* you were relaxed and safe – slow, smooth and deep – this sends the signal to your body to relax and de-stress.

Exercise
BREATHE!

Pay attention to your breathing as you go through your day. Are you breathing deep down into your abdomen? Are your ribs expanding with each breath? Are your breaths slow, smooth and even? All three answers should be Yes. If you are breathing rapidly, unevenly or shallowly (into your upper chest), you are almost sure to be in the stress response. Likewise, if you are periodically holding your breath, you are suppressing painful emotions. Sit quietly with yourself and – without judgement – notice what you are feeling.

A simple meditation:
For a simple meditation, close your eyes and focus on the sensation of your breath as it moves in and out of your nostrils. When you get distracted by thoughts – and you will, again and again – gently pull your attention back to your breath. Allow your mind to become more still. It generally takes at least eight minutes to get into a meditative state, so aim to meditate for fifteen or twenty minutes, daily or twice daily if possible. When your mind tells you that you are 'not doing it right', or that you have more urgent things to do, treat those thoughts as the distractions they are, and bring yourself back to your breath.

Breath technique to ease anxiety:

Here is a simple breath technique for reducing anxiety (and other negative emotions such as anger or frustration):

1. Inhale through your nose as slowly, deeply and smoothly as you can, without strain.

2. Exhale through your nose as slowly, deeply and completely as you can, focusing on your navel.

3. Before you inhale again, pause by saying to yourself, 'One thousand. Two thousand.'

4. Smoothly repeat steps 1–3, until your breathing has slowed down and you feel calm.

If you wish, you can also breathe in positive qualities such as joy, compassion, hope or peace, and breathe out any tension, worries or discouragement, while doing steps 1–4.[70]

STRESS IS A VERB, NOT A NOUN!

Research has shown for decades that stress makes us more vulnerable to illness and disease – but we often talk about stress as if it was something that *happens* to us. The well-known Holmes and Rahe Stress Scale from the 1960s suggests that events such as moving house, getting divorced, getting married or having a baby are inherently stressful in a very predictable way. The new biology makes it clear that *stress is something we do to ourselves* – through our negative thoughts and beliefs, and through the choices that we make.

We can turn almost any event into a comedy or a tragedy, depending upon how we perceive and handle it. A divorce can be a mutual relief as a relationship relaxes into a more appropriate and friendly form, freeing the children from tension and allowing you to expand in new ways; or the marital tensions can continue beyond divorce into years of battles over money and children, along with burning resentment, guilt and dependency. Having a baby, likewise, can be a priceless joy or a miserable prison. Moving house can be a cinch and a pleasure, or entail months or even years of house-hunting, clutter-clearing and exhausting renovations. Just like a disease, stress is a verb rather than a noun. If you are under stress, you are *stressing* yourself.

Whenever you see stressful circumstances as beyond your control, or as inevitably stressful, it is that *belief* which creates stress. Whenever you see someone as doing something wrong – or see yourself as behaving badly – it is that judgemental *thought* which throws you into the stress response. Whenever you expect a situation to be stressful, or worry about what might happen, you tip yourself into the stress response. The question is: *How are you stressing yourself?* What unquestioned beliefs or fears are causing your stress?

Whatever the situation, you have the ability to choose thoughts that take you out of the stress response. As soon as you tell yourself, I would be happy if only . . . ('If only my child wasn't sick, if only my wife hadn't left me, if only my husband would change, if only I had money in the bank, if only I didn't have this tumour, if only I wasn't disabled, if only I was younger, if only my sister hadn't died, if only this project was over, if only I could move house'), you are dis-empowering yourself. Unless you are facing a hungry tiger, it is your *thoughts* that are stressing you out. And your feel-ings won't change until you change your thinking. Nothing changes until you do.

Barbara came to see me with chronic fatigue syndrome. She was a senior physiotherapist with a heavy caseload, who went home from the hospital to care for a son with cystic fibrosis and a blind husband. It had been so long since she had even considered her own needs that she looked bemused when I asked what she really wanted from life. 'I just want to be well, so that I can look after my family and patients again,' she said, as if it was obvious. When I gently asked again, 'What about *your* needs?', she broke down in tears and quickly saw that she was exhausted by the unremitting demands. Even though it meant she was living a half-life, being ill was her only way of saying no and cutting down to part-time work. Illness was preferable to her former existence.

When we explored her childhood, Barbara realised that, as the eldest of five children with a depressed mother, she had been looking after others since she was a young child – giving the care and love to others that she had always been longing for herself. Being a carer made her feel good about herself, but it did not meet her own needs for care and attention. Her body eventually decided that being ill was the best possible option. Barbara began to see that the stress was not coming from *outside* her – from uncontrollable circumstances – but was coming from within. She needed to make self-nurturing and life-affirming choices for herself, and put herself on her own list of priorities. As she did so, her energy slowly began to return.

One of the simplest ways to take yourself out of the stress response is to relax – and follow your bliss. I generally recommend that you aim to spend at least two hours each day in which you are a human 'being' rather than a human 'doing'. Even if you have young children or a demanding job, it is essential to carve out time for yourself.

Exercise
R-E-L-A-X

If you show signs of chronic stress, you can help to prevent future health problems by devoting time each day to unwinding. Nurture yourself. Write a Bliss List of whatever helps you to relax deeply, and to shift into that timeless right-brain space in which you feel blissfully happy and at peace. Then build those practices into your everyday life. Some examples might be: meditation, yoga, running, dancing, tai chi, taking a nap, lying in the sun, gardening, walking the dog, being in nature, playing the guitar, having a massage, making love, listening to music, baking cakes, singing, photography, watching feel-good movies, reading or writing poetry, stroking your cat, going to an art gallery – or just sitting and daydreaming happily in your favourite chair.

Notice whether you spend time 'zoning out' or numbing yourself – for example, watching mindless TV, aimlessly surfing the internet, or shopping for the sake of it – rather than truly relaxing and wading into that delicious ocean of happiness. Keep tuning into your body throughout the day, and asking yourself, 'Am I relaxed right now? How am I feeling? Am I enjoying this?'

When we are stressed, we tend to dissociate from the body and our emotions. By tuning into your feelings and bodily sensations, you send the message to your body that it is not in danger, and it can relax. (If you notice resistance to taking time out, or tell yourself you are too busy or that others come first, later chapters will help you explore the old beliefs or inner voices that are holding you in the stress response.)

YOUR BODY READS YOUR MIND: THE MESSAGE OF EPIGENETICS

So far, this might not sound like revolutionary stuff. Stress makes us sick. Big deal! But it is a very big deal. Once you understand how the stress response works, and how it affects the body, you are stepping into the new paradigm. Although conventional medicine doesn't seem to have cottoned on to this yet, the stress response leads us into a psycho-energetic universe. The new biology shows how mind literally turns into matter, and why emotions are the key to our health – and there is no turning back from there. *This marks the dawn of a medical revolution.*

If you don't have a scientific background, please read this section carefully even if you feel inclined to skip over it, because the new biology provides much of the scientific basis for conscious medicine. Read it several times if necessary. For those who say it is just flaky to suggest that we create – and can uncreate – almost every health disorder from arthritis to lupus to tonsillitis, this will give you some hard facts to throw back at them. And it will help you understand how the mind impacts upon the body, turning what is invisible and energetic into what is visible and solid.

Until recently biologists believed that our destiny is written into our genes, and that our DNA controls all cell functions. In this view, DNA is fixed from birth, your body does its own thing and you are just along for the ride, despite decades of anomalous phenomena that bring this idea into question. For example, identical twins (with identical DNA) can have dramatically different health and life spans – one twin might have bipolar disorder, for example, while the other does not – so clearly the genes we have at birth do not even determine our health, let alone our behaviour.

At the start of the twenty-first century, the Human Genome Project discovered (with some embarrassment) that the total number of genes in humans is a mere fraction of what was expected. We only have slightly more genes than a chimpanzee, and not many more than a tiny marine worm. This suggests that we have to look beyond the idea of fixed genes – and even beyond the physical body – to explain the complexity of human health and behaviour, which is exactly where the new biology takes us.

Bruce Lipton, a former Stanford University researcher and medical school professor, is one of the foremost pioneers of the new biology.[71] Three years ago, I attended a workshop with him in San Francisco, which was a mind-blowing few days. He is a cellular biologist whose groundbreaking research on stem cells in the 1980s began to point towards biology being controlled by the *environment*, rather than by our genetic inheritance. In other words, he found that the central dogma of molecular biology – that we are controlled by our genes – was incorrect! At the time, he had no idea that this would lead him inexorably towards psychology, and beyond that to spirituality – but like all heretics, he was questioning old assumptions and thinking outside the box.

When I studied A-level biology in the 1970s, we were taught that the nucleus of a cell is the command centre – that since it contains the DNA, it must be the 'brain' of a cell. Biologists blindly assumed that the control mechanism of a cell must lie in the 'solid stuff'. Since all cell activity is governed by proteins, which are manufactured from DNA, they assumed that DNA must be at the top of the chain of command. They also assumed that genes are self-activating – that they can mysteriously turn *themselves* on or off.

To a left-brain materialist, the question of whether the CEO of cells might lie in the invisible realms of energy-consciousness would not even cross their mind. Sorry, let me re-phrase that: it would not even cross the neural pathways of their prefrontal cortex! Such a question would mean thinking outside the box of scientific materialism, on which conventional medicine is based.

Thanks to Bruce Lipton and others, we now know that the true 'brain' of the cell – the information processor – is the cell membrane. A cell can live without a nucleus for several weeks. You try living without a brain for several weeks! However, if you destroy the cell membrane, the cell dies almost immediately. It is the membrane that passes instructions on to our DNA – which, in turn, is just a passive blueprint.

The new biology is showing that our DNA is not in charge of the body. It is merely a factory worker, which takes instructions from the cellular membrane, which in turn is responding to signals from the environment. This finding has given rise to the exciting new field of epigenetic research – the study of how the environment affects how genes are expressed. Many other researchers have confirmed Bruce Lipton's findings. So the old question of whether a disease is due to heredity or the environment turns out to be a red herring. Even our genes are controlled *by the environment*!

Why is epigenetics so crucially important? And how does it pave the way towards conscious medicine? Because it shatters the old materialist paradigm. The key to this lies in how the cell membrane (or mem-brain) makes its decisions. It is picking up signals from the environment – not from DNA. The membrane contains receptor proteins that vibrate rather like tuning forks in response to signals from outside the cell, and then give instructions for action to effector proteins. These effector proteins, in turn, control proteins and genes – which put biochemical responses and physical behaviour into action, such as releasing histamine in response to pollen, or reaching for a tissue when you are about to sneeze. (Keep hanging on in there if you are not scientifically minded. The best bit is about to come!)

Now, while some receptor proteins in the cellular membrane are sensitive to *biochemical* stimuli such as oestrogen or histamine, other receptors have been found to be sensitive to *energy fields*. They respond to vibrational frequencies – including sound waves, temperature, light waves, radio waves and *thoughts*. Thoughts generate waves of energy. It turns out that our thoughts – which are part of the invisible world cast out by science in the seventeenth century – operate as energy fields. Bingo!

Do you see how crucial this is? It means that our cells and DNA can respond to our *thoughts*, and not just to physical molecules. I leapt around the room with excitement when I first realised this! (Mind you, I am rather strange like that!) For me, it created a bridge between science and metaphysics – between biology, psychology and spirituality.

At one level, it is blindingly obvious that the mind affects the body, and that your body can 'read your mind'. If you want to raise your left hand, you simply have that intention and your hand goes up in the air. How does this happen? Until the last few years, we simply did not know. Epigenetic research has plugged that gap between mind and body, and so paved the way for conscious medicine. It bridges the gap between conventional medicine and conscious medicine, taking us from the solid world of the materialist to the psycho-energetic (or conscious) universe of the new paradigm.

DNA AND CONSCIOUSNESS

Einstein's famous equation $E=mc^2$ showed that matter and energy are interconvertible. The new biology shows how that conversion happens within the bodymind system. Thoughts are energy fields which impact on the body via the cellular membrane, triggering proteins that in turn activate DNA. This is crucial in understanding how the mind affects the body.

The new biology shows that it is our consciousness that controls our biology, turning the stress response on or off, moment by moment. We are not controlled by our genes, but by our *perception* of the environment. Our DNA is merely a worker on the factory floor, which manufactures proteins as required. The cellular membrane is a middle manager, paying attention to signals from the environment. (Do you feel safe, or under threat?) What is more, the signals from thoughts are found to override biochemical signals from the body. *The CEO of the body is our consciousness.*

Remarkable research at the Institute of HeartMath has shown that while in a state of heart coherence (see Chapter 2) people can twist or untwist DNA, while it is being observed under a microscope along the corridor or even in a distant laboratory. Some people can even twist DNA in, say, one out of three numbered test tubes, according to precise instructions. Let us be clear that they are twisting or untwisting DNA *using their minds*! And they are influencing DNA other than their own – which opens up the possibility of distant and surrogate healing. (Surrogate healing is when person A stands in for sick person B, accepting the healing on their behalf.) DNA responds to our thoughts, even at a distance. This blows conventional medicine right out of the water – but thanks to epigenetics, we now have a scientific model that explains how it is possible.

In another HeartMath study, twenty-eight researchers were each given a vial of human DNA, and asked to hold it while focusing on either positive or negative emotions. When they focused on positive emotions such as love, joy, gratitude and appreciation, the DNA responded by relaxing and unwinding its strands. When they held negative emotions such as fear, anger, guilt or frustration, the DNA tightened up and became shorter; some of the genes were shut down, limiting the range of possibilities we can choose from.[72] No wonder we talk about feeling 'wound up' or 'shutting down' under stress, and 'unwinding' when we relax and de-stress. Our language mirrors what is happening in our DNA. The more stress we are under, the more we shut down our options, repeat old patterns from the past and block our personal growth. Our genes are damaged – and eventually we become sick.

MOLECULES OF EMOTION

Biologist Candace Pert suggests that the body *is* our subconscious mind.[73] The body mirrors all that we are holding at a subconscious level; and since body and mind are inseparable, it makes more sense to talk about the bodymind (see page xxii). A dynamic network of communication within the bodymind – known as the psychosomatic network – unites the nervous system with the endocrine, immune, respiratory, digestive and other systems. Her pioneering research showed that this network is linked up by information-carrying substances – peptides, hormones and neurotransmitters – which she calls the 'molecules of emotion'. Much of the information never reaches our conscious mind, but we *feel* it through our emotions.

Whenever we feel the negative emotions associated with stress – such as frustration, guilt, loneliness or despair – our bodymind is being pumped full of biochemicals that are damaging to our health. When we feel positive emotions such as unconditional love, joy, passion, hope and appreciation, our bodymind soaks in healthy biochemistry. This is why falling in love has often led to miraculous healing – and why long-term meditators tend to live longer and healthier lives. Feeling good switches off the particle response, and allows your bodymind to heal – or to remain healthy.

Here is an exercise for starting and ending your day in a positive, heart-centred space – and releasing those healthy 'molecules of emotion' into your bodymind:

Exercise
LIVING FROM THE HEART

When you wake in the morning, spend a few minutes focusing on all that you feel happy and grateful for – whether it is your relationships, your home, your work, your health, your pets or whatever. Today, it might be your warm and comfortable bed, or being able to take a hot shower, or having delicious and nourishing food in your kitchen, or hearing the birds sing, or seeing a blue sky. It does not matter what you focus on, as long as it brings up emotions such as love, joy, appreciation and gratitude. These heart-based feelings set up your neurochemistry for a good day ahead.

Then briefly set your intentions for today. Whatever your plans, what do you hope to experience or achieve today? What are you looking forward to? What do you plan that is fun-loving, self-nurturing, creative or joyful today? What will you contribute to the lives of others? Before your feet even touch the bedroom floor, you can set yourself up for a happy and healthy day.

At the end of the day, before you go to sleep, focus on the beautiful moments from that day: a hug with a friend, the soft raindrops that fell on your face, the first daffodils of spring, the orange-streaked sky at sunset, the appreciation from a customer at work . . . Let go of anything that is troubling you, and deliberately focus on what you appreciated today. Fall asleep smiling, and with a warm heart – and you will wake up feeling good too.

(Note: If you are in extreme distress, this exercise will not be possible – and might even make you beat yourself up, or feel worse. The reasons for this will become clear in Chapter 7.)

WE ARE NOT VICTIMS OF OUR GENES

Let's make it clear how the new biology can transform the world of healthcare. In *The Biology of Belief*, Bruce Lipton points out that less than 5 per cent of us are born with faulty genes which result in having a disorder from birth (such as Down's syndrome or cystic fibrosis). The rest of us have genes that are perfectly healthy at birth. As he says, this means that more than 95 per cent of disease is caused by stress. It is stress that turns healthy genes into sick genes.

Our biology is controlled by our perception of the environment. The body is constantly taking its lead from whether we see our environment as safe and loving (from the wave response), or stressful and threatening (from the particle response). We are not helpless victims of our genetic inheritance. Genes cannot turn themselves on or off. We do that ourselves. What makes our genes faulty is chronic stress – which is created by our thoughts and beliefs. *In other words, our cells and genes dance to the tune of consciousness.*

If you are faced by a hungry tiger or a runaway bus, your body will react with the fight-or-flight response, and return to normal as soon as the emergency has passed – and this does not create unhealthy stress. Unhealthy stress comes from the stress response being *inappropriately* and *chronically* triggered, when you are not in immediate physical danger. That is, it comes from your thoughts.

This means that all stress is caused by negative beliefs. As Bruce Lipton puts it, beliefs control our biology. Let me remind you, this is not the view of a clinical psychologist like me, but a molecular biologist. This is what he has learnt from studying cellular biology, and being unafraid to question the old materialist paradigm. Disease quite literally comes from dis-ease.

Some young women who believe their own fate lies helplessly in their genes have had healthy breasts removed because relatives have had breast cancer. In the light of modern epigenetic research, such surgery is based on a false assumption about genetic determinism. In future, these anxious women might be given a book to read about the new biology, along with sessions of energy psychology to relieve their fear and shift their negative beliefs – instead of having a healthy body mutilated.

Even if you do have a congenital disorder, there is evidence that consciousness can affect this too. For example, there is a famous case of a sixteen-year-old English boy who consulted a surgeon about a severe case of warts. After taking a sample for biopsy, the surgeon decided that the warts were too extensive for surgery, so he referred the boy to a doctor who practised hypnosis, which is often effective for warts. Dr Mason suggested to the boy under hypnosis that his unhealthy, thickened, disfigured skin disappear and be replaced by pink, healthy, normal skin – and began to see results. However, the biopsy then revealed that this was not a case of warts but a severe case of congenital ichthyosis, also known as 'fishskin' disease. Dr Mason decided to continue the hypnosis anyway, since he reasoned that it could do no harm. The boy's skin soon improved until it was 60–70 per cent healed, and for the first time in his life, he had normal-looking skin. This improvement was still maintained four years later.[74]

What does this tell us? Again it confirms that consciousness is the CEO of the body, and that it can even overrule congenital defects – as long as we *believe* it can. If this boy had not grown up believing that he simply had warts, but instead was told that he had a genetic disorder, the outcome might have been very different. But it might well be that belief is what blocks the healing even of genetic disorders – and that not only the 95 per cent of stress-triggered disease but even much of the remaining 5 per cent of congenital disease can be healed (or at least improved) using conscious medicine.

AGEING AND STRESS

What about ageing? Isn't disease sometimes related to simple wear and tear on the body, and growing older? It might sound logical, but research suggests that – with a few exceptions – the oldest cells in the human body are seven to ten years old, while many cells live for only a few days or weeks.[75] The cells that line the surface of the gut last only about five days. The epidermis cells of the skin are recycled every two weeks or so. Red blood cells live for about four months. A liver cell lives for about a year. This means that your body is ten years old at the very most! How aged and decrepit would you expect a ten year old to be? Would you expect a ten year old to show signs of wear and tear? Probably not!

Have you noticed how people can suddenly look older after a stressful period in their lives? As many researchers are now saying, ageing is not about how old you are, but about how much time you spend in the stress response. The human body seems to be designed to live for at least 120 years. If you stay out of the stress response, you will look and feel younger – and can even reverse many of the physical signs that we associate with ageing. Letting go of your negative beliefs about ageing will also help!

The body is pure energy-consciousness – and when you are in the wave response, time expands and your body regenerates itself. Forget about having toxic Botox injections or cosmetic surgery! Just focus on de-stressing your life, releasing trauma, being appreciative and filling your days with joy and bliss. The wave response is not only a natural anti-wrinkle cream. It is also the best form of preventive healthcare there is.

SHIFTING OUR PERCEPTIONS

Conventional medicine sees the body as faulty, stupid or inadequate when we become ill, and in need of correction with drugs or surgery. This is because it sees the physical level of reality as the *causal* level. The new biology shows that disease starts in the mind, then gets hard-wired into the body. The stress response slowly damages our physical body (and our genes), and sets up emotional and physical disease.

In the twentieth century, seeing a disease as psychosomatic was tantamount to saying that it was imaginary, that it was 'all in your mind'. We are now realising that, apart from a tiny proportion of disease which is present from birth, every illness is psychosomatic. In a psycho-energetic universe, what matters most is what we think and feel. This is the world of conscious medicine.

Albert Einstein said that 'The field is the sole governing agency of the particle.' In other words, the invisible world – mind, energy, spirit – is what shapes and controls the visible world of matter. This invisible world is now being reclaimed by the new physics and new biology, and it lies at the heart of conscious medicine. The old paradigm suggests that the body is a biochemical machine controlled by genes. The new paradigm says that *the body is an energetic reality shaped by the field of consciousness.* It is our perception and beliefs that control our biology.

We are physical beings, and we can support our physical health at that level – with good nutrition, rest and exercise – but the primary work of healthcare and medicine is to shift our *consciousness.* In truth, I prefer the term healthcare, since the very word 'medicine' keeps us focused on disease rather than wellness. But we have to build bridges from conventional medicine to new approaches, and I see the term 'conscious medicine' as one of those bridges.

Once you think in healthy and positive ways, it becomes natural to take care of yourself physically, remove yourself from toxic and stressful environments, and gravitate towards relationships and activities that make you happy. When you deactivate the stress response, you switch into nature's 'default mode' – the relaxation or wave response. This promotes your normal state of vibrant health and well-being, and whatever your disease – whether it is depression, hypertension, infertility or back pain – you begin to heal. You simply have to let go of the stress response, and live more habitually in the wave response.

If it feels so good when we are in the wave response, why don't we all just relax, chill out and get happy? Why don't we simply get out of stressful situations or relationships, think positively and take good care of ourselves? Because that is easier said than done – for reasons we will explore in the next chapter. As Candace Pert says, the body is our subconscious mind – and our subconscious is stuffed full of beliefs, attitudes and habits that were set up in early childhood, or which came from painful, frightening or traumatic experiences. The particle response throws us back into these subconscious patterns, and keeps us frozen in the past. Happily, these old patterns and traumas can be released – this is what conscious medicine is all about – but first of all, we have to recognise the underlying problem. Then we begin to see that *every* symptom, whether emotional or physical, offers an opportunity for growth and change.

Chapter Four

FROZEN IN THE PAST

In this infinite sea of potentials that exist around us, how come we keep recreating the same realities?

Joe Dispenza[76]

In 1978, Dirk Hamer, the son of a German doctor, was holidaying on a yacht in the Mediterranean when he was shot while asleep by an Italian prince who had gone crazy. He died four months later. Shortly after, his father Geerd Hamer found he had testicular cancer – and his wife also developed breast cancer – and he guessed that there was a link between his son's tragic death and the cancer. He then interviewed women with ovarian cancer – the female equivalent of testicular cancer – and found that, without exception, these women had undergone a traumatic loss or separation before the onset of cancer.[77]

Through intensive medical research over many years, Geerd Hamer found that specific diseases were linked with specific traumas that he called 'biological conflict-shock'. The onset of disease would be marked by having cold hands and feet, disturbed sleep and loss of appetite, and being preoccupied with the problem day and night. The person would usually feel isolated or lonely at this stage, and could see no way of resolving the issue. (These are two common signs of the particle response.) Curiously, it is usually when a resolution is found – either inwardly by making peace with what happened, or through an outer resolution such as finding a new partner or job, or adopting a child – that pain, infection or physical disease eventually shows up. In extreme cases, a heart attack or epileptic fit might arise during the 'healing crisis'.

Geerd Hamer found that the 'scar' of a trauma would show up on a brain CT scan, and he could eventually predict the location of disease in the body, whether current or healed, and what sort of trauma the person had been through, on the basis of a CT scan alone. For example, colon disorders were linked with indigestible anger; a detached retina would arise from 'fearing attack from behind'; bladder problems pointed to territorial conflicts and boundary issues; hearing loss was linked with not wanting to hear something; skin disorders such as eczema were triggered by separation from a loved one; the gall bladder showed problems when there was anger over boundaries being violated; thyroid disorder was linked with an inability to get something one wanted, or to get rid of something unwanted, along with feelings of powerlessness. Lung disorders, according to Hamer, arose from fear of death. This led to the idea that a diagnosis of cancer could *in itself* trigger secondary tumours in the lung, if the person was 'frightened to death' as a result.

These controversial ideas grew into the German New Medicine, which subsequently developed into the diagnostic approach known as Meta-Medicine.[78] Although I have some reservations about linking specific disorders with specific emotional traumas (see Chapter 8) the Meta-Medicine model does fit well with what I have learnt from thousands of clients. Disease begins with trauma, which leaves a person feeling unsafe or unloved – and the body 'speaks' to us about unresolved issues.

Stephanie came to see me because she had fibroids. Her doctor was recommending treatment that might leave her unable to have children, so she was looking for an alternative. A recent scan had shown that there were two fibroids, one slightly larger than the other. Fibroids are often triggered by a painful relationship with a man involving grief and separation – so I asked her, 'If there were two painful episodes with men from your past, what would they be?' She knew in an instant. Her much-loved brother had died suddenly. A few years later, an ex-boyfriend had committed suicide shortly after she ended their relationship, leaving a suicide letter that blamed her for his misery and despair; she sat at his hospital bed while he slowly died. These were her two trigger events, which had made her feel unsafe in the world and disconnected from love – feeling like a particle rather than a wave. Although she had seen a counsellor about these events, talk therapy often reinforces trauma rather than healing it, so the two traumas were still stuck in her energy system, and had eventually shown up physically as two fibroids.

THE LINK BETWEEN TRAUMA AND DISEASE

The field of energy psychology has long recognised the links between disease and trauma. When training as an EFT practitioner, you are repeatedly reminded to look for *specific events* from the past. Instead of working on a general issue such as 'my father was abusive', you might address 'that day when my father threw my teddy into the fire', or 'the night that he came home very drunk and slapped me'. EFT and other forms of energy psychology seem to be one way of releasing trauma, discharging it from our energy system, and helping us move into the relaxation response. Once trauma is healed, symptoms often disappear miraculously.

In recent years, many health practitioners have noticed that allergy is linked to trauma. A woman who was severely allergic to red grapes remembered that she had been eating red grapes when she heard that her mother had been killed in a car accident. Her body associated the grapes with extreme stress, and so had reacted to grapes as if they were 'dangerous' ever since. Another woman who was sexually abused by an uncle when she was a child was given a packet of crisps each time as a reward. She became allergic to salt.[79] When the original trauma is discharged, the allergy tends to go away.

I experienced this myself when I realised that my allergy to mould and dust stemmed from being locked in a wardrobe by my brother at the age of three. After I neutralised the trauma using energy psychology, I could suddenly tolerate dusty environments and mould without becoming sneezy and wheezy, despite decades of allergic response. When the body is given new information, it is no longer frozen in the past and feels safe again.

Conventional medicine tends to ignore the links between emotional trauma and disease. It limits itself to the physical level of reality, and so ignores the world of emotions and relationships – despite the vast evidence relating these to our health. As one of my family doctor friends points out, this is not because doctors are blind to the connection, but because they have no tools or training for *tackling* emotional issues, other than the prescription pad. A model based on materialism reduces everything to the physical level of reality.

A couple of years ago, I walked into the sitting room where my son was watching a TV programme about skin disorders. A woman was showing rough patches of eczema on her arms to a doctor, and saying, 'It began when I had a miscarriage four years ago'. The doctor diagnosed eczema, and told her that if she rubbed steroid cream into it, it would heal the skin disorder. A few minutes later, the scene repeated itself almost exactly. Another woman pointed out pustules and blemishes on her face and back, and said, 'It began when my father died.' Again, the emotional trigger was ignored, and she was prescribed long-term antibiotics for her acne.

The doctor was behaving quite appropriately and professionally within the medical model, which focuses on finding the correct diagnosis and medical treatment rather than looking for the cause of dis-ease. The drugs he prescribed might or might not have suppressed the symptoms. However, drugs would not deal with the emotional *cause* – and unless this was resolved, conscious medicine would expect the underlying problem to show up again, either emotionally or physically.

Most often the true root lies in childhood, and recent events have merely triggered unresolved trauma from the past. I remember a woman I saw soon after I qualified as a clinical psychologist. She was hospitalised with severe endogenous depression, which means depression with no known cause (or 'coming from within'). I talked to this woman on the ward, and asked what had been going on before she became depressed. 'Nothing really. Life as usual. Well, a neighbour died – but I hardly knew him at all.' I knew this death must be significant, since she had mentioned it. Probing for clues, I asked her what the neighbour's name was. 'William', she said. 'Who else have you known called William?' I asked. 'My father', she said, as her eyes filled with tears.

There was the trigger. Her father had died when she was five years old, and her neighbour's death had triggered unresolved grief from childhood. It turned out that this woman often had bronchitis as a child. Every cold or bug would go to her chest, and she would be bedridden for a while. Bronchitis is usually a disorder of the lung meridian, which traditional Chinese medicine links with grief.

Finding out what triggered a dis-ease is not always necessary for healing, but it can lead you back to the original trauma – along with the negative beliefs that were set up at that time. You can then use a variety of tools to heal the past, or change the beliefs. Finding the root can also help you to make sense of an emotional or physical symptom, which in itself can be healing. When we make connections, it often restores a sense of wholeness. Instead of feeling like the helpless victim of a symptom or disease, we see that it is meaningful.

Exercise
FINDING THE DIS-EASE TRIGGER

Whatever the dis-ease, whether emotional or physical, look for the root of the problem. This often means asking a series of questions:

1. When did you first notice the symptoms?

2. What was happening in your life just before that? What was bothering you? What changes were going on? (Note: For serious diseases or chronic complaints, which can be set up over a long period, you might need to look at what was happening in the previous two to three years or more. I find that the majority of people just 'know' what triggered their illness when asked.)

3. How did that make you feel (e.g. sad, lonely, criticised, abandoned, helpless, frightened, guilty, furious, invisible, inadequate, ashamed, unloved, disappointed, frustrated, resentful, betrayed, bewildered, unwanted, confused)?

4. When was the earliest time you remember feeling that way?

5. What negative belief or decision arose from that experience (e.g. I am not safe in the world. Men abandon me. I am not good enough. I must hide my feelings.)? If you are not sure, just take a guess. Or imagine that you are talking to that part of you that does know.

Once you know what triggered a disease, you can tackle it by writing about it in a journal, writing an imaginary letter to the person involved then burning it, using EFT or other forms of energy psychology, 'shaking it out' (see page 81), doing inner journeys using visualisation, for example to meet your inner child, or a future self or guide who can help you heal the past – or directly changing the negative beliefs that were set up by that event.

THE FREEZE RESPONSE

Most people are familiar with the fight-or-flight response. However, there is a third response that can be triggered by stress. Whenever you feel threatened, *yet cannot take any action to deal with it,* it leads to a state of traumatised helplessness. You are like a rabbit frozen in headlights. There is nothing you can do. This is known as the freeze response – and it seems to be crucial in understanding why human beings are uniquely susceptible to trauma. It explains why people find it so hard to change – feeling stuck and unable to resolve issues, clinging to situations that are causing stress, repeating the same patterns and making the same self-destructive choices. It locks us into stress, and so paves the way for chronic disease.

Whereas the fight-or-flight response prepares us for action, the freeze response paralyses us. If you watch an animal being chased by a predator, it might suddenly 'play dead'; or it might run until exhausted, then when pounced upon it becomes stock still. This is the freeze response. At this point, endorphins flood into its system, providing instant pain relief and a 'natural high' if it is going to be eaten. Becoming immobile might also give it a better chance of survival, since few hunters will eat an animal that already seems to be dead. It is also likely that its consciousness leaves its body in preparation for death – just as when we are involved in a serious accident in which death seems imminent. Countless people have reported an 'out-of-body experience' when facing death, or even when getting shocking and traumatic news – a state in which they are free from any fear or pain.

If the freeze response becomes chronic, stress is internalised – and we are in deep trouble. This state was first recognised by Sigmund Freud and Josef Breuer, in the early days of psychoanalysis. During the First World War, when soldiers were fighting helplessly in the trenches, it became known as shell shock. More recently, it has been called post-traumatic stress disorder (or PTSD). Many doctors, biologists and psychologists now suspect that PTSD is far more pervasive than we once thought – perhaps almost universal – and that chronic shock and trauma have a crucial role to play in emotional and physical dis-ease.

Chronic illness and disease are uncommon in the wild. Unless they are caged or domesticated, animals tend to either get sick and die, or quickly recover from illness. So why do so many human beings suffer from chronic and degenerative conditions? Why are we seeing so many autoimmune diseases? Why are so many people anxious or depressed? One answer to this is that we are *collectively* suffering from shock and trauma, and passing it on to the next generation. We get stuck in the particle response, and do not discharge trauma in the healthy and natural way that animals do.

Peter Levine is a psychologist, medical biophysicist and former stress consultant to NASA.[80] He observed that wild animals that have been traumatised into the freeze response, yet survived the ordeal, will always shake violently afterwards. They literally shake the trauma out of their energy system. They might also show odd movements such as running while lying down, as if they are 'completing' their escape. After this, their physiology returns to normal, as if nothing ever happened. In fact, research suggests that trauma builds resilience – and that avoiding change and stress is not necessarily good for us. Both animals and humans become stronger after trauma, *as long as it is discharged*.

UNDISCHARGED TRAUMA

It was a young woman called Nancy who first helped Peter Levine realise that trauma was held in the body as well as the mind. Nancy was suffering from intense panic attacks and agoraphobia, and felt unable to leave her house alone. When Peter guided her into a state of relaxation, this triggered a full-blown anxiety attack. She became paralysed, and appeared to stop breathing. Intuitively he exclaimed, 'You're being attacked by a tiger. Run towards that tree!' To his amazement, she let out a bloodcurdling scream, and her legs began to tremble rhythmically as if she were running.

Nancy continued to tremble, shake and sob convulsively for almost an hour – and recalled a childhood incident from when she was three years old. She had been hospitalised to have her tonsils removed, and was strapped to a table while she was given ether. Feeling suffocated, helpless and unable to move, she had been deeply traumatised. (Surgical operations and dental treatment are a frequent source of childhood trauma.) After that session of shaking, with her childhood trauma discharged,

Nancy had no more anxiety attacks – and went on to complete her doctorate degree. She also reported feeling more happy and alive than ever before.

I have had personal experience of 'shaking medicine'.[81] During some of my healing sessions with Tjitze de Jong, who specialises in cancer, my body would spontaneously jerk and twist and go into circling motions around my spine. Sometimes the jerking was so violent that it felt like having a *grand mal* fit. At the same time, emotions connected with the events that triggered the cancer would come up to be released – intense grief and sadness, anger, guilt, anxiety, bewilderment and confusion. Sometimes aftershocks of the physical shaking would continue for a day or two afterwards, as my energy system re-balanced itself.

Neurologist Bob Scaer,[82] building upon Peter Levine's work, believes that most disease results from undischarged trauma – in other words, going beyond fight–flight into the freeze response and getting stuck there. If it is not discharged, trauma remains locked in your energy system, and you cycle between the fight–flight and freeze responses. You might have emotional symptoms such as being anxious, hypervigilant, unable to relax, hypersensitive, overprotective, fearful and avoidant, along with characteristic feelings of shame, guilt and inadequacy. You might be drawn to endurance sports or thrill-seeking behaviour in adult life, re-enacting the physiology of the earlier trauma. You might also develop tics, nailbiting, clumsiness, stammers, nightmares, memory loss, palpitations, self-mutilation, eating disorders and addictions, as well as chronic pain or almost any chronic disease. Even hunching in old age arises from stress and trauma rather than ageing, says Bob Scaer, and is due to habitually holding a defensive posture to protect your vulnerable heart and abdomen.

So next time you have a shock – whether emotional or physical – let your body shake! And if you have traumas from the past that need to be released, shaking medicine which taps into your innate healing wisdom is one way of removing trauma from your bodymind.

Exercise
SHAKE YOUR BOOGIE!

Set aside an hour or so when you will not be disturbed –
ideally, somewhere you will not be overheard. Write down
two or three events from the past that you suspect might be
stuck in your energy system. These might be serious traumas
from adult life – such as a car accident, or your child being
hospitalised, getting a life-threatening diagnosis, or your
partner abruptly walking out – or more minor traumas from
early childhood, such as wetting your pants in nursery school,
going to the dentist or getting lost in a market square.
(The younger you are, the more easily you can become
traumatised.)

Put on some drumming or dancing music with a strong
rhythmical beat, then let your body do its own thing.[83] Focus
your mind on a trauma from the past, then shake to the music.
It does not matter if you have no memory of that time, but
simply know that it happened. Your body knows what to do, so
trust it to lead the way. Listen to your body. Notice your bodily
sensations. Get out of your own way, and let your instinctive
movements release the trauma from your body. Let yourself
shake, run on the spot, squirm, twist, unwind, lie down and let
your body move itself, scream, go wild. Let loose! Shake your
boogie!

(Note: Unless you are working with a therapist, only use this
approach for minor to moderate trauma. If you are dealing with
severe trauma such as childhood abuse, rape, war trauma or
serious road accidents, I strongly recommend that you see a
qualified therapist who uses an energy-based approach to
healing. Avoid traditional talk therapies, which can reinforce and
deepen the trauma.)

SHOCK AND STRESS

Neuropsychologist and writer Stephanie Mines grew up with domestic violence and abuse that left her in a chronic state of shock. She would suddenly freeze, become speechless and go into a foggy numbness, along with many other symptoms ranging from trembling and panic to feeling trapped. Stephanie had grown up with chronic feelings of shame, guilt and inadequacy – which she later learnt were signs of shock. It wasn't until she had young children herself, and left a difficult marriage, that she came to recognise what was 'wrong' with her, and began to heal herself using energy-based approaches.

In her book *We Are All in Shock*, Stephanie Mines distinguishes between two different forms of shock – sympathetic and parasympathetic. Sympathetic shock corresponds to being in a chronic fight–flight response, and is marked physically by hyperactivity, sweating, darting eyes, inhibited digestion, muscular tension or pain, disturbed sleep, and an increase in heart rate, blood pressure, blood glucose and metabolic rate. It can also lead to various heart conditions. Psychologically you might have emotional outbursts, be prone to compulsive talking, edgy laughter, over-busyness, and bouts of agitation or even panic attacks. You become a stress junkie, which is a vicious cycle. You might suffer from addictions – such as alcoholism, workaholism or codependency – which are part of the fight–flight response. It might be difficult to reach orgasm. You are likely to be irritable, attacking or even aggressive under stress, or want to run away. Others might see you as driven, tense or controlling. Sympathetic shock is like a 'raging fire', and reddened skin is one outward sign of it. It is like keeping your foot on the accelerator.

Parasympathetic shock is linked with depression, tiredness and fatigue, and an increased need for sleep. This corresponds with the freeze response. Physically the body produces more mucus, tears and inflammation, and your heart rate and blood pressure decrease. You feel less able to handle stress – whereas in sympathetic shock you might even seek it out. Psychologically you might be socially withdrawn, and feel resigned, defeated or in despair. When faced with emotional intimacy, you become stiff and frozen, so you avoid it whenever possible. Sexual desire is lost or minimal. You might suddenly disconnect from emotions, or abruptly withdraw from relationships. Others might see you as weak and passive, or cold and distant. Parasympathetic shock is comparable to a 'frozen body of ice', and your skin tends to be pale. It is like keeping your foot on the brake.

Like Bob Scaer, Stephanie Mines notes that although you might be primarily in sympathetic or parasympathetic shock, many people cycle between these two states – with one foot on the accelerator, and the other on the brake – in a chronic state of stress. In both states, there are pervasive feelings of shame, guilt and insecurity. You feel sure there is something wrong with you.

Shock also affects your relationships, making you withdraw from others, attack them or defend yourself against them. It is hard to connect deeply with anyone – or even with nature – when you are in shock. However, the real problem is the painful *feeling of separation*, which in itself is a sure sign of shock. Feeling separate means you are stuck in the particle response. You have lost touch with your wave self, which always has a deep sense of loving connection.

If you live with chronic stress for too long, you might head towards burnout – which is the end-stage of both sympathetic and parasympathetic shock. At this point, your adrenal glands are exhausted, levels of the stress hormone cortisol fall away, and you can no longer cope with stress in the way you used to. Your energy level dips, and you need more rest and sleep. Now you become at high risk of disorders such as chronic fatigue syndrome (ME), fibromyalgia, underactive thyroid, multiple allergies, rheumatoid arthritis, depression, lupus and other autoimmune disorders, and (for women) an early menopause and severe menopausal symptoms. A famous example of burnout would be Florence Nightingale, who spent fifty years housebound and mostly bedridden with fatigue after her work in the Crimean War; she was suffering from the end-stage of chronic shock.

Most clients I have seen with fibromyalgia – a diagnosis characterised by widespread muscle pain, stiffness and fatigue – have lived with chronic stress and tension for many years, and often went through childhood abuse. Bernadette's story was fairly typical. Her father was in the army, and he was away for long periods. When he returned, to a distant and unhappy marriage, he drank heavily and sometimes became violent. Although Bernadette was never hit herself, she watched her mother and older sisters being thumped and bashed against walls, or even thrown downstairs, and she lived in fear of him. When her father was away, the situation was not much better. Her mother blamed the children for keeping her trapped in the marriage, and would lash out verbally or lock them in a cupboard without any apparent provocation. Bernadette's only refuge was school, and even there she was sometimes bullied. She married at the age of seventeen to escape the family, but not surprisingly, found herself with a man who was alcoholic and violent. By the time she divorced him, twenty years later, she had been taking Prozac for depression for several years, and had a diagnosis of fibromyalgia.

If you suspect that you might be suffering from chronic shock from the descriptions above, it can be helpful to identify whether you tend towards sympathetic or parasympathetic shock – or spend equal times in both states – since this points towards the inner shifts and lifestyle changes which you need to make. In either case, energy-based tools can also help to retrain your neurochemistry out of the habitual stress response.

Exercise
HEALING SHOCK: COOLING FIRE, WARMING ICE

If you lean towards sympathetic shock, you will be an adrenalin junkie. You need to slow down, and use practices that force you to be still and quiet – such as meditation, yoga, journalling and walking (rather than jogging, working out or running marathons). Spend time in nature. Chill out more. Become aware of the fears that drive you. Notice when you are overreacting to others, and bringing the past into the present. Be clear about your own boundaries. Make genuine eye contact with people.

If you are prone to parasympathetic shock, you need to find the courage to be visible. You might be vulnerable to abuse. Notice your pattern of withdrawing, giving in or taking refuge when you feel anxious. Learn to express your feelings more openly and honestly, as they come up. Commit yourself to being authentic. Reclaim yourself through creative expression – perhaps art, writing, pottery, creative cookery or garden design. Be aware of your own uniqueness and individuality, instead of merging with others or sacrificing yourself.

ECHOES FROM THE PAST

In conscious medicine, the primary cause of emotional and physical dis-ease is stress and trauma – which leads to negative beliefs and the particle response. Although I focus more on physical disease in this book, the same principles apply to psychological problems. No one has a chemical imbalance or genetic disorder which *causes* depression, bipolar disorder, anxiety or any other mental health problems. Both emotional and physical disease stem from disturbances in the *invisible* world – the world of energy-consciousness – which then ripple down to the physical level.

Bipolar disorder, for example, is a mental health problem that is commonly seen as 'caused' by faulty genes or disturbed biochemistry. Therapist and author Sasha Allenby used to struggle with bipolar disorder, along with multiple addictions and chronic fatigue syndrome (also known as ME). Then she discovered energy psychology and other forms of healing, and began to recover. At a workshop on Matrix Reimprinting,[84] Sasha recalled a traumatic incident from childhood in which some inappropriate photographs were taken of her. Although she had managed to obtain and destroy these photographs as an adult, there was still a frozen and traumatised self locked away. Talking about the memory triggered the stress response, and she began to descend rapidly into a black hole of depression – which she knew from long experience would last for weeks.

Fortunately, an experienced practitioner noticed Sasha's distress and helped her to heal the event. In her imagination, the frozen self from the past was given a box of matches, and encouraged to burn the photographs. To Sasha's amazement, the depression lifted immediately – and this marked the abrupt end of her bipolar disorder. It has never returned. A serious condition that had lasted twenty years, and which most doctors see as genetic or biochemical in origin, was totally resolved in half an hour – by healing the event that first triggered it.[85]

In Matrix Reimprinting, the 'self' that dissociates under stress is known as an ECHO (Energetic Conscious Hologram). It is literally an echo from the past that has remained frozen in time – initially as a way of protecting the self. Dissociation was the best way of coping at the time. Every time you go into the freeze response, at any age, you dissociate and an ECHO splits off. However, these ECHOs hold traumas in your subconscious – or more accurately, in your energy field. This means that part of you is forever re-living that event, along with the negative beliefs and decisions that were made at that time, with all the knock-on effects for your physiology and health.

The good news is that you can visit these ECHOs, using guided imagery that directly accesses the subconscious mind, and heal the trauma. The subconscious does not distinguish between what is real and what is imagined – so you can create new memories, provide resources that your younger self did not have, or make new decisions. Your frozen selves can thaw, so that you no longer have a hairline trigger for the stress response. It will be harder for anyone to 'push your buttons', and you are more likely to remain conscious and respond with love, whatever the situation. This will prevent future health problems – *and* you can live more fully in the present, instead of reacting habitually from the past.

Soul loss

In shamanism – probably the oldest form of medicine – this splitting-off of traumatised selves is known as soul loss, and is seen as a primary cause of disease.[86] In modern psychology, we call it dissociation or splitting. It is a protective mechanism designed only for dire emergency, yet it can become chronic – leaving us frozen in the past.

When I worked in the National Health Service, I saw a young woman who had been sexually abused, who used to put herself in the keyhole of her bedroom door as soon as her father crept in and lifted up her bedclothes. She had found an effective way of using the freeze response, so that she was not in her body while 'it' was being abused. However, it soon became a habit to leave her body whenever she felt under the slightest stress – which was most of the time. She cycled between panic and feelings of emptiness. The lights were on, but no one was home. When you're out of your body, you are also out of your life.

I recently saw a woman with coeliac disease – a severe intolerance to gluten. When Martha was three years old, she had a stomach bug that passed on to her pregnant mother, who went into premature labour. The baby died, and when her mother came home from hospital, and Martha excitedly asked, 'Where's the baby?' she was pushed aside and told to be quiet. Somehow she came to believe that the baby's death was her fault – that she was bad and toxic. Since this message was something that she 'could not digest', she became a sickly child who never seemed to thrive. Many years later, she was diagnosed with coeliac disease.

In our session together, Martha revisited the scene of her mother coming home from hospital – and asked young Martha what she would have liked to happen. This time, in a re-imagined scene using Matrix Reimprinting, her mother was overjoyed to see her again, and reassured her that the baby's death had nothing to do with her. This new 'memory' was then broadcast to her digestive system, throughout the cells of her body, and into her whole energy field. Her subconscious received the new message that she is lovable, that she is allowed to be here, and that she is safe to be around. Although there were still other traumas to heal, the shame, guilt and fear that had been built into her digestive system from that incident were healed. Her frozen self had returned to a warm fireside, and a great burden was lifted.

For many people, getting in touch with the body, feelings and sensuality is one of the keys to recovering from shock and trauma. Trauma makes us dissociate from the body. As you reconnect with your senses and are willing to feel again, it gives those dissociated parts the message that it is now safe to 'come home'. For some people, body-centred practices such as yoga and breathwork, or sensual creative arts such as pottery and gardening, might be enough to soothe the neurochemistry and slowly bring you out of chronic stress and dissociation over a long period. Other people might need to release trauma more directly and consciously, using energy psychology, body-based psychotherapy or other forms of conscious medicine. (See Resources for Health and Well-being at the back.)

TRAUMA IN CHILDHOOD

Compared to almost any animal, human beings have a very long childhood, and we are highly dependent on our parents or caretakers. This means that many of us learn to tune into others' emotions as a survival strategy from an early age. Any sign of disapproval, criticism, rejection, prolonged separation or threatened abandonment in the early years of childhood might be perceived as an emergency, and lead to the fight-flight freeze response. Now that we have nuclear families rather than close-knit communities, there might be no other loving person to turn to, so our very existence can feel threatened when a parent is not happy with our behaviour, or pays no attention to us. The stress response is triggered – and until the trauma is released, it remains stuck in our bodymind indefinitely. In later life, facing others' disapproval – instead of being a minor event – might feel like a life or death emergency.

Let's suppose that, when you were three years old, your mother was suddenly taken into hospital and you did not see her for several months. That day, you had played in the mud and messed up your clothes. Your unwell mother, struggling to cope, was cross with you. Then she disappears and you are told that she is very ill. What does your three-year-old self conclude? That you have been very bad and made your mother angry and sick, so she has abandoned you. *Emergency!* What might you decide as a result? 'I have to be good and perfect, or I will be abandoned.' Or 'I must please others, or something terrible might happen.' Or even, 'I am a bad and evil person, and I can make people ill.' This happened to a close friend of mine. When his mother eventually returned home, he did not seem to recognise her – a sign of a deeply traumatised child.

He grew up to be a doctor, trying to heal the sick to compensate for 'making' his mother ill, to recover his sense of power, and overcome the childhood belief that he was somehow bad and toxic. He was terrified of anyone being angry with him, and jumped through hoops to please others and avoid upsetting anyone, regardless of his own needs and wishes. Catching the faintest whiff of disapproval would send him scurrying into the stress response. Not surprisingly, he went through bouts of depression, as well as chronic anxiety, guilt and workaholism – with physical symptoms such as irritable bowel syndrome and frequent headaches – and his personal relationships were deeply troubled.

Trauma arises whenever we feel both *threatened and help-less*, so a young child is readily traumatised. Being hit, criticised or shouted at by a parent ('You stupid child!', 'You spoilt brat!', 'You're so clumsy!', 'Don't be a cry baby!', 'Bad girl!', 'Don't be a nuisance!') can throw you into fear, damage your self-esteem and trigger chronic stress that slowly damages your physiology. The younger you are, the more easily you are traumatised. Being left alone to cry when you are a baby – or even being kept in an incubator at birth – might set up a lifelong fear of abandonment, with knock-on effects for all your adult relationships, as well as your mental and physical health, until that early memory is healed.

Any event that makes you feel threatened – physically or emotionally – can be traumatic, especially in the first seven years of life. Many of my clients have found that ordinary childhood events such as wetting their pants in nursery school, ripping a coat which reduced an impoverished parent to tears, feeling that a brother or sister was favoured over them, or being mocked for wearing glasses, have left them deeply shamed, fearful or insecure, with repercussions which can ripple on for decades.

Children who feel unloved seem to be most vulnerable to trauma. In one study 95 per cent of students who reported low levels of parental love and care were later diagnosed with serious disease in midlife, compared with 29 per cent of those who rated their parents as loving and caring.[87] Almost every client I have seen with life-threatening disease as a young adult went through severe childhood trauma – usually taking the form of early death or (perceived) abandonment or neglect by a parent, and/or emotional, physical or sexual abuse.[88] Some were the result of an unwanted pregnancy – even if they were later loved – and so received an injunction to die while still in the womb.[89]

Up to the age of seven, whatever you witness or experience is downloaded directly into the subconscious mind. It is not processed by your conscious brain, which is still developing. It simply gets filed away as the truth. From then on, future events will be filtered and distorted by this new belief or experience.

Perhaps you see your parents being polite with each other through gritted teeth, and you conclude that 'When there is a problem, you avoid talking about it,' or, 'If you are angry, it is best to hide it.' Then you repeat that dysfunctional pattern in your adult relationships. Or your mother shouts at you for not coming when she calls, transforming herself into a terrifying demon, and you decide that 'If mother is angry, it is my fault'. This might slowly generalise over time into 'I am responsible for other people's happiness and well-being' or 'I am faulty, and must hide my true self from others or they will reject me.' Now you have a subconscious belief that will create stress in almost every situation.

If you lived with chronic stress and tension in childhood, you are likely to have a trigger-happy amygdala, which responds to the most benign of situations by pressing the red alarm button. At best, you will go into fight mode, which leaves you hyperactive, driven and unable to relax. At worst, you might become a frozen automaton, barely able to make decisions, insecure and paralysed by fear. You might seem to function normally to the outside world, but you are sleep-walking through life — living in survival mode, and unaware that you are locked into chronic stress.

As an adult, you are likely to pass on your beliefs and behaviour to your children (or other children around you), just as your parents passed on their family patterns to you. A woman who felt unsafe around men in childhood, for example, might be reluctant to let her children play out alone in the garden, telling herself that a paedophile might walk past. She might never speak of her irrational fears to her children, or might even see herself as being rightly protect-ive and motherly — yet she is energetically passing her fears on to the next generation, with all its consequences for emotional and physical health. Another mother might pass on beliefs in a safe and loving universe, positive views of men, and seeing people as creators of their lives rather than victims — leaving her children far less likely to have a trigger-happy amygdala as they grow up.

Research has found that babies adapt to their mother's stress levels while still in the womb — and that by the age of six months after birth, a base level of the stress hormone, cortisol, is set.[90] A stressed mother can give birth to a child who is already primed for emergency, and whose forebrain is less well developed. Before they even walk or talk, children can be programmed to live in fear. Nature is preparing the baby for a dangerous environment — even if the 'danger' is all in the mother's head, and comes from her own childhood.

Some children readily become upset or have temper tantrums from an early age – a sign of high cortisol, and flipping readily into fight–flight. Other young children are placid, quiet, unresponsive and 'easy' – which can be a sign of low cortisol. This is an adaptation to extreme stress based on the freeze response, when chronic stress seems unavoidable and there is no point in even preparing for fight or flight. Either way, the family baton of stress is passed down to the next generation.

BELIEFS FROM THE PAST

Our beliefs are the key to our health and happiness. When we talk about inherited disease, we are probably talking mostly about inherited patterns of *thinking*. Particle thinking. Obstetrician-gynaecologist Christiane Northrup notes that the black sheep of families – those who do not follow in the family footsteps – do not tend to get the diseases that 'run in the family'.[91] Remember that genes are activated by *consciousness*. What we inherit from our parents is their beliefs and emotional patterns. It is up to us to break any chain of pain, and pass healthy beliefs and attitudes on to our children.

Children do not just learn from what we say. They learn by watching what we do, and tuning into our emotions. So whenever you make conscious choices based upon love, freedom and joy – rather than subconscious choices based upon fear, guilt, habit or duty – you are not only protecting your health for the future, but giving a gift to the next generation. And since all consciousness is interconnected, as you let go of your own fear-based beliefs, you also help to heal the world.

One crucial factor for health and happiness is whether you believe in a loving God or a judgemental God. A study of those diagnosed with HIV/AIDS found that belief in a loving God was a hugely protective factor in their illness. Those who believed in a judgemental God were far more vulnerable to opportunistic infections and early death.[92] If you believe in a judgemental God – or were fed such beliefs in early childhood – you will readily fall into criticism, blame, shame or guilt, all of which take you out of the wave response, and you will live with a constant sense of threat and anxiety. Belief in 'original sin' or a judgemental God is a major health risk.[93]

Here are just a few examples of the negative beliefs that might be set up in childhood:

❖ Life is a struggle

❖ I am not good enough

❖ I have to be perfect to be loved

❖ The world is a dangerous place

❖ You cannot trust anyone

❖ I must hide my feelings

❖ I must be in control

❖ I have to keep smiling to stay safe

❖ I have to hide (or be invisible) to stay safe

❖ Love hurts

❖ I'm unlovable

❖ I'm not important

❖ I'm stupid

❖ I'm helpless

❖ I'm a failure

❖ I'm a nuisance

❖ I can never get it right

❖ I will be abandoned

❖ No one ever notices me

◇ I am responsible for other people's happiness

◇ Other people are responsible for my happiness

◇ I'm not in charge of my own life

◇ Everyone else's needs come first

◇ I'm guilty and deserve to be punished

◇ God only loves me when I am good and perfect

◇ There's no point in trying

◇ I'll always be second best

◇ There is never enough to go round

◇ Better the devil you know

◇ As you get older, you get sicker

◇ Men are . . .

◇ Women are . . .

Any negative belief becomes a self-fulfilling prophecy (as we shall see), so we get 'evidence' of it everywhere. We prove it to ourselves, making the belief even stronger. We repeat the same situations, over and over again – and so family patterns pass down the generations. Change your beliefs, and the evidence changes too!

Remember that stress is a verb and not a noun. Stress is not about what happens to us, but about what we do to ourselves. Undischarged shock and trauma can leave you highly vulnerable to stress. Anything that vaguely reminds you of the original trauma may trigger the stress response, flooding your body with adrenalin and corticosteroids – the stress hormones – to prepare your body for an emergency. Our biology is controlled primarily by our perceptions of the environment. However, our perceptions are filtered through our *beliefs*.

How you respond to a situation depends not on what happens, but on how you *interpret* what happens. Our beliefs are like wearing spectacles of a certain colour, which distort how we view everything that happens. Your spectacles might selectively 'see' criticism, or watch out for threatened abandonment, or they might see the world as friendly and benign. We tend to see what we expect to see. For example, one man whose boss shouts at him might react with panic, cover up and deny the shameful incident, and work feverishly through the night in an attempt to regain his boss's approval. (Approval-seeking is part of the flight response.) Someone else might react to the same event with anger, blame and self-righteousness – 'How dare he speak to me like that? What is *wrong* with that man?' – which is the 'fight' side of the stress response. They might then contemplate making a formal complaint against their boss (fight mode), or even resigning from their job (flight mode). A third person might shrug it off. 'Watch out – he must be having a bad day!', they wink at their colleagues as they cheerily relate the story. The first two have been triggered into the particle response, while the third has not.

Why do people react so differently to the same event? Because they are filtering the same experience through a different set of beliefs and attitudes. They are wearing different spectacles. For many people, the traumas of the past reverberate into their present – which means they are easily pulled into the particle response. Their amygdala is triggered, and they overreact on autopilot. There are many ways of healing this pain, but the first step is to recognise that it is a problem.

Negative beliefs from childhood can be readily reprogrammed, as long as you know how to access the subconscious mind. Simply deciding to change a belief doesn't work. The subconscious needs to feel safe and relaxed before it will listen to anything new – so one way to address the subconscious is to relax deeply, *then* use affirmations or inner journeys or self-hypnosis CDs (see Resources, page 330).

The subconscious learns through repetition, so the more often you say or think something, the deeper the neural pathways become for that thought, and the easier it becomes to think that thought in future. This is why affirmations can be effective if you use them consistently over a period. (We will look at why affirmations can fail in Chapter 7.) The subconscious is also visual, so using inner journeys (through visualisation) is a good way to communicate with it. And since it is connected to your body and your right brain, techniques that involve touch and movement, or which connect both hemispheres of the brain, tend to work well.

Kinesiology and the bodymind

Kinesiology – a form of biofeedback that involves muscle-testing – is another powerful tool for both asking questions of the bodymind, and for re-programming the subconscious. I've trained in various forms of kinesiology over the years, and often use these techniques at workshops and with clients. It is used in many new healing techniques such as Psych-K, the Lifeline Technique and BodyTalk. (See Resources for Health and Well-being, page 325.)

There are various ways of muscle-testing yourself, but the most reliable way is to work with a partner, and test an arm muscle. It is a curious fact that our muscles go weak when we make a statement that is not true, or which our subconscious mind does not believe, or when we hold anything negative or stressful in mind. Stress, negativity and lack of authenticity short-circuit our energy system.

Most people are amazed when they experience this for the first time. They try hard to hold up their arm after saying 'My name is Harry' (when it is not), but their arm goes weak. Or you can test for 'I want to heal' if someone is ill – and very often, the muscle-test will be weak, showing that their bodymind does *not* want to heal. A weak test shows that energy is short-circuited. That is, their subconscious mind is in conflict with the statement. This makes muscle-testing an excellent way of accessing information from the subconscious mind, or bodymind.

Whether or not you went through obvious childhood

trauma, you are likely to have some negative beliefs that are limiting your life – and which could be a health risk. Changing your core beliefs is a huge step towards staying more consistently in the wave response, and taking stress and trauma out of your energy system. And a stress-free energy system means a happy and healthy person!

Here are some ways of shifting your core beliefs using energy tools. This works far more rapidly than using spoken or written affirmations, since it allows you to talk directly to your subconscious mind. Changing your beliefs can have a profound impact on your life – and it feels so good that you are likely to want to keep using this process, until you have tracked down any beliefs that are keeping you stuck or frozen. Sometimes shifting just one core belief has a domino effect that can change your life!

Exercise
CHANGING YOUR CORE BELIEFS

Put aside an hour or so when you can work with a friend or partner. Drink some water beforehand, and keep water available.

How to muscle-test with a partner:

Hold one arm out, parallel to the floor. Your partner stands to one side, holding your shoulder lightly while pressing down briefly just above your outstretched wrist with their other hand. Say 'Be strong' or 'Hold' before testing the muscle. Look down at the floor while you are being tested. Do not make eye contact. A strong (Yes) test – a muscle that has a strong bounce, or feels strong – shows that energy is flowing well.

To establish muscle-testing, your partner should:

1. Check whether you have a preference for which arm to use, or any arm or shoulder injury.

2. Ask you to say 'My name is [your first name]' – which should

give a strong test. Then to say, 'My name is [choose a name of opposite sex]' – which should give a weak test. Then say 'Yes, Yes, Yes', and muscle-test; then 'No, No, No', and test. This should give a strong, then a weak test.

3. If all muscle tests are weak, you should both drink more water. If all tests are strong, you both need to use the Whole Brain Posture (see opposite) for one to two minutes.

Make sure your partner is not testing for muscle strength by pushing too hard or for too long. They should be simply testing for a strong bounce when they press briefly. Once you have established clear tests, your partner has established a good connection with your subconscious mind and can then check out your beliefs using muscle-testing. You need to repeat the above every time you want to work with beliefs.

How to muscle-test on your own:

If you have to work alone, one method of asking a question or testing a belief is the Sway Test. While standing up, state the belief, or ask a yes-no question, then allow your body to sway forward (for Yes) or backwards (for No). It is uncanny how this works, but you have to remember that 'your body is your subconscious mind'. It can control the right muscles without your conscious mind knowing the answer.

Muscle-test for each of the following statements. These are twenty core beliefs that will support your health and well-being:

1. The Universe is friendly and loving.

2. I deserve to be happy and loved.

3. I am safe in the world.

4. I am in charge of my own life.

5. I love and accept myself as I am.

6. I am a necessary and important part of Divine Intelligence.

7. My body is my friend.

8. I trust my body to heal itself.

9. I am authentic and true to myself in my relationships.

10. I see the best in everyone and everything.

11. I forgive others for all the bad things that have happened to me.

12. I forgive myself for all the choices I have made.

13. My needs are as important as anyone else's.

14. There is plenty of time.

15. I can trust other people.

16. I take 100 per cent responsibility for my life.

17. I am divinely guided in every moment.

18. I expect the best to happen.

19. I welcome growth and change in my life.

20. My life is unfolding perfectly.

If you test weak on any of these beliefs, use any of the methods below to re-programme your subconscious mind. The first method below is very often enough to shift things. Any or all of the other three can be used to strengthen the new belief. You can also use the techniques below to install any positive belief of your choice into your subconscious mind (for example, I am creating healthy relationships. Money flows easily into my life. My body is now healing itself. I want to heal.).

a) **Whole Brain Posture** – If you are right-handed, cross your right ankle over your left ankle. Then hold your arms in front of you, and cross your right wrist over the left wrist, palms down. (Or vice versa if you are left-handed – or if it just feels right to do it that way.) Now curl your fingers down towards each other, and clasp them together. You can rest your twisted arms on your lap, or curl them under and rest them on your chest, whichever feels more comfortable. Hold this posture while you repeat the new belief to yourself, either out loud or silently, a few times.

Now be aware of what happens. Just pay attention. You might notice voices in your head that argue with the new belief, and you might wish to give those voices a positive new perspective. Memories might come to mind. You might feel energy shifts in your body. Whatever happens is fine. Stay focused on what you are doing, and repeat the belief occasionally if it feels right.

After a few minutes, you might take a deep breath, or notice yourself relaxing, or you might sense a shift in energy, or just 'know' that you are done. It rarely takes more than five minutes. Then open your eyes, uncross your ankles, and hold your hands in front of you, with all your fingertips touching in the chapel position. Look down through your fingers at the floor, and repeat your new belief. Hold your gaze for ten seconds to anchor the new belief.

b) **Cross-crawls** – Walk on the spot, lifting each leg high and touching the opposite knee with your hand with each step. Twist your waist to get a crossover effect. Do this for about 30 seconds or until it feels right to stop, while repeating the new belief out loud, over and over again.

c) **Ear-rolls** – Unroll the fold of your ears with your fingers, starting where your ears join your skull and moving up and around your ear. Do this for about thirty seconds, while repeating the new belief again and again.

d) **Figure of 8s** – Inscribe a large infinity sign (an elongated figure of eight on its side) with one of your thumbs, while following your thumb with your eyes. Keep your head still. Make sure your eyes do not 'jump' at any point. If you are working with a partner, they should watch your eyes carefully. If they notice a jump, slow down and repeat that section again. Keep saying the belief out loud throughout. Keep going for a minute or two, or until you feel 'done'.[94]

Keep using the methods above until you get a very firm Yes to a muscle-test on each positive belief. (It is possible for beliefs to shift somewhat but not fully at first – though even a small shift is worthwhile.) In the days that follow, watch out for signs that your beliefs have shifted.

THE TRIUNE BRAIN

Let's look briefly at how stress and trauma affect the brain, keeping negative beliefs from the past running constantly like old tape-loops, which means that you attract similar events and traumas in later life, and patterns keep on repeating – including illness which 'runs in the family'.

According to neurologists, the brain has a triune structure. In other words, it has three different parts:[95]

1. The most primitive part of the brain, known as the hindbrain or reptilian brain, comprises the brainstem and cerebellum. This is responsible for well-practised skills, conditioned behaviour, automatic reflexes, and hard-wired beliefs and attitudes. It is essential for skills such as walking, making breakfast, brushing your teeth and other everyday activities. Once it is triggered into action, the reptilian brain is habitual and automatic. This is why you can arrive at your destination while driving and have no memory of driving there. Your lizard brain was doing the driving!

2. Then there is the limbic brain, or mid-brain, which is responsible for the fight-flight-freeze response. This is also known as the emotional brain, and it holds all your subconscious beliefs. If you grew up in a stressful environment or went through childhood trauma, your limbic system will be easily triggered into the stress response.

3. Finally, there is the neocortex or forebrain, which is the seat of our conscious awareness and higher thinking. It is the neocortex – and the frontal lobes, in particular – which give us free will and creativity, and make us fully human. (See Chapter 5.)

The limbic brain includes the amygdala, which decides whether your environment is safe or threatening. In other words, it decides whether to respond to any situation from love or fear. Research has shown that the amygdala perceives situations *before* the neocortex, or conscious brain – which means that you can react with fear, and switch into a fight-flight response, before you are even aware of what is happening. (Tools such as energy psychology soothe the amygdala so that we become less easily triggered into fight–flight, even when reminded of past traumas.)

Let's suppose that you were hit by your angry father in childhood, and that your father had a beard and red hair. In later life, whenever you are faced with a man who raises his voice, you will flip into the stress response. The HPA axis then triggers a cascade of neurochemical events, and your lizard brain automatically takes over. You will react as if this man was your father – perhaps overreacting with an angry or emotional outburst, submissively giving in or feeling paralysed – without even knowing what you are doing. This fear response might become generalised over time to apply to any man with a beard, or any man with red hair, or anyone with the same first name or accent as your father, or anyone who expresses anger, or any man who is an authority figure or with whom you have a close relationship – or even to any man, or any situation in which you are alone with another adult.

Once you 'get triggered', you are no longer making conscious adult choices. You no longer have any emotional intelligence. Even the most innocent remark might be filtered through your childhood beliefs, and become potentially threatening. Your anxious thoughts run away with themselves, and quickly create havoc in your body. You react as if you were a young child, using defensive strategies which you probably learnt or observed before the age of seven – such as going silent, trying hard to please, running away, getting busy, putting on a smile and pretending everything is fine, or blaming and criticising others. You are no longer in the present moment, but living in the past – and in a state of fear which is where a lot of people spend most of their lives.

For someone who lives with chronic stress, it is not uncommon to 'wake up' in their forties, fifties or later – perhaps due to a serious diagnosis or other crisis – and wonder where their life has gone. Their limbic and reptilian brain have been running their lives, based on subconscious programming set up in early childhood. They have been mindlessly repeating the past.

When we are under chronic stress, we are *biologically programmed* to avoid the risk of anything new, to cling to what is familiar for security, to become more conventional and conservative – even if that familiar job or relationship is what is causing your stress.[96] In other words, the stress response turns you into a lizard! You begin to listen to what I call 'lizard voices' from the past (see Chapter 7). Then your natural and healthy tendency to reach towards your dreams and desires – to move towards the future, rather than repeating the past – is switched off.

The more you repeat the same daily routines, the more your conscious brain switches off – so you fall asleep even more. Your personal and spiritual growth is blocked, and your physical health is now at risk. Chronic stress can wreck your life in every direction. But it is never too late to wake up and begin to change and grow. The more you deliberately shift into the wave response, the more you reclaim your potential.

In the next chapter, we look more fully at the qualities of the wave response, so that you can begin to recognise that state – and shift into it more and more consciously.

Chapter Five

MOVING INTO THE WAVE RESPONSE

Love is the subtle web that maintains connections.

Darren Weissman[97]

Yesterday I went into the garden to feed my free-range chickens in mid-afternoon. It is a snowy winter, and the landscape is turned to white. My head was buzzing with all that I needed to do – urgent emails to respond to, the website to update, a snow-filled driveway to clear, a broken gate to mend, dinner to prepare for guests, this chapter to write – and a client was due to arrive soon, if she could make her way along the icy roads. I felt rushed and hassled and disembodied.

I called my three chickens (whom I adore) and as they scuttled towards me, a wave of love swept through me – and my whole awareness shifted. As the chickens pecked at the bread in my hands, I looked around at the winter wonderland, the branches groaning with sparkling snow, a soft mist in the distance, the pale orange sun sinking behind the mountains – and I was overwhelmed with the beauty of it all. How lucky I am to be here! How lucky I am simply to be alive! The words of the poet Rilke came to me, 'Being here is so much.' I smiled to myself, realising I had just shifted from being a particle to being a wave. I was in love with life, and bathed in joy and gratitude. Time felt boundless, and I didn't have a problem or pressure in the world. I had merged with the infinite ocean of love.

It has gradually become easier and easier for me to make this shift, regardless of what is happening in my life. An invaluable piece of wisdom I learnt many years ago is that 'The steps to getting there are the qualities of being there'.[98] In order to become a healthy person, you start taking on the qualities of a healthy person, step by step – even if you can only visualise it at first. In order to become enlightened, you start taking on the qualities of a more enlightened person – stepping into the shoes of a wiser self. In order to become more loving, you act *as if* you love yourself and others.

This might sound circular, but it works. It creates a virtuous cycle that makes it progressively easier to stay there. You make different choices. You focus on the positive. You begin to see yourself differently. Your habitual neurochemistry and neural pathways change. Even if you occasionally slip back, it no longer feels comfortable and you soon catch yourself. You forge a new riverbed. Your consciousness shifts. You slowly evolve into a new self.

In order to step into the wave response – which promotes health, happiness and growth – you need to consciously take on the characteristics of someone who is in the wave response. So in this chapter, we will look at some of these wave-like qualities.

THE FRIENDLY UNIVERSE

'Is this a friendly universe?' Einstein suggested that this is the most important question we can ask ourselves. It is central to being in the wave response. In the wave response, you are connected with your higher self, your expanded consciousness, the self that is inseparable from the universe. You connect to the flow of Source energy, and move into a state of heart coherence. Once you are there, you *know* that this is a friendly and loving universe. You tap into universal abundance. You shift from fear, scarcity and limitation to boundless love and potential. You know there are solutions to every problem. The wave response takes you beyond belief to intuitive *knowing*.

When you are in the wave response, you intuitively know that:

✧ I am safe

✧ I am loved

✧ All is well

Read these statements again, and repeat them to yourself right now. Take them in. How do they make you feel? What do you notice happening in your body? As you move into the wave response, your body relaxes. There is no threat, no problem, no scarcity, no reason to worry. The stress response now switches off. Normal growth, maintenance and healing processes are restored in every cell in your body. Your consciousness expands as blood returns to your forebrain.

Instead of scrabbling to get through your to-do list for the day, you are now more likely to take a long stroll in the park, where you muse on bigger questions such as what to do with the rest of your life, what your dreams are and whether you want to make changes. You are open to intuitive messages. You make life-affirming choices. You feel waves of joy and delight. You have a sense of freedom, inner peace and empowerment. You feel deeply connected to others, to nature and to the world. Your creativity returns, along with your spirituality. You are fully present in the moment. You are in love with yourself, with others and with life. And while you remain in that state, any disease in your body will naturally be healing.

THE BRAIN'S FRONTAL LOBES

As we saw in the last chapter, stress deactivates the frontal lobes in your brain. This has serious consequences, since it is the frontal lobes that make us fully human. Whenever your frontal lobes are asleep, you lose your ability to feel truly alive and joyful, and to make conscious and life-affirming choices. You revert to subconscious conditioning, and repeat habitual tape-loops of thoughts and behaviours. Instead of making free-will choices, you revert to mere pattern recognition. You are a hamster on a treadmill, rather than a human being. As neurologist Joe Dispenza puts it, 'When the frontal lobes are asleep, so are we.'[99]

It is only from the wave response that you are visionary and creative about the future. Only then do you have spiritual awareness. Only then are you truly joyful. Without the frontal lobes, you are a push-button automaton who was programmed in childhood – and your health and happiness are in jeopardy. So how can you make sure that your frontal lobes are switched on?

Here are some of the qualities linked with the frontal lobes:

✧ Focus and intent

✧ Joy

✧ Empathy and compassion

✧ Sense of freedom

✧ Adaptability

✧ A strong sense of self; individuality

✧ Clarity and decisiveness

✧ Making choices that match your goals and desires

✧ Creativity

✧ Being able to imagine new possibilities, and ask 'What if?'

✧ Being proactive rather than reactive

✧ Learning from mistakes, and doing it differently next time

✧ Good concentration

✧ Being able to plan for the future

✧ Spiritual awareness

✧ The ability to stay present with yourself and your inner world

✧ Having faith and trust in the future – regardless of the current reality

✧ Living your potential

Needless to say, for optimal health and well-being you need your frontal lobes to remain active. How can you do this? Remember that the steps to getting there are the qualities of being there – so as you choose to do what your frontal lobes naturally do, you become someone with active frontal lobes. That means you are living from the wave response rather than the particle response. Whether you are a health practitioner or have your own health issues – or you simply want to stay healthy and live life to the full – it is crucial to keep your frontal lobes turned on.

One of the simplest tools for soothing the stress response and activating the frontal lobes is the ESR (Emotional Stress Release) technique. Cradle the back of your head with one hand, with the other hand across your forehead. Breathe deeply into your abdomen until you feel strong pulsing under the hand on your forehead – showing that blood is returning to the frontal lobes. This might take between fifteen seconds and a few minutes. It is a great tool if you suddenly find yourself under stress, and you cannot think clearly.

Here are seven more ways of keeping your frontal lobes fully active:

Exercise
WAKING UP YOUR FRONTAL LOBES

1. **Do something different.** Avoid clinging to habit and routine. This sends your frontal lobes to sleep, since they are no

longer needed. Change is good for the frontal lobes. It wakes us up. Staying in the same home, same job, same relationship, choosing the same hobbies and social circles and holiday destinations is a sure-fire way to switch over to lizard voices, and revert to your subconscious beliefs and family-ar patterns. Lizard voices like stability and security! They like thinking the same thoughts day after day. And when we are stressed, we avoid the discomfort of the unknown.

The fact that so many people change careers, end marriages and move frequently these days is, in part, due to becoming more conscious and self-aware, and less likely to remain stuck in unfulfilling situations. Society has become more supportive of change, and less likely to expect people to stay in an unfulfilling job or marriage for life. (If you do stay in the same job or relationship, it must keep evolving and growing, and bringing out more and more of your potential if you are going to thrive.) Aim to do something different each day. Keep learning something new. Welcome change into your life!

2. **Seek out stimulating ideas.** The frontal lobes love to play with ideas, and deal with abstract and challenging questions so switch off that soap opera, and read a book about quantum physics instead. Choose interesting films, books, lectures and conversations, or sign up for a course.

3. **Use your imagination.** Daydream about the future. Visualise what you want. Sink into happy memories, or even create some new ones. Take inner journeys and explore the imaginary realms, as the shamans do. Only humans can do this – and we don't do it when we are in the stress response. If you are not actively imagining the future, you are likely to keep on repeating the past.

4. **Follow your bliss.** Fill your life with joyful activities and loving relationships. When we are in survival mode, we do not seek happiness and joy. We simply do what is required, and keep our heads down. So actively seek bliss, joy and sensual delights. (See overleaf.)

5. **Do anything creative.** It might be painting, pottery, photography, sculpture, drama, writing, poetry, cookery, dancing or any other form of creative self-expression.

6. **Meditate regularly.** The frontal lobes are the home of our Witness self – which is a part of our consciousness that allows us to monitor our own thoughts and inner state. It allows us to remain mindful and self-aware. The witness self is activated by regular meditation, since we notice our thoughts rather than identifying with them during meditation. We learn to detach ourselves from our busy 'monkey mind'. As you develop this ability to stay present to yourself, whatever is happening, you are less liable to repeat subconscious patterns and 'lose yourself'. (For a simple meditation using the breath, see the Breathe exercise in Chapter 3, page 56.)

7. **Make time for personal and spiritual growth.** It might be something as simple as keeping a journal, daily prayer, using affirmations or reading inspirational books – or it might mean attending workshops, seeking out a therapist, or finding an active spiritual community where you feel at home. Whatever it is, make sure it keeps evolving and changing. Don't let it become a fixed habit or routine, or you risk falling asleep again.

FOLLOW YOUR BLISS

The mythologist Joseph Campbell famously urged us to 'follow our bliss' – and that is the best possible advice if you want to be healthy. Bliss is a natural part of the wave response. We are designed for happiness – and the more deeply we go into the wave response, the happier we feel. Joy increases our levels of DHEA, the anti-ageing hormone, making us look and stay younger. Being happy makes us more creative and intuitive. Falling happily in love has cured countless health disorders. Happiness and health go hand in hand. Despite what some religions have taught, the world is not meant to be a vale of tears. We are meant to be happy. As biologist Candace Pert puts it, bliss is hard-wired into our physiology.[100]

It isn't enough to release toxins, such as trauma, negative beliefs and toxic patterns in relationships. We also need to add nutrients – whatever feels joyful and life-affirming – to our lives. We need to have positive reasons for getting out of bed each morning. Moving towards joy and away from pain makes you healthier, smarter and younger. It is what healthy cells in your body do – and they know what is best for them.

We have special neurons in the brain known as 'mirror neurons', which pick up and copy whatever we see around us – so it is wise to show those neurons lots of happiness, fun and good times. We resonate to the frequency of those around us, so it makes sense to choose happy and positive people to be around, and to avoid watching doom-laden news, angst-ridden soap operas or tragic documentaries. If you must watch a soap opera, choose *Friends* rather than *ER*! We pick up the vibrational frequency of whatever we focus upon, and our brain cannot tell the difference between what we are experiencing and what we are seeing or hearing about, or even imagining. For your health's sake, choose what makes you feel good, rather than triggering the stress response. (There is a list of feel-good movies in Resources for Health and Well-being on page 329.)

Why do we sometimes move away from joy and towards pain? Because of our habitual neurochemistry (which asks to be 'fed' with family-ar emotions such as fear, guilt, resentment or overwhelm), and also because we are trying to seek love and stay safe in childlike ways – by pleasing others, conforming to social expectations, or keeping our head down. We are trying not to upset anyone by being exuberantly happy, alive and free! How often are children told to 'calm down' or 'be quiet' when they are bursting with joy? And what is the message? 'Your happiness makes me unhappy.' Or when children are angry or sad, they are told 'Don't be silly' or 'Big boys don't cry' or 'That's a nasty face!' – instead of their feelings being honoured and valued. What is the message? Don't upset others. Don't feel your emotions. Do what I expect. Pretend to be happy. Put on a smile – and stuff your feelings down.

Many of us learn to squash ourselves in early childhood,

when a sharp word or look of disapproval from a parent might be enough to stop us reaching for that bar of chocolate, or splashing in that inviting pool of mud. We learn to hold ourselves back. We learn that parts of us are good and acceptable, and other parts are bad and unacceptable. We decide that we are only lovable when we are being 'good' – so we learn to hide what is 'bad', and pretend it is not there. We tuck it away in our Shadow, and later project it on to others. By learning to be shiny and pure in the eyes of others, we conform to social expectations and lose touch with our authentic self – and we retreat from bliss. We disconnect from who we really are.

Trying to please others is probably the single most important factor that keeps us out of alignment with our higher self.[101] It is therefore a huge health risk. Whenever we seek approval, we are being guided from outside ourselves, and stop paying attention to what *feels good*. Instead of feeling what we feel, we look at the faces around us to work out what we are *supposed* to feel or do – and lose touch with our emotions and inner guidance. This throws us into conflict, and activates the stress response. Instead of aiming to be happy, we are trying to 'be good'.

It reminds me of a woman diagnosed with terminal cancer who was treated with EFT, and rapidly began to improve. However, she stopped practising EFT and her health declined again. When her therapist probed as to why, he found that her family and friends had already held a goodbye party for her, and she didn't want to 'upset' them by not dying! Thankfully she soon saw the absurdity of this – and went on to recover from the cancer. But how many of us similarly twist ourselves into pretzels trying not to upset others, instead of pleasing ourselves and living life to the full?

A LOVING UNIVERSE

When we align with our higher self, which loves us unconditionally, we remember that the purpose of life is joy (see my earlier book, *Life is a Gift*). We are not here to prove ourselves good and worthy, nor are we here to save the world. We are here for a glorious adventure in consciousness. Life is supposed to be fun! Every day should be filled with wonderful experiences, loving encounters, natural highs and sensual delights. When we learn to trust in a loving universe, we know that love and freedom and joy are our natural state of being. Feeling less than fabulous is an anomaly caused by the particle response. It is a wake-up call that is gently reminding us to get back on track – and get happy!

When you value yourself and honour your own needs, you reach towards whatever you most desire – whether it is travelling to India, building your own home, setting up a business, becoming a singer in a rock band or adopting stray cats. Self-love means that you believe in yourself, follow your dreams, and trust that you can turn your dreams into reality.

Many people have conflicting beliefs such as 'I want to love and be loved' and 'Relationships are dangerous', or 'I want to be free' and 'I want approval from others'. These inner conflicts will block your dreams and rip you apart until you deal with them – and will become a health risk. The task is to give up whichever belief comes from your past. Whichever belief feels more joyful, light and expansive is the one that comes from your higher self – so that is the belief to programme into your subconscious. (You can use the techniques in Chapter 4 to do this, see page 97.) Then you move towards your dreams – and towards health and well-being.

Physician Leonard Laskow[102] – who gave up his conventional medical practice when he discovered the healing power of unconditional love – sees the positive intent that underlies most illness as the desire to love and be loved, along with the desire to be free to make your own choices. Love and freedom are twin keys to healing. They are two sides of the same coin, like energy and consciousness. Particle thinking often sees them as incompatible – and suggests that love means compromise and sacrifice, giving in for the sake of peace, or caring for others at your own expense. From the wave response, love and freedom always go hand in hand. Then we give up scrabbling to please others, and learn to be true to ourselves.

In a conscious universe, we can have whatever we want, as long as we are not getting in our own way. *Ask and it is given*, says the Bible. No questions asked. Our higher self always aligns itself with our dreams and desires, and calls us towards that new future. And since the universe does not take sides, it has everyone's needs in mind. Following your dreams works out well for everyone else involved. This is the heart of what it means to live in a conscious and loving universe.

THE HEALING POWER OF LAUGHTER

In 1964, Norman Cousins flew home from a trip abroad with a slight fever. Within a week, he found it difficult to move his neck, arms and legs. There were signs that he was in a critical condition. He was soon diagnosed with ankylosing spondylitis – a disease of the connective tissue that is said to be chronic and degenerative. His spine was disintegrating, and he was told to expect to be in a wheelchair within a few months to a year. However, he reasoned that he was suffering from adrenal exhaustion due to stress as a newspaper reporter, after many years of high pressure and constant travelling. He discovered that the huge doses of painkillers he was prescribed would be putting his adrenal glands under even more stress – and since conventional medicine could only offer pain relief and a poor prognosis, he took his healing into his own hands.

He decided to check out of hospital and into a hotel room, came off all his tablets, and 'prescribed' heavy doses of laughter for himself. He watched Marx Brothers films and *Candid Camera*, read comic books – and soon found that ten minutes of laughter would give him two hours of pain-free sleep. He also took large doses of vitamin C as an anti-inflammatory and blood oxygenator (and it is widely rumoured that he used homoeopathy too). Within days, he was feeling better.

Within weeks, his symptoms had improved markedly. Within a few months, he was back at work, and his health – with some minor limitations – was almost back to normal. He had found a simple and natural way of switching into the wave response.[103]

The inspiring film *Patch Adams* tells the true story of a renegade medical student who (outrageously) believes that making patients laugh and helping them feel happy is good for them. Despite his excellent grades and the loving gratitude of the patients, he is nearly thrown out of medical school. The real Patch Adams – doctor, clown and social activist – went on to found a holistic medical community in Virginia that offered free healthcare to thousands of people. He is now gathering funds to set up a free hospital, and still believes that the most revolutionary act in the world is to be happy.

In the past twenty-five years, research has shown that laughter boosts the levels of natural killer cells in our immune system, lowers our serum cortisol levels and increases salivary immunoglobulin (IgA), which helps protect against viruses. In other words, it soothes the stress response, releases endorphins and boosts the immune system. Tears of laughter also have a different chemical composition to tears of sadness, with a higher level of toxins, which suggests they might play a role in detoxifying the body.[104]

Whatever makes you laugh, grab it with both hands. It will release your stress response. Whether it is a favourite comedy series, an enjoyable activity that touches your funny bone, or a friend or lover who makes you laugh until you cry, laughter is worth every minute you devote to it. A belly laugh each day can be seen as part of your routine preventive healthcare – and it can even help you to heal. Laughter is good medicine.

THE HEALING POWER OF NATURE

As I write this book from my ground-floor office at home, I look out over my woodland garden, which is crammed with life. I can sometimes see my three chickens, my cat, roe deer and grey squirrels in a single glance, while my bird table is visited by a host of birds from jays and woodpeckers to wrens and chaffinches. It feels like heaven on earth to me. A recent visitor said it felt like 'the garden of Saint Francis', as deer and other wildlife gathered around us near the dovecote. I am a short stroll away from woodland and waterfalls, and (in my eyes) the most beautiful lake in the world, Rydal Water. Or I can hike further up the lane towards Nab Scar and the Lakeland fells. Enticing footpaths are all around, and the stunning scenery changes with the seasons. I am very blessed. For me, nature is the great healer – and whenever work or life crowds in on me, I spend time in nature and it soon restores my sanity.

When asked who my greatest spiritual teacher is, I sometimes reply (only half-jokingly) it is my cat, Mystic. Like most cats, Mystic has mastered the art of living in bliss. He sleeps on the rug in front of the woodburning stove, wanders down to his food bowl, sits meditating on my desk or takes an excursion around the garden. He stretches out in the sun. He takes another nap. He rolls over and asks for a tummy-rub. He gazes out of the window. On the rare occasions that he can be bothered to hunt for a shrew or mouse, he is alert and excited for half an hour, then returns to licking his paws, before finding a warm place – or preferably a lap – in which to curl up and snooze. I only have to stroke or gaze at Mystic for a few moments to relax and smile. (My son Kieran says that, in his next lifetime, he is coming back as a cat!)

Nature is almost permanently in the wave response, which is one reason why being in nature is so healing for us. What we call 'instinct' in animals is simply their natural connectedness to the zero point energy field, or universal energy, to the Oneness. This is how a flock of terns or a shoal of fish can swoop and turn in perfect unison. Or how dozens of blue tits can appear on my bird table as soon as I fill it with their favourite seed, as if by magic. In nature, animals only rush about for the brief periods when they are in the fight-flight response as hunter or prey, or while they are feeding young. At other times, they are generally relaxed and in tune with the universe.

I remember hearing the remarkable yachtswoman Ellen MacArthur[105] talking about her long solo sailing trips. The interviewer asked whether she ever felt lonely when she spent weeks alone at sea. Ellen seemed puzzled by the question. She had the birds and creatures of the sea, the ocean itself and her much-loved boat for company. How could she possibly feel lonely? Sailing obviously shifted her into the wave response (no pun intended!) – and from there, we feel a deep sense of connectedness with All That Is.

As I know from my own experience, feelings of loneliness or separation have nothing to do with being alone, or being separated from anyone you love. We feel lonely only when we are out of touch with our true self. I have felt utterly lonely at a party, and blissfully connected while 'alone' in nature. At other times, I have been out in the wilds yet immersed in painful thoughts that have made me feel lonely and separate, and unable to take in the beauty of the landscape. Loneliness is based solely upon being in the particle response – which makes us feel disconnected. One of the characteristics of the wave response is that we tend to feel closer to nature and appreciate it more, since we are tapping into our more earth-centred and body-centred right brain.

Ecopsychology is a recent movement – forged by writers such as Theodore Roszak, James Hillman, Chellis Glendinning and David Abram – which believes that much of our dis-ease stems from our disconnection from nature.[106] As we deeply connect with nature, we heal imbalance and dissociation within ourselves. Nature has so much to teach us about how to be human beings rather than human doings, and how to come out of the stress response – and many books have been written about lessons from gardening, lessons from the wilderness, lessons from animals and so on. Many of these lessons from nature are about learning to relax and chill out, and go with the flow, or about loving and accepting yourself as you are. One reason why I love flower essences for healing is that they help us reconnect to nature, and tap into its healing powers.

It is hard to imagine a daffodil fretting because it is not a bluebell, or striving to bloom for longer this year than last. Nature does not strive to be different, or to achieve more and more. It simply is what it is – perfect and blooming in its own way, just as we are. Paradoxically as we slow down and strive less, we tend to achieve far more. We are aligned with the forces of the universe from the wave response, so miracles and synchronicities abound and new doors open. More importantly, we *enjoy* life more, since the wave response releases our joy and creativity and aliveness.

Spending time in nature can help us to awaken. It helps us to reassess our priorities, to slow down the pace of our lives, to worry less about money and possessions, to focus more on the quality of our lives, and to value what comes free in life – from a beautiful sunrise to a loving hug. It helps us to care more about how we feel than about how much we achieve. (A serious illness can have exactly the same effect, which will be part of its gift – but you can reap these rewards *without* having to get the diagnosis.) Next time you are stressed, sit in the welcoming arms of an oak tree, relax deeply – and ask for its wisdom. It will have all the time in the world to chat with you!

IMAGERY AND THE BRAIN

A whole host of well-known physicians have recommended imagery in healing – such as Carl Simonton, Larry Dossey, Bernie Siegel, Norm Shealy and Dean Ornish – as well as psychologists such as Jeanne Achterberg who has specialised in this topic. Patients who recover quickly from surgery often report having done significant healing work in their imagination while lying in bed, such as 'seeing' their broken bones knit together or 'watching' their internal wounds heal.[107] Imagery works. If you vividly imagine a positive scene, it will trigger the healing response and guide your bodymind towards your desired outcome.

Back in the 1980s, there was a lot of publicity about using

imagery in healing cancer – and people were often advised to see vicious sharks eating the cancer cells, or an army of soldiers shooting them. Then it was realised that seeing cancer cells as dangerous enemies was less helpful than seeing them as weak, helpless and confused – which is more accurate – so imagery became more benign. For example, the cancer cells might be seen as ice cubes being melted by candles, laser beams or log fires. This is much more likely to trigger the wave response than picturing a vicious battleground!

My tendency is to find whatever imagery works best for that individual – but to lean towards images that are fairly neutral and matter-of-fact, rather than desperate or war-like. This is less likely to trigger fear and anxiety, which could block the imagery from being effective. I also encourage people to see many inner helpers when they journey inside their body, so that they have a strong sense of being supported and cared for.

When I was working with cancer in my own body, I saw the cancer as pieces of coal that were being mined inside a large mound (symbolising my breast). Coal miners would chip out the coal, which was transported out into the garden on a railway track, then burnt on large fires. Eventually the coal mine was free of blackness, and its walls were sparkling with jewels, and a skylight had been built into the ceiling so that sunlight flooded in. One day when I visited the mine, the miners were sitting around drinking tea, with their pick-axes on the ground. I asked them what was happening, and they said there was no more coal. So I knew the cancer was no longer active. I then checked into the mine from time to time to make sure it was still sparkling with jewels and light. Another image I used for a while was of polar bears eating black fishcakes (cancer cells) on a snowy landscape – which made the fishcakes very easy to find.

You can use imagery for almost any dis-ease. For example, one of my clients saw workers squirting oil into her creaking and painful joints; another client saw miniature massage therapists working on the muscles in her eyes, which were distorting her vision and creating astigmatism; another client watched as inner healers repaired his stomach ulcer, and filled the hole with healthy new cells. Yet another client – a driven, workaholic woman with hypertension and a long history of drug abuse – looked into her arteries, and saw over-busy ants which were 'scuttling around as if they're on amphetamines', so she gave them dope to smoke instead, and watched them begin to lean against the artery walls and put their feet up!

In a study in New York, people with one-sided paralysis after a stroke watched their own brainwave activity on a screen when they moved their healthy limb, then *imagined* that they could produce the same brainwave activity while trying to move their paralysed limb. With a little practice, using the feedback from the screen, they became able to move their paralysed limb again.[108] Until fairly recently, it was thought that the brain began a slow decline after childhood, and that brain cells could not be replaced. We now know that the brain shows amazing 'neuroplasticity' – and can keep on changing, learning and adapting even in very elderly people, or after horrific damage or injury, as long as you set a clear intention.[109]

Whatever you imagine, your body believes is real – and it will come into alignment with your desires. This is another of those wondrous skills of your frontal lobe, which allows you to imagine a future that has not yet happened. When we are not in the stress response, human beings tend to become visionary about the future – and instead of repeating the past or doing what is expected, we are creative and innovative.

If you spend just ten to fifteen minutes each day visualising what you desire – whether this is a positive state of health, or a happy daydream about your future, or basking in feel-good memories – it can have a significant impact on your health. (Yes, visualising *anything* that feels positive will help you to heal from disease, since it takes you out of the stress response.) This is good preventive healthcare – and it feels delicious!

FIND YOUR HIGHER PURPOSE

For many people, the wave response brings a strong sense of higher purpose, which in itself has great benefits for our health. Many of us long to make a positive difference and to play a part in making the world a better place – and countless people have recovered their health through having a vision that they long to fulfil, which takes them beyond their individual concerns and connects them with a global dream. Again, this activates the frontal lobes since it means visioning the future. Also, connecting with a global dream means tapping into our intuitive (wave) knowing that we are all One, and moving beyond the (particle) pain of feeling separate.

Edward Bach, for example, who developed the Bach Flower Remedies, was unconvinced that his training in conventional medicine held the key to health. He watched people suffering from harsh medical treatment, and passionately yearned to discover a more gentle and nature-based approach to healing. He also felt sure that the personality of the patient was far more important than the disease itself. When handed his medical degrees, he remarked that it would take years to forget all he had learnt! He adored nature – yet avoided even going to the city parks while he lived in London, fearing that the call of nature would distract him from his serious vocation.

As a young man, Edward Bach became very ill. His poor health barred him from serving in the First World War and by 1917 he was told that he had three months to live at most. Believing that he had little time left, he worked day and night, feverishly researching into homoeopathic remedies for health. His laboratory became known as 'the light that never went out'. Over the months, he slowly grew stronger and fitter, and eventually he was surprised to notice that his health was better than it had been for many years.[110] He realised that his fervent sense of purpose had restored his health. It was when he followed his heart and moved to the countryside that he created his famous Bach Flower Remedies – which became the forerunners of all our modern flower essences (including my own Lakeland Essences).

When you align yourself with a dream or higher purpose, you are connected with your higher self, and therefore aligned with health and well-being. It does not have to be a dream of earth-shattering importance. It might be as simple as wanting to watch your children or grandchildren grow up, or even seeing the daffodils come up again (though it needs to feel within reach of your current vibrations – or what you can comfortably imagine – so if you have been told you only have three months to live, aiming to see your next birthday is a better choice than aiming for your hundredth birthday). It needs to be a future that you strongly want to experience – and without any contradictory thought that says, 'Yes, but I cannot have that' or 'It isn't possible' or 'I don't deserve that' or 'But the doctor said . . .' No tail-enders that say, 'Yes, but . . .' Just a simple and heartfelt statement of what you desire.

You do not have to 'discover' a higher purpose, as if it was a task assigned to you by a committee before you entered this lifetime. You have to *create* your sense of purpose. You do not have a mission to fulfil. Nor does God give you extra marks for helping deprived children in Bangladesh, or frown on you for manufacturing rubber ducks! The Universe is non-judgemental and supportive. If you choose a purpose, it will knock itself out to send you the events and circumstances that will help you fulfil that purpose – as long as you are not throwing out tail-enders that block it.

Finding meaning or purpose in an illness can help enormously in the healing process, since it gives you a positive focus. It is one reason why I found myself dancing around my kitchen soon after getting a cancer diagnosis! I knew that this could help me fulfil my dream of writing and teaching about conscious medicine. I also knew that it would push me to deal with the personal issues that had blocked my relationships, and set up the cancer – and I trusted enough in a loving universe, and my awareness of conscious medicine, to know that the outcome would be positive.

If you decide that healing from an illness will allow you to achieve a dream, or to help others, or to change your lifestyle in positive ways, or that it will free you to become the person you have always wanted to be, then the universe immediately lays the foundations of that golden path for you. We get what we focus upon. As your thoughts become coherent in focusing on that new goal, and you look *beyond* the illness to that bright future, you shift more and more into the wave response – and healing comes naturally.

FREEDOM AND UNCONDITIONAL LOVE

The wave response also takes us into that expansive state of awareness that connects us with unconditional love – and this in turn brings true freedom. If you are happy *because* things are going well for you, or *because* others are behaving as you wish, then you will always feel anxious, vulnerable and insecure, since your happiness is conditional. Part of you will be waiting for the other shoe to drop. When you are in the wave response, you are happy without condition. Paradoxically – for reasons we shall see later – this allows circumstances to change for the better.

Conditional love says 'I will be happy if/when . . .' Unconditional love says, 'I am happy' – while also visualising and expecting the best possible outcome, knowing that life is a journey and is forever changing, and trusting the universe to come up with unexpected solutions, whatever the situation – even if told that you are sick or dying. This is crucial when faced with a serious diagnosis, since the paradox is that being happy even *with* that diagnosis will allow you to recover more easily. (Even if the time has come to die – and we all do eventually – it will allow you to die with inner peace and grace.)

If you see the universe as loving and friendly, then everything that happens in your life can be welcomed as a friend. If an event or situation feels good, it can simply be enjoyed. If anything 'bad' happens – a disease appears in your body, or your partner leaves, or your boss criticises you, or your roof develops a leak, or someone crashes into your car – you know it is just a friend in disguise. Instead of pushing against it, you welcome and embrace it. You trust that nothing ever 'goes wrong' within the big picture. When things look bad, it is only because you cannot see the bigger picture yet. The story is still unfolding. This positive attitude towards life will help you stay aligned with your higher self, whatever happens. It is a key to living with unconditional love.

When you are in the wave response, you intuitively know that you create your life from the inside out, not from the outside in. Instead of waiting for other people or circumstances to change so that you can feel better, you aim to change your own consciousness. As we shall see in the next chapter, this allows you to truly love yourself, others and the world – which takes most of the stress out of life. Finding fault anyone or anything – even because you want to make the world a better place – will always throw you into stress. Learning to love unconditionally has been the greatest lesson I have learnt in recent years, and it has transformed my life.

In Chapter 6, we look at one of the primary sources of stress in our lives – as well as (potentially) our greatest source of joy and fulfilment: our personal relationships. And we see how the wave response can transform your relationships – helping you to shift from distant, tense or stressful relationships, which are a risk to your mental and physical health, to deeply loving relationships that promote your health, happiness and growth.

Chapter Six

EVERYTHING IS A FRIEND

You can't take sides against anything. If you would just be one who is for things, you would live happily ever after – if you could just leave the 'against' part out.'

Abraham[111]

When Lester Levenson was forty-two, he had a plethora of health problems – an enlarged liver, kidney stones, heart and spleen disorders, perforated stomach ulcers and depression. After his second heart attack, his doctors gave up and sent him home to die. However, Lester was a successful businessman, and he loved a challenge. He began to explore spiritual teachings, and eventually hit upon a method that brought him relief from his pain and symptoms. Whatever he felt, whether emotional or physical, he would welcome and embrace it – and then let it go. He noticed that it was only when he *resisted* a symptom or emotion that it persisted. If he dived into it, then became willing to let go, it would quickly pass.

This approach became a constant form of meditation for Lester, and he felt better and better. Within three months, he had totally recovered his physical health – and also found a deep sense of inner peace. His method later developed into the Sedona Method (which I trained in several years ago, in the beautiful mountain city of Sedona). Lester lived for another forty-two years – and that profound inner peace never left him.[112]

What was the secret to Lester Levenson's recovery? He found a natural way into the wave response. He stopped going into fight or flight – either battling against his sick body and troubled emotions, or trying to resist or run away from them. Instead he embraced whatever came up as a friend. Then it vanished like the morning mist. *Let it be – then let it go.* He had stumbled upon a way of holding himself in unconditional love, which is central to the wave response. It is also a key to making relationships work.

As many people have found, if you simply *accept* pain – whether emotional or physical – and relax into an awareness of it, it often melts away. Likewise, accepting a problem is often the first crucial step towards resolving it. What we resist persists. Surrendering to anything releases resistance, and allows blocked energy to flow again.

Everything becomes softer when we are in the wave response. Things are less solid and fixed, more fluid and flexible. Nothing seems such a big deal. You see gifts in every situation. You become more curious and exploratory. Problems dissolve, and unexpected solutions are found. You move out of the world of duality – right and wrong, us and them, black and white, good guys and bad guys – into a world of oneness and connectedness. A world of unconditional love.

I have studied various forms of shamanism over the past twenty-five years but when I trained in Hawaiian shamanism in Kaua'i (or Huna) nearly twenty years ago, I felt I had come home.[113] The Huna wisdom sees the universe as a loving place, in which everything is a mirror of the self. Instead of battling against enemies and overcoming them with strength, courage and determination, it embraces them. It sees no separation between me and not me. If you fight anything 'out there', you are merely pointing arrows at a mirror – and they bounce right back at you.

In a loving universe, nothing is ever going wrong, if only

you see a big enough picture and look at it through the eyes of the wave response. Everything is a friend. Anything that is uncomfortable has a helpful message for you. It simply means that your lower self (or bodymind) is not in alignment with your higher self. For me, this attitude is a key to coming out of the stress response.

This does not mean that you turn belly-up, and pretend everything is fine as it is. It is not about pretence, denial or giving up. It means that you are authentic about how you feel, and take responsibility for whatever is happening in your life, and accept your starting point. You love and accept your current reality, coming to peace with what is – while holding a clear vision for the future. Then you come into alignment with your higher self, which is relentlessly positive, loving and visionary. And as we shall see, this can transform your personal relationships.

MAKING PEACE WITH YOUR 'ENEMY'

When you are in the particle response, you are in a war zone. You are either fighting against an enemy, fleeing from it or frozen in terror. You become a predator stalking its prey – or a fearful and vulnerable prey that must watch out for danger. You are on tenterhooks, with adrenalin pumping through your bloodstream. It is not a peaceful state, and is not conducive to healing.

Your 'enemy' might take many forms, inner and outer: a headache, a bout of indigestion, a common cold, a painful twinge in your head, a rush of sadness and grief, the government, the economy, your boss, a tight deadline, the weather, planning regulations, the local council, your ex-partner, your unruly teenager . . . the list goes on for ever. You are pushing against someone or something you see as bad, wrong or unwanted. You and 'it' are seen as separate. You are in competition, and you want to win – or at least keep yourself safe. You are on the battlefield of attack or defensiveness. And battlefields are stress-laden places to be.

Conventional medicine goes into battle with illness and disease. It shoots the messenger – silencing warning signals from the body that something is awry, that energy-consciousness is not flowing freely. It battles against viruses and bacteria and inflammation and tumours. It views disease as an enemy that needs to be shot down. Zap it, cut it out, irradiate it! No questions asked. *Could it be that the paradigm that conventional medicine is built upon is the very world view that makes us sick – a fear-based, materialist model based on separation from love and oneness?*

As Albert Einstein said, you cannot solve a problem from the same level of thinking that caused it. So we cannot resolve disease, which is caused by the stress response, using an approach based upon that same level of thinking: thinking like a particle, and having a battle mentality. It is like trying to melt an ice cream using an ice cube. You have to shift into a different level of awareness. Hot air, for example, could melt that ice cream. Yes, hot air is invisible stuff – but then, that is just what is needed. A different category of 'stuff', which comes from expanded awareness. Mind-stuff. Invisible stuff like thoughts and beliefs. Invisible stuff like love.

Perhaps we are now seeing so much illness that conventional medicine can do little about – such as chronic and degenerative disease, depression and autoimmune disorders – because this forces us to shift to a higher level of consciousness? When we cannot resolve a problem in our familiar old ways, we eventually surrender and let go, then come up with more creative solutions. We are often led out of the stress response – away from fear, struggle and limitation – and towards unconditional love, joy, freedom and expansive possibilities.

Arielle Essex is a therapist–healer and life coach who discovered in her twenties that she had a brain tumour that would leave her infertile. Since she had recently decided to stop focusing on her career and have children, this seemed a cruel blow at first. The brain tumour was inoperable, leaving her no choice but to find an unconventional approach to healing. As she explored spiritually, she felt sure that God was not cruel or punishing, and that she must have created this for a reason. When she looked within, she found a lot of subconscious resistance to becoming a mother, and realised that her body had been 'protecting' her from having children. Her journey of self-healing continued, and after nine years of inner work and transformation, she had changed herself and her life radically – yet the tumour still remained.

At this point, Arielle realised that she had been seeing the tumour as an enemy and wanting to get rid of it, without acknowledging that it had led her on a profound spiritual journey of growth and awakening. She thanked the tumour, and gave it permission to stay for the rest of her life if it wished. At long last, she was at peace with it. The next time Arielle saw her doctor, she was amazed to find that the test results had suddenly changed. The tumour had vanished.

From a conscious medicine perspective, the body is intelligent and conscious and infinitely helpful, and nothing is incurable or terminal – unless you *believe* that it is. Unless you are stuck in fear-based, limited, particle thinking. Unless you are stuck in undischarged trauma and unresolved conflicts. Unless you are pushing against an illness, and treating it as an enemy – which is one reason why desperately *trying* to heal so often fails.

It does not matter what the statistics are. Statistics can never tell you what will happen for *this* unique individual with his or her own habits of thought, beliefs, desires, intentions, relationships, background and higher purpose. Statistics do not take account of the real creative force in the universe, which is *consciousness*. And the more consistently you hold yourself in unconditional love – seeing everyone and everything as a friend – the more readily your body can heal itself.

ARE YOU IN THE DRAMA TRIANGLE?

Relationships can be the source of our greatest joy and growth, as well as our deepest unhappiness – with huge implications for our health. For better or worse. It is our relationships that are most likely either to throw us into the stress response, or to relieve the stress response. So creating healthy relationships – based on unconditional love, freedom and authenticity – is a crucial key to health and happiness.

As a clinical psychologist, one of the most useful models I ever came across was the drama triangle. Every dysfunctional interaction or emotional drama in our lives is said to occur around the drama triangle. People sometimes mistakenly believe that you need three people to create a drama triangle – but it can occur between two people, or even in your own head. It involves playing power games of attack or defence, and seeing yourself as separate from someone or something that is a threat. You are on a battlefield. A medical diagnosis often sets up a drama triangle – which can then block the healing process.

There are three roles you can play within a drama triangle: Persecutor, Rescuer or Victim. These are inner voices or sub-personalities that everyone has. They are part of the legacy of growing up. Two of these voices are parental voices – the Persecutor (critical parent) and the Rescuer (over-responsible parent) – while the third inner voice, the Victim, is like a helpless and frightened child. These are the dark Shadow side of the father, mother and child, respectively. (Our Shadow comprises those unacknowledged parts of ourselves which we hide and push away.)

All three voices are desperately trying to seek love, inner peace or security – while secretly feeling unsafe or unloved. What does this tell you? That's right. All three voices are in the stress response. After all, when we are in the wave response, we always feel safe and loved – regardless of what is happening or how anyone else is behaving. So how can you recognise these three voices of the drama triangle?

The Drama Triangle

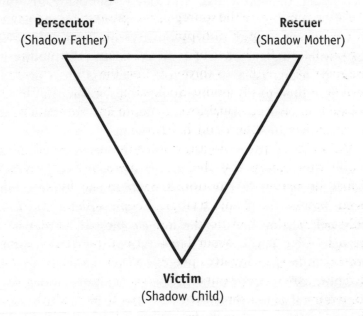

The Persecutor
(Shadow Father)

Rescuer
(Shadow Mother)

Victim
(Shadow Child)

The Persecutor tries to feel safe by controlling, criticising or blaming others. It is judgemental and self-righteous, and needs to be seen as perfect and beyond reproach. It has a false sense of superiority, which covers up its hidden shame and insecurity. The Persecutor gets an adrenalin rush from being angry and righteous, so it needs an enemy to compete with. It is in the 'fight' mode of the stress response, and sees attack as the best form of defence. It can be bossy and authoritarian – and even bullying, threatening or abusive. It tends to feel 'entitled' to have its needs met, or to have other people behave as it wants them to. The Persecutor can be the hardest pattern to see in ourselves, since we feel justified in our anger and blame, or believe we are obviously 'in the right'! When this voice is turned against the self, it becomes the inner critic who makes us feel guilty, inadequate or 'in the wrong'.

The Rescuer tries to soothe ruffled feathers, care for and protect others, and keep the peace at any cost. It is over-responsible for others' happiness and well-being, and tends to be over-loyal, over-caring, over-protective and often controlling. It wants everyone to be happy, and sacrifices its own needs in the process. It is sometimes called the hero-martyr or responsible-parent voice within us. It tends to foster dependency, disempowering others by taking on a parental role, protecting them or doing what they need to do for themselves – and calling this love. It sees itself as wiser, stronger or more resourceful than others, and often attracts 'lame ducks' or needy people.

If you are a Rescuer, you will feel over-responsible for others – whether it is your partner, children, family, friends, clients, employees or the world at large. The hidden belief of the Rescuer is 'If only I take care of everyone else, I will be loved.' The reality is that it feels stressed, burdened or unappreciated. This is the flight mode of the stress response, and it means that you disappear and 'lose yourself' in relationships (or work). It tends to be the strongest inner voice in carers and helping professionals, and it is easy to mistake this apparently caring voice for love.

The Victim tries to get its needs met by being helpless, dependent, hurt, frightened, vulnerable or childlike. It tends to blame other people, situations or what happened in the past for how it feels, and why its life is so stuck and frozen – or might beat itself up for being stupid, or making bad choices. It looks up to other people, especially those in authority, and wants their approval. It often turns to others for help and guidance, but it plays 'Yes but . . .' games if they slip into Rescuer and try to be helpful or make suggestions. This corresponds to the freeze response – so while we are in Victim mode, we tend to feel numb, passive, insecure, helpless and unable to make positive decisions. Or we might feel depressed, hopeless, trapped or despairing. Or we might try to manipulate others into protecting or rescuing us.

Within conventional medicine, illness or dis-ease is treated as the enemy – and the Persecutor voice is turned against it. There is no question that the illness is 'bad and wrong', and should be eliminated. The doctor, nurses and other health practitioners serve as knights in shining armour, who will valiantly rescue the patient from this dangerous or unpleasant enemy. The patient plays the role of a helpless and passive Victim – perhaps of bacteria, viruses, faulty genes, unexplained pain, invading disease or 'accidents'.

This is an ingrained model of healthcare, and many patients accept and even welcome it. The problem with this way of thinking is that it exacerbates the stress response, and so blocks the natural process of healing. It puts the patient in a dependent childlike position, which cuts them off from their inner wisdom. It makes it unlikely that they will listen to their body's intelligence, and learn and grow from the experience – so they might get symptomatic relief, but will not find true healing.

The roles within a drama triangle can rotate at lightning speed – so well-meaning doctors or therapists can suddenly find themselves persecuted by an angry patient or family who blames them for 'getting it wrong'. Or sometimes doctors turn into persecutors when the patient fails to play a passive Victim role. Any communication tends to be distorted, since you are playing a role rather than being real and authentic. Old dramas from childhood or the past have usually been triggered, which means that the players are no longer conscious – and the healing response is blocked.

BEYOND THE DRAMA TRIANGLE

Once you move beyond the stress response, you embrace everything as a friend. The more deeply you connect with your higher self, the more you know that this is a loving universe, in which nothing can ever go wrong, if only you enlarge your consciousness enough to see the bigger picture. This isn't to say that having a skin condition or a migraine is somehow 'good and right'. It is simply beyond right or wrong, good or bad. When you are beyond the stress response, your consciousness moves beyond judgement and duality. No blame, no guilt. No attack, no defence.

Any illness or disease is a mirror of what is happening in your consciousness, like everything else in your life. When a symptom appears, instead of anxiously dashing to a doctor in an effort to get rid of it, you might say, 'How interesting! I wonder what this is trying to tell me.' The body is designed to be healthy if only you can get out of its way – and this means staying off the battlefield of the stress response. It means holding yourself in unconditional love – loving whatever is – while holding a clear vision of where you are going. Then you can make clear decisions about how best to handle it.

In a conscious universe, we get whatever we focus upon – so what we resist persists. If you focus on having hyper-tension or multiple sclerosis, and go into fierce battle mode to find a healing approach that works, you are stabbing yourself in the back. Fight against anything, and it fights back. As any martial artist knows, there is far more power in *yielding* to the blows of your opponent – while also being clear about where you are going. The martial artist understands the power of non-resistance. A willow tree that bends in the wind can be stronger than a mighty oak that resists it. Your opponent vanishes as an 'opponent' once you focus clearly on what *you* want, holding to your own strength and power, and even using their strength to augment your own. There *is* no 'enemy' in this world view – just an opportunity to build your strength and clarify your vision.

Let's take the example of being harassed by a neighbour who keeps pushing your boundaries, invading your space or making excessive noise, and insists that *you* are the one with the problem when you complain. It goes on day after day, and you feel resentful and anxious. You see the other person as an enemy. The problem is that you then have to defend yourself or try to keep out of their way, or go into attack mode, perhaps spreading the word about how nasty they are, or even taking them to a tribunal. Such approaches are unlikely to resolve the issue. You are on a battlefield.

Another option is to see this harassing person as a friend. What might happen if you simply agreed with them? If you thoughtfully (and genuinely) agree with someone who is criticising you, it takes the wind right out of their sails! Try it. No resistance. No pushing against. Uniting with them instead. Or you can ask yourself: what is the opportunity here? If you had invited this person into your life as a friend and teacher, what might they have come to teach you? What are the helpful lessons in this situation? What are they mirroring in you? Do you criticise or harass yourself – or others? Are you 'taking it personally', because your own childhood buttons have been pressed? Are you poor at maintaining boundaries yourself?

If you look honestly at *yourself*, rather than seeing the other person as 'in the wrong', what might you learn? How might you think or behave differently from usual, and break your old habits? Once you have grasped the pearls from an irritating oyster, the situation will usually change – or it will no longer push your buttons.

Treating everything as a friend doesn't mean you want to hang out with a difficult neighbour, colleague or relative. It just means that you know they have a 'message' for you – that they match some unhealthy habits of thought of yours. Likewise you probably don't want to hang out with a tumour or broken ankle or kidney stone for too long, but you can accept that it has a hidden gift for you. It is a wake-up call. Instead of pushing against it (fight), you can relax and embrace it. You are not denying it or running away from it (flight), nor are you sinking into helplessness and despair (freeze). Instead you are becoming like a willow tree, powerful in its yielding – and listening to the voice of the wind.

HOW LOVE CAN HELP YOUR HEALTH

Countless research studies have shown that loving relation-ships are linked with positive mental and physical health, and better recovery from illness. A study of 150 married couples found that those couples who were most supportive of each other had the healthiest hearts. Those who felt angry or hostile towards each other had more hardening of the arteries – in other words, they had literally become hard-hearted.[114]

However, any relationship might be better than none at all. In a study of people who had heart attacks, those who lived alone were almost twice as likely to have a second heart attack within six months. A study of people aged 65 and over found that those who reported low social support were nearly four times as likely to die prematurely from all causes within two and a half years. And it is not only our relationships with people that matter. In a study of people hospitalised with a heart attack or chest pain, only 6 per cent of pet owners were dead a year later, compared with 28 per cent of non-pet owners.[115]

I could quote endless research studies like this – but you get the picture. Loving relationships seem to be good for us. However, we must not confuse correlation with causation. As we saw earlier, you cannot assume that a healthy diet or moderate exercise *makes* us healthier. You have to factor in why someone *chooses* a healthier diet or takes regular exercise. Why is someone making self-nurturing and conscious choices? It might be that the same factor which allows you to create healthy relationships, or even makes you choose a pet, is also good for your health: namely, relaxing into the wave response so that you are in a heart-centred state of oneness and unconditional love.

Once you have created healthy relationships, they further boost your mental and physical health, and bring you out of the stress response. It is a virtuous cycle. Relationships mirror your state of consciousness – just as your body does. So let's look at how the particle response plays out in intimate relationships.

STRESS IN RELATIONSHIPS

Personal relationships become dysfunctional when one of you habitually goes into a fight-flight response, then drags the other person into the stress response too. Perhaps one partner arrives home late, and the other becomes angry, blaming, controlling or critical (fight). Then the other fights back and starts a row, or becomes defensive, submissive and guilt-ridden, or just walks away and refuses to talk (flight), or even 'flees within', becoming numb, unresponsive and speechless (freeze). Or perhaps one of you expresses a need for time to yourself, and the other becomes critical, attacking or guilt-tripping. ('I've waited all day to spend time with you!' 'I never get any time to myself, so why should you?')

When you perceive what the other says or does through the filter of negative childhood beliefs – such as 'I am not good enough', 'I am unlovable' or 'Men abandon me' – it 'pushes your buttons'. Suddenly you feel unsafe or unloved, and you are triggered into a family-ar stress response. You no longer see the person in front of you. You are no longer even conscious. You are living from the past. Your overreaction then flips the other person into their stress response. Then you're both in a downward spiral.

Since these fight-flight-freeze cycles are so painful to be in, dysfunctional relationships often become more and more superficial to avoid intimacy – perhaps focusing on practicalities and parenting, or escaping into work. Emotions are suppressed and denied, and neither person's deeper needs are met. Both are in a chronic flight response, afraid of being real or honest with each other, while pretending everything is fine. The relationship is frozen in time. Other couples get hooked on the adrenalin/endorphin highs of frequent rows, threats of separation and making up. Others pretend to agree, 'merging' with each other to avoid conflict. I sum up these stress patterns as making relationships SAD – Superficial, Aggressive or Defensive.

Whatever the dysfunctional pattern, the stress and tension are a long-term health risk. And the patterns get passed on to the next generation. Here is how the stress response shows up in relationships (of any kind):

FIGHT – Anger, blame, criticism, self-righteousness, judgement, control, nagging, making demands, making threats, disapproval, jealousy, paranoia, possessiveness, justifying yourself, feeling 'in the right'. (This is the Persecutor/Critical Parent stance.)

FLIGHT – Guilt, shame, insecurity, self-judgement, approval-seeking, martyrhood, giving in, self-sacrifice, keeping the peace at all costs, avoidance of intimacy, withdrawal, refusing to talk, being defensive, feeling 'in the wrong'. (This can come from Rescuer/Over-responsible Parent or from Victim/Appeasing Child.)

FREEZE – Disengagement, despair, depression, fear, panic, numbness, denial, dissociation, speechlessness, feeling lost or empty, weakness and fatigue. (This is a Victim/Frightened Child position.)

Where is love? It is nowhere to be found. Love comes from connecting with your wave self, which is on a higher frequency than the particle response, so its voice cannot be heard. All that can be heard is the voice of fear and judgement. You circle each other like predator and prey. No wonder that some people learn to avoid close relationships altogether.

Toxic relationships are characterised by what psychotherapist Susan Forward calls the FOG (Fear, Obligation and Guilt).[116] This is a symptom of stress. Getting lost in this FOG makes it easy for others to manipulate you, so that you feel trapped and controlled. Fear makes you feel like a vulnerable particle – so you focus on how to protect yourself or the other, how to defend yourself, or how to attack, making the other feel guilty, obligated or anxious so that you stay in control. You avoid possible negatives, rather than moving towards the positive. Fear makes us avoid the unknown, which is why it keeps us so frozen – whereas love knows that 'you are part of me', and allows us to connect and to grow.

Why do people stay in unhealthy relationships, which constantly trigger the fight–flight–freeze response, and in which they can never truly relax and be themselves? Because they have fallen asleep. They have chosen a partner with whom they can re-enact their childhood – even if it was a childhood of abuse, neglect, abandonment, criticism, martyrhood, distance, insecurity or fear – because that is the partner who feels 'right' to them. They are either replicating their parents' relationship, or their own relationship with one parent. Even though it is painful, it fits with their habitual neurochemistry of stress. It feels family-ar, and they are loyally repeating their family patterns.

Conventional relationships come from the same world view as conventional medicine. Just as medicine tries to control the body from the outside in, marriage vows or family ties are often used to control people. 'If you do what suits me, I will be happy.' People fall into patterns of compromise and sacrifice, pretending to agree and shrinking themselves to fit the relationship, or telling themselves that marriage is tough and they have to stick it out. The longer people stay in conventional relationships like this, the more strongly the habits are reinforced – and they might remain stuck and frozen for decades. Mental or physical health problems become inevitable.

Unhappy relationships are glued together by the stress response itself. Remember that the reptilian brain favours loyalty – since it prefers what is familiar, and urges us to keep things stable. This is why an abused child will cling to an abusive parent, and might have to be dragged away kicking and screaming. When we are under chronic stress, we mistake familiarity and dependency for love, and avoid change at all costs. It is a vicious cycle. So the paradox is that the worse a relationship is, the harder it is to leave it – even though it might be blocking your growth and threatening your health.

The fight-flight response is useful when you are facing a hungry tiger, but it makes a hopeless mess of personal relationships. While you're in the stress response, you have zero emotional intelligence. You are lost in the FOG of stress. Your frontal lobes are switched off, and you think like a lizard. And even if you do leave, you take your problems with you – so it is crucial to change your subconscious beliefs and habitual neurochemistry after leaving, otherwise you might re-create the same relationship with someone else.

The good news is that it only takes *one* of you to 'wake up' and remain firmly in the wave response. Then you can build a healthy and loving relationship together – or move towards a healthy and amicable separation.

DIVORCE AND AVOIDING THE STRESS RESPONSE

In this Age of Consciousness, many people are moving away from conventional relationships and towards conscious partnerships that make their hearts sing and spirits dance. When unhealthy stress patterns have built up in a marriage over many years, or you have simply grown apart, divorce allows you both to grow and move on. If you do decide to separate or divorce, then your primary aim should be staying out of the stress response.

If you see divorce as a tragedy that leads to a 'broken family', or as damaging for your children, then it will become so! Or if you 'justify' divorce by constantly pointing out how awful your partner was (*fight mode*) – or feel guilty about leaving, and over-compensate by giving in to your ex-partner's demands (*flight mode*) – this will bring more of the same pain for years to come. Instead focus on what was good and positive between you, and the positive qualities of your ex-partner, while acknowledging that you no longer bring out what is best in each other, or do not match well as a couple. This is no one's fault. Being together probably helped you both to clarify what you really want in a partnership – and a better future awaits you.

In most cases, one partner is more ready to end a marriage than the other. If you are the one who leaves, you need to do so without guilt – trusting that you are following your higher guidance, and that if the relationship was truly loving and worked well, you would want to stay. No blame, no guilt. This is the key to an amicable divorce – as I know from my own experience. Following our dreams and desires always *feels good*. And in a loving universe, it always works out for everyone.[117]

When I decided to end my own marriage, I knew that it was the right choice for me, and now that my ex-husband is happily remarried to the woman of his dreams, he knows that the choice was right for both of us. The universe is not taking sides when it sends us guidance. It wants to fulfil *everyone's* needs and desires.

Divorce can trigger health problems if it is not handled well. Last month, I saw a lovely man whose prostate cancer was triggered when his wife left him for a younger lover, while mocking him over his own sexual failings. David's mother had been the single parent of four children, all with different fathers, who told him that men were 'only good for one thing'. When his wife reminded him that he could not even get this 'one thing' right – he suffered (unsurprisingly) from impotence – it threw him into shame and insecurity which dated back to his early years. David had grown up believing that he was not worthy of love, and his marriage repeated his relationship with his mother. Their divorce was bitter, and the legal wrangles expensive. And the stress hit his prostate gland.

HUNA HEALING

A simple but powerful tool for healing relationships – whether past or present – is known as Ho'oponopono. This is an ancient Hawaiian approach to healing relationships, which I first came across while training in the Huna wisdom in Kaua'i. It is based upon knowing that everything that comes to us is a mirror of the self – including what happens in our own body, and even how others behave. This stops you pushing against another person or against your body, and brings you back into thinking like a wave.

Exercise
HO'OPONOPONO FOR HEALING HEARTS

This is an ancient Hawaiian approach to healing relationships of all kinds – relationships with everything – so it can be applied to personal relationships or to illness. (I've even used it to heal a crashed computer!) If you use it for illness, you can direct your thoughts towards your body in general, a sick organ, or a symptom or disease.

The simplest way to practise Ho'oponopono[118] is to say silently, like a prayer:

✧ I'm sorry

✧ Please forgive me

✧ Thank you

✧ I love you

Or you can even shorten this to 'Thank you. I love you.' And *feel* it!

Apologising does not mean feeling guilty or taking the blame. It means taking back your power as a conscious creator of your reality. If you apply it to people, it means recognising that their behaviour mirrors your own vibrations. If you apply it to dis-ease, it means recognising that your bodymind would be healthy if you were not getting in its way by setting up resistance. And that is OK. You are doing the best you can, and are on an eternal journey towards expanding awareness.

RELATIONSHIPS IN THE WAVE RESPONSE

In a warm, loving and supportive relationship, you readily bring each other out of the stress response. You 'hold' each other emotionally – without taking it personally if the other is feeling hurt, angry or insecure. You know how to soothe and reassure each other. You become waves in the ocean together. You deeply relax and breathe fully in each other's presence. This is why loving and being loved feels so good. It provides a comforting haven to return to. Even if it is challenging at times, the love is steady and unconditional. Fear makes us contract, run away and resist change – whereas love makes us expand, embrace each other and move towards growth.

In the eyes of unconditional love, the other is never the enemy, never a threat – always a friend. Instead of circling each other from a distance, you deeply connect – while remaining aware of your own uniqueness. There is nothing to hide, nothing to avoid, nothing to run away from. You feel able to be honest and authentic, discovering yourself through the other. There are no demands or expectations, no jealousy or possessiveness. You are free to be who you really are. You bring out what is best and deepest in each other. Love makes us more conscious.

The key to healthy relationships (of any kind) is to mind your own business – which means keeping *yourself* out of the stress response. If you blame anyone else for how you feel, you are stuck in the stress response (fight mode). This is conditional love. You are seeing the other person as 'the problem' – which leaves you feeling angry, hurt, helpless or disempowered.

Likewise, if you take responsibility for how someone else feels, you are also in the stress response (flight mode). You might feel guilty, resentful, defensive or submissive, or want to keep the peace. Then you are imprisoned by the other person, and will resent them for it. Once you understand the true role of emotions, as we shall see in the next chapter, it becomes easier to steer clear of these relationship landmines.

From a higher perspective – beyond the stress response – everyone is in charge of their own happiness. If either of you feels bad, it is not because of the other person (or the situation), but *because your stress response has been triggered*. Once you reconnect with your higher self, you gaze through rose-tinted glasses – seeing what is best in the other, instead of seeing what is 'wrong' with them, so that you set them free to be who they really are. You also become more aware of your own patterns. And instead of being filled with blame, guilt or regrets – which are all signs of the stress response – you focus on what you desire for the future.

BEYOND BLAME AND GUILT

What I teach in my *Wild Love* workshops is: 'You are responsible for everything you create in your life – *including how
others behave towards you.*' It can be tempting to give others
the responsibility for how they behave – and might even
sound like 'common sense' to do so – but that means you
feel like a helpless victim. If you have ever tried to change
someone else – to make your partner more romantic, or your
teenager tidier, or your mother-in-law less interfering – you
will know that it is a mug's game!

You cannot control anyone else. But you can control how
you think about them, how you think and feel about yourself, and how you speak to others – shifting out of old
patterns of blame, guilt, fear or insecurity.[119] Are you being
judgmental, blaming or controlling? Are you repeating patterns
from your own childhood? Are you focusing on what is
'wrong' with them, instead of what is right? Are you holding
yourself responsible for their emotional baggage, or trying
to 'fix' them? Are you projecting parts of yourself that you
feel uncomfortable with? Are you clinging to a relationship
that isn't working out of fear, guilt, obligation or inertia? Are
you making demands or feeling 'entitled' to have them behave
in a certain way? You can only change yourself – and that
changes everything.

The 'blame game' really messes up relationships – and it
means you are giving your power away. The single most
important rule for healthy relationships is to take responsibility for your own feelings and needs. It isn't 50/50 in a
relationship. That is merely a cop-out that still allows room
for blame. ('If he/she hadn't behaved that way, I wouldn't
have reacted as I did.' 'If he/she was more loving, I would
be too.') You are 100 per cent responsible for your experience. This does not mean that you are to *blame* for others'
behaviour. However, you are responsible for how you perceive
and respond to it – and as we shall see in Chapter 7, you
are also responsible for bringing that behaviour out in them.
You are always gazing into a mirror.

In my own journey through cancer, my primary focus was resolving the relationship that had triggered the cancer. I knew this mirrored inner blockages I wanted to break through. After the cancer diagnosis, I slowly renewed my loving friendship with the man I had fallen in love with. However, it was an emotional rollercoaster as we strived to keep our friendship stable in the face of his long-troubled marriage. The strict limitations of our friendship tore me apart, and I ended it twice – but we both found it too hard to be apart for long.

Eventually after months of heart-searching, he confided in close friends and family that he was in love with me and wanted to separate from his wife. We agreed to spend the rest of our lives together, and kissed for the first time. It felt like a dam bursting, with long held-back passion and honesty bursting forth – and I was deeply in love.

However, when he expressed his desire for an amicable separation at home, it caused a major row – and he suddenly changed. The warm and loving man I knew vanished over-night, and he became anxious, guilt-ridden, dissociated and frozen (the stress response personified). He said he needed more time – and after several more weeks of torment, he phoned to say he would be staying in his marriage after all. The pattern of five years earlier had repeated itself all over again.

Until now, the tumour in my breast had been small, trouble-free and mostly inactive. I had only felt twinges of discomfort in my breast when I was in turmoil over the rela-tionship, and had no symptoms of illness. Within a week of his abrupt pulling back, I was suddenly in severe pain at night, as if shards of glass were being thrust into my chest. I felt weak and tired, and knew that my body was now 'cancering' in a big way. The tumour was growing rapidly. It was a highly stressful time. I suddenly felt helpless and unloved – which I knew was carcinogenic for me – yet I could not allow myself the luxury of wallowing in hurt, grief or anger. Every negative emotion would be damaging my biochem-istry, and allowing the cancer to thrive. Nor could I risk denying my emotions. I had to accept my feelings, while reaching for the wave response. I knew I had to bend like a willow in the wind – and that this was a huge opportunity to practise all that I now knew.

Rather than 'pushing against' what was happening, or worrying about him, I had to focus on my own issues. I had to take my power back – by taking responsibility for his behaviour towards me, and for how this mirrored my habits of thought and childhood issues. I knew that I was gazing in a mirror, and had never seen my own patterns in such sharp relief. The problem was not his behaviour, but *me*. With the help of energy healing and energy psychology, I healed traumas from the past in new ways, got my energy flowing again and stabilised myself in the wave response. Amazingly, I found my way back to unconditional love – and now trusted that everything was unfolding perfectly.

Within two or three weeks of his decision, the pain began to fade away, my energy returned and the tumour softened. All of the symptoms disappeared. My energy healer confirmed what I already knew – that the cancer was no longer active, and had gone into retreat. And all of these rapid changes in my body, for better and worse, happened solely because of shifts in my energy-consciousness. (Diet, exercise and other physical factors remained the same throughout.) For me, this was a powerful experience of conscious medicine in practice.

Whenever I felt painfully separate from love, I knew that I was in the particle response. Then my body expressed that malignant belief through the cancer. When I consciously reconnected with love and trust – without anything external changing – my body healed itself. I knew how to do that now. And I had learnt so much about myself, about the particle/wave response and about unconditional love throughout this whole journey.

No one can press your buttons (that is, trigger the stress response) unless you have old habits of thoughts that need to be explored, or unresolved traumas which need to be healed, or denied parts of the self which you have squashed and projected. Everyone and everything that comes to you is your friend and teacher – whether it is a difficult relationship, a bankruptcy or a tumour. It mirrors some part of you. And once you have embraced it, learnt the lessons and healed the energetic patterns, you can step into a new future.

In the old Newtonian universe, a billiard ball can be the innocent victim of another billiard ball. This makes room for blame, guilt and criticism. But in a conscious universe, everything is connected. You are responsible for your own experience – and you can only change your body, your relationships or your life from the inside out.

TRANSFORMING RELATIONSHIPS WITH TURNAROUNDS

One of the most useful tools I know for shifting relationships out of habitual patterns, and breaking out of drama triangles, is Byron Katie's exercise on turnarounds.[120] This helps you take responsibility for what you are feeling, and realise that the only person who needs to change is you! It reconnects you with your inner wisdom, and reminds you that you are always looking in a mirror. Then any challenge becomes a source of growth rather than stress.

Exercise
TURNAROUNDS

Choose someone – dead or alive – whom you are holding any negative feelings towards. Then fill in the blanks below. (You might want to write out or photocopy this exercise so that you can use it again and again.) Don't hold back – express your anger or pain as if the situation is happening right now, even if it is in the past.

1. Who angers, frustrates, saddens or confuses you, and why?

   I am...........................with [name]................
   because..
   ....

(E.g. I am angry with Jack because he betrayed and abandoned me. I am angry with David because he doesn't listen to me and argues with what I say. I am frustrated with Mother because she is so dependent on me and won't make her own decisions.)

2. How do you want them to change? What do you want them to do?

    I want [name] .... to ....

    ....

    ....

    (E.g. I want Jane to see that she is wrong. I want her to apologise. Or: I want Sam to be more loving towards me. Or: Tom should take better care of himself.)

3. What is it that they should not do, be, think or feel? What advice could you offer them?

    .... should/shouldn't ....

    ....

    ....

4. What do they need to do in order for you to be happy?

    I want [name] .... to ....

    ....

    ....

5. What do you think of them? Make a list (e.g. lazy, selfish, irresponsible, controlling).

    ....[name] is ....

    ....

    ....

6. What is it you don't ever want to experience with that person again?

I don't ever want to ....

....

....

Then for every statement above, go inside yourself and ask the following four questions. Go deeply. This is meditation:

1. Is it true?
2. Can you absolutely know that it's true?
3. How do you react, what happens, when you believe that thought?
4. Who would you be without the thought?

Byron Katie, founder of The Work, strongly suggests that you do not try the turnarounds without first walking yourself through these four questions. It is crucial that this does not become an exercise in self-blame, but rather about seeing the innocence of the other person, along with your own innocence.

The Turnarounds – Now comes what I consider to be the best bit! This is where you turn around whatever you wrote above until you get one or more Aha! moments. This is based on an awareness of relationships as projections of our own beliefs and unexpressed Shadow side, and any uncomfortable thought not being aligned with our higher self. Play with turning around every statement above in different ways until you get a positive shift in your emotions, or a smile comes to your face. Is this new statement at least as true as the original statement, or even more true? Does it set you free if you look at this relationship through these new eyes?

Examples of turnarounds:

'Jack betrayed and abandoned me' might turnaround into: 'I betrayed and abandoned Jack' or 'I betrayed and abandoned myself'.

'Mother is so dependent on me, and she won't make her own

decisions' becomes 'Mother is so independent' or 'I am so dependent on Mother, and I won't make my own decisions'.

'David should listen more to me' becomes 'I should listen more to David' or 'I should listen more to myself' or 'David shouldn't listen more to me'.

'Jane needs to apologise' becomes 'I need to apologise to Jane' or 'I need to apologise to myself' or 'Jane should not apologise to me'.

'Sam should be more loving towards me' becomes 'I should be more loving towards myself' or 'I should be more loving towards Sam' or 'Sam should not be more loving towards me'.

'Tom should take care of himself better' becomes 'I should take care of myself better' or 'I should take better care of Tom' or 'Tom should not take better care of himself'.

Now use the space provided below to formulate your own 'turnaround'.

....
....
....
....
....
....
....
....

BEING YOUR OWN BEST FRIEND

Most relationships are troubled because of negative beliefs and decisions set up in the first seven years of life. These were originally designed to protect you, and to make sure you are safe and loved. However, a decision that is 'protective' for a three year old – such as deciding to be good and perfect, or never to trust strangers, or to hide anger or sadness, or always pretend everything is fine – becomes a form of self-sabotage when you are an adult. The original intention was positive, but being defensive or protective means you are in the stress response, which damages your health and your relationships. It can turn you into your own worst enemy.

If you decide that you are unworthy of love at the age of five, it can affect your relationships for decades to come. You are likely to choose partners, bosses and even friends who mirror back your 'unworthiness', and deepen your insecurity. Our beliefs become self-fulfilling prophecies. Likewise if you decide that it is *your fault* if a parent is distressed or angry, and that you are not being good enough, you will be easily controlled by guilt in later life – and might find it hard to love and nurture yourself. This can be reflected in eating a poor diet, not taking exercise, not getting enough sleep, working too hard (in order to 'feel good') or simply not having much fun.

Our relationships with others mirror our primary relationship – with self – and if we don't see ourselves as worthy of love, caring and attention, nor will those around us. If you love yourself conditionally, then others will do the same. It is rather like those fairground mirrors in which you are surrounded by reflections within reflections of yourself, appearing on all sides and receding into the far distance. Negative beliefs and undischarged traumas create stressful relationships, and set up defensive strategies that make relationships even worse.

Your relationship with your body is one of those reflections. If you see your body as a potential enemy, and battle against it when it displays symptoms of dis-ease – or criticise it for being the 'wrong' shape or size, or less than perfect in your eyes – then you are likely to choose healthcare strategies which are unlikely to work in the long term, since you are thinking as if you're on a battlefield. Even when you are sick, your body is always your friend. It is doing the very best it can, given the thoughts and beliefs you are feeding into it. Treating yourself as your best friend – and caring for your body as a much-loved friend too – is one of the best healthcare strategies there is.

EVERY PROBLEM IS A GIFT

The universe is always on your side. Any unwanted situation simply mirrors something you need to explore about yourself. Old habits of thought; lizard voices from the past. It can also help you clarify what you want for your future. It can push you to develop strengths and resources which would otherwise have lain dormant, and make you dream bigger dreams for your future.

Every problem, challenge and trauma – including illness and disease – has a higher purpose when seen through the right eyes. From the wave response, it is all part of the adventure of being alive – and just like a wave, it will have its highs and lows. Every challenge is an opportunity to learn and grow, and to look for the hidden gifts so that we can surf that wave and reach the next high point. Life is always full of ups and downs. It is how you navigate those ups and downs that make all the difference. Getting off the battlefield of the 'stress response' turns life into an enjoyable and even magical journey.

In the next chapter, we will look at why *thinking* in positive ways is not necessarily enough to prevent or heal disease. What really matters is how you *feel*. And how you feel, in turn, reflects how well your energy is flowing – whether you are crashing painfully into ocean waves, or surfing them with joy and exhilaration. When Source energy is flowing freely, you approach everything that happens in life with unconditional love – seeing it all as a gift. Then you are living from the wave response.

Chapter Seven

STAIRWAY TO HAPPINESS

You could stand here sick with ten illnesses today, and tomorrow have no evidence of any of them. Your body has the ability to replenish itself that fast. But most of you do not have the ability to change your thoughts that fast.

Abraham[121]

So far, we have looked at how the new science is leading us inexorably towards a new approach to healthcare, and why having a healthy body means having a healthy mind. We have also explored how and why healthy relationships support our mental and physical health. Now we are going to look at the crucial role that *emotions* play in our lives – and how they offer an early warning system that can prevent disease, or guide us towards healing. Feeling good is – in a quite literal sense – feeling God.

THE STORY SO FAR

Let's review the principles we have covered so far:

✧ At a deeper level, the universe is not solid and material. According to the new science, this is a psycho-energetic reality. Everything is energy, which is shaped and moulded by consciousness

✧ Within the new paradigm, everything is 'caused' by what is happening in the unseen realms – the invisible realms of energy-consciousness. Everything unfolds from deep reality into surface reality. Our lives are created and moulded by our own consciousness

✧ The body has its own intelligence, but consciousness can override this. Our biology is not controlled by genes, but by our perceptions, thoughts and beliefs

✧ We have two primary ways of thinking – like a fearful and separated particle, or like a loving and connected wave

✧ The particle (or stress) response, when chronically activated, sets up disease. The wave (or relaxation) response allows the bodymind to heal or remain healthy

✧ Undischarged trauma leaves you feeling unsafe or unloved – which readily triggers the stress response. You are frozen in the past

✧ While you are in the stress response, your frontal lobes are deactivated. You 'fall asleep', and cling to what is family-ar. You revert to childhood programming, and repeat the same repetitive thoughts, habits and routines. Your growth and potential is blocked – and your emotional and physical health is progressively damaged

✧ When you push against anything (including disease), you are in battle mode – and what you resist persists

✧ Illness is not a 'design fault' in the body. It is a helpful messenger about inner conflict

✧ The key to releasing the particle response is becoming more conscious and self-aware, and moving towards joy and unconditional love – by breaking old habits of thoughts, releasing trauma and changing your subconscious beliefs

✧ Once you trust in a loving universe, and embrace everything as a friend, you switch on the wave response. Then your consciousness expands, you relax – and your body can heal itself

So what role do our emotions play in a conscious universe? And what is the relationship between emotions, energy and health?

EMOTIONS AS GUIDANCE

As we saw in Chapter 3, the particle and wave responses lie on a continuum. You might be 30 per cent particle and 70 per cent wave, or 80 per cent wave and 20 per cent particle in any moment – depending upon what you are focusing upon right now, and your habits of thought. The more the particle response is switched on, the more separate and small you feel, and the worse you feel emotionally. You feel unsafe and separate from love. At worst, you might feel frightened, despairing or even suicidal. The more the wave response is switched on, the more connected you feel – to everyone and everything. You feel expansive, free and unlimited. When your heart sings and your spirit dances, you're fully in the wave response. This has also been called nirvana, bliss or the 'oceanic feeling'. Moving towards this state is a key to health and healing. *And our emotions indicate where we currently lie on the particle–wave continuum.*

Within the old paradigm, emotions are pretty much irrelevant to health, and rather a nuisance in our lives. They can make life uncomfortable at times, but are not to be taken too seriously. Since the old paradigm focuses on physical reality, it sees emotions as a reaction to what happens in the 'real world'. If you feel angry, it is because someone out there has behaved badly. If you feel guilty, it is because *you* have behaved badly. If you feel sad, it is because you have lost something or someone, or something bad has happened. If you feel frustrated, it is because events are not turning out as you wanted them to, or not quickly enough. And so on.

From the perspective of conscious medicine, this is misleading or even nonsensical!

Nine years ago, when I began practising EFT (see Chapters 1 and 9) and other forms of energy psychology, I had to re-think almost everything I learnt about emotions from my training in psychodynamic psychotherapy (which looks at the patterns and defences we carry from the past). The guiding principle of EFT is that 'Any negative emotion arises from a disruption in the body's energy system'.[122] I knew this was consistent with traditional Chinese medicine (TCM) – but although emotion can be translated into e-motion, or energy in motion, I wasn't used to thinking about emotion in energy terms.

From a background in clinical psychology, how could I translate from an energy-based system into a consciousness-based model? How did energy and consciousness fit together? I grappled with the ideas for years, and slowly it all clicked into place. Piecing together ideas like a jigsaw is what I really love doing – and as I gradually integrated different models from the new physics, new biology, alternative medicine, psychology and spirituality, I began to see an overall model for conscious medicine.

'Any negative emotion (or physical symptom) arises from a disruption in the body's energy system.' What does this really mean? It suggests that there is a natural flow of energy when we are in a healthy state, and when this flow is blocked or distorted, we feel bad. We might feel worried or sad or resentful or frustrated – but this is just a signal that our energy is not flowing as it should be.

Can you see how this fits with the new biology, and the stress response? Negative emotion means that the stress response is switched on – which disrupts our energy flow – and since that is bad for the physical body, emotion is an immediate warning signal that grabs our attention. Our emotions are like traffic signals – red, amber or green – which indicate the state of our energy flow.

Six years ago, I came across the spiritual teachings of Abraham,[123] which are now reaching millions of people.

Abraham is a collective consciousness, or aspect of Divine Intelligence – expressed through a woman called Esther Hicks, while she holds an expanded state of consciousness – who offers universal teachings about reality creation, why we are here and how to make our lives work well. I studied these teachings intensively, and my understanding of emotions moved into a whole new dimension.

Abraham explains that emotions are designed to be our primary form of *guidance*. When you feel unconditional love, joy, passion, enthusiasm, gratitude, appreciation and other positive emotions, your thoughts are aligned with your higher self. This means that Source energy is flowing freely through you, which (not surprisingly) makes you feel good. When you feel worry, disappointment, doubt, loneliness, anger, guilt, insecurity, fear and other negative emotions, it means that your current thoughts are not aligned with how your higher self thinks. The 'split' between you and your higher self feels uncomfortable, blocks your energy flow and produces negative emotion.

Emotions tell you how large the gap is between your ego and your higher self. Small gap equals positive feelings; large gap equals negative feelings. Aha! Energy psychology, Chinese medicine and Eastern philosophy, the new biology, new physics and spiritual teachings began to come together for me with this insight – like a shifting kaleidoscope that began to settle into a harmonious new pattern.

Emotions are not telling you what is happening 'out there', and whether it is good or bad. Your emotions tell you *which voices you are listening to*. Are you listening to a voice of love and connectedness, or a voice of fear and judgement? If you feel bad, it is only because you are looking at things in a screwy way – through the eyes of your particle self. The stress response is switched on, and you are thinking more like a (fearful, separate) particle, and less like a (loving, connected) wave. And that puts your health in jeopardy.

Our emotions do not arise from what is happening in physical reality then, but from our *thoughts* about what is happening (or has happened, or might happen). Our emotions come from our *perceptions* of the environment – filtered through the distorting lens of our childhood and past experiences.

From this viewpoint, if you are feeling angry, it is not because someone is behaving badly, but because (unlike your higher self) you are *judging* someone as behaving badly, and also choosing to focus on that 'bad' behaviour. If you are feeling guilty, it is not because you have done something wrong, but because (unlike your higher self) you are *judging* yourself – often through the eyes of others. If you are feeling sad, it is not because you have lost something precious, but because you are focused on what is missing and feeling disconnected. If you deliberately change your thoughts, your emotions will change too.

In other words, your emotions do not depend on how anyone is behaving, or what is happening, but on how you are choosing to *think* about it. And how you choose to think about it depends on your childhood experiences, your underlying beliefs, and whether or not you are in the stress response.

WHICH VOICES DO YOU LISTEN TO?

Shamanism tells us that we have three selves – the subconscious, conscious and higher self (or body, mind and spirit respectively). When these three work together in harmony, your energy is strong and coherent, and the result is vibrant health, happiness and loving relationships. This inner harmony corresponds to what the Institute of HeartMath calls a state of heart coherence (see Chapter 2) – that is, synchronisation between your heart, brain and autonomic nervous system.

When there is a clash between your subconscious and conscious mind, your subconscious tends to win out. After all, it can process a million times more information per second than the conscious mind, and trigger the stress response before you're even aware of what is happening. It coshes your conscious self over the head, leaving it out cold on the floor, while your primitive brain takes over dealing with life.

Let's suppose that you receive only messages of unconditional love in the early years of life – that your parents adore
you and each other, and see the world as a safe and loving
place to be, and that your household is full of joy, laughter
and appreciation, and free from any tension, anxiety, blame,
shame or guilt. If so, your subconscious mind will be aligned
with your higher self – and you will only go into the stress
response (briefly) when you face immediate physical danger.
However, no one has a childhood like this!

In a normal childhood we go through many emotional
traumas and pick up countless fears and negative beliefs. And
in fact, much of our growth and creativity comes from the
tension between our subconscious and higher self. Trauma
seems to build strength and resilience, once we move beyond
the freeze response, so an idyllic childhood might *not* be the
ideal start to life. It could leave us placid but fairly stagnant,
with a limited range of inner resources.[124] (Since I believe
that we choose our parents before we are born, this might
be why so many people's higher selves choose tough child-
hoods – to grow and evolve through experience.)

So here you are, with a subconscious generously stuffed
with faulty beliefs, habits of thought and family patterns
passed down the generations. The task of your conscious self
(ego), which is suspended between the subconscious and
higher self, is to choose which voice to listen to. The voice
of love, or the voice of fear? How many of your 60,000
thoughts per day are anxious, defensive, stuck, critical, guilt-
ridden or repetitive? How many of your thoughts are loving,
joyful, enthusiastic, appreciative, forward-looking and creative?
How often do you think about the worst that could happen,
rather than the best that could happen? How often do you
beat yourself up, rather than loving and supporting yourself?
Which voices do you listen to?

How to recognise your lizard voices

If your subconscious mind is filled with fear and shame, your
conscious self (or ego) will be frequently thrown into the

stress response. Instead of hearing your higher self, you listen to the stressed voices of your subconscious: the voice of your inner child, critical parent or over-protective parent, voices of habit and convention and duty, voices of fear and guilt and negativity. Lizard voices from the past.

Since they come from childhood, lizard voices tend to look up to 'experts' (such as doctors) and anyone in authority, and will override your intuitive guidance in order to follow others' advice. Lizard voices warn of possible risks and dangers and threats. They urge you to play safe and repeat the past. 'Don't rock the boat!' say lizard voices. 'Better the devil you know!' 'Put others first.' 'Respect your elders!' 'Don't take any risks!' They favour loyalty and stability, even if it doesn't *feel* good, so that they can carry on repeating family-ar patterns. Lizard voices are focused on survival, on staying safe, on getting through the days, on being good and perfect – rather than on happiness, growth and creativity.

Healthy cells in the body move towards nutrients, and away from toxins – and so do healthy people. But what if you have a subconscious belief that life is a struggle, that you do not deserve to be happy, that love hurts, or the world is not a safe place to be? Then you will tend to move towards relationships and situations that reinforce those beliefs – which trigger the stress response, and confirm your negative beliefs. You might find yourself pulling away from relationships that are potentially nourishing and supportive. Or you will stay in a job you do not enjoy, while telling yourself that you have no choice, at least it pays the mortgage, and it is only twenty years to retirement. You sabotage yourself. You move towards toxins, and away from nutrients. It feels family-ar and somehow comforting, even if it is painful. Your primitive brain and habitual neurochemistry govern your choices.

How to recognise the voice of your higher self

The voice of your higher self feels very different from those lizard voices. It calls you towards the future – towards expansion and growth. It calls you towards unconditional love, freedom and joy. It is the voice of inspiration and creativity. It is like a breath of fresh air. Sometimes I call it a phoenix voice, because it helps us transform like the phoenix – becoming a firebird which rises from its own ashes, evolving into a higher being which can fly.

The voice of the phoenix is drowned out by the particle response. This isn't because your higher self has stopped speaking to you. It is just that you cannot hear it when you are stressed out. You are like a radio tuned to a lower frequency. However, it is always speaking to you *through your emotions*. This is your moment-to-moment guidance system. And if you are listening to this, you will know that any negative emotion (or physical symptom) is a wake-up call, a warning sign that you are listening to lizard voices from the past.

One of my favourite ways of shifting our antennae from lizard voices to the voice of our higher self is using power animals.[125] Power animals are archetypal energies that can symbolise personal qualities you want to release, as well as those you want to tap into. Here is an inner journey to help you to re-tune your radio so that you are less likely to hear what your lizard voices are broadcasting – and even if you do, you are more likely to decide to change station.

Exercise
FINDING A NEW POWER ANIMAL

Make yourself comfortable, and relax deeply – then imagine that you are in a natural landscape, whether it is a beach, a forest, a meadow, a mountain or a riverside. Use all your senses to make the scene come alive. When you are ready, turn to your left and begin to walk in that direction. You are now walking into your past, towards all the stress-laden patterns passed down the generations, the old habits of thought, the old ways of being that perhaps served you at one time, but which no longer support you in fulfilling your potential, or helping you find happiness and inner peace.

Look ahead of you now, and you will see an animal, bird or water creature appear. Trust whatever image comes to you now, without judgement, trusting your subconscious to send you the animal that best symbolises these old patterns. Greet this animal in a friendly and loving way, knowing that it has been doing its best to serve you. It has been trying to protect you in some way, to ensure that you are safe and loved. It is the voice of fear within you. Speak to this animal now, and ask how it has been trying to serve or protect you. Find out how it thinks, so that you will be able to recognise its voice if it speaks to you again. Thank it for serving you up to now – and tell it that it can now go into retirement. It might feel like an old friend – but it is time to let it go, so that you can move on. Say goodbye to it now.

Now turn back and walk in the opposite direction, towards your future. Keep walking until you see another animal coming into view – again trusting whatever image comes to you. What strengths or qualities does this animal represent? Say hello, and listen to what this animal wishes to say to you. What messages does this animal give, when you are listening to this new inner voice? Then merge with your new power animal – allowing it to step into you, or you step into it. It might need to shrink so that this can happen. Absorb it into your energy field, allowing it to shift your thoughts and beliefs as it does so. Then absorb it into every cell in your body.

Feel the power of this new voice as you invite it into your life. This is the voice of love. How will this new power animal help you handle life? How might you think or behave differently, with this new voice guiding you? Commit yourself to listening to this voice within you, more and more, until it becomes natural to think in this new way, until it becomes who you are. And be aware whenever you hear your old voice from now on – and laugh at it gently and with love. When you are ready, bring your awareness back into your body, and into the room – feeling wonderfully alive and at peace with yourself.

(A guided version of this inner journey is available on my CD, *Your Future Self.*)

VOICE MANAGEMENT

Sharon consulted me about severe migraines that began twelve years earlier, when she was heading towards finals in medical school. The migraines were becoming more frequent and severe. I led her through the power animals journey, and she found that her old power animal – the voice from the past – was a golden labrador puppy, eager to please and hyperactive. She said this summed up how she ran her life! She forever ran around looking after everyone else's needs. The only time she took care of herself was when she had a migraine – and even then, she might push herself through a busy surgery, rather than let down her patients and colleagues. (Migraines are often associated with a driven, perfectionist personality.)

Sharon's new power animal – the voice of her higher self, leading her towards a new future – was a roe deer, a symbol of gentleness and unconditional love. The deer urged her to love herself, first of all, and become a healthy role model for her family and patients. It reminded her that she used to love water-skiing, and that she had always wanted to learn how to draw – two activities which would help her come back into balance. Soon after, Sharon decided to go part-time, and explore parts of herself that had been put aside when she became a hospital doctor – and reported that the migraines had become much less frequent, shorter and milder. She still listened to that labrador puppy at times – but she now knew that the migraines were a reminder to take care of herself, so she saw them as helpful friends rather than as a problem.

When I attended a workshop with Lewis Mehl-Madrona, the medical doctor-cum-shaman (see Chapter 2), he said that 'life is all about voice management'.[126] He helps people to tell different stories about their lives – to shift from seeing themselves as 'victims' of medical diagnoses or betrayal or redundancy or troubled relationships or endless demands to seeing themselves as heroes within their own adventure. Our fear-based voices are unable to see the bigger picture like this. Fear makes you contract. So when you are asked to see an illness or other challenge as an ongoing journey, in which you are the scriptwriter and hero, you have to expand to a higher level of consciousness.

Seeing life as 'all about voice management' makes sense in terms of the new biology. Which thoughts you are running through your head controls how you feel, what choices you make in life, how your relationships work, and whether or not your body heals or remains healthy. So it makes sense to choose those voices wisely and consciously.

Cassie came to see me with a diagnosis of breast cancer. She had cut down her work as a management consultant to a minimum, but her days were now packed with her intensive healing programme – a raw food diet, daily coffee enemas, meditation, yoga classes, visualisations, affirmations, running, seeing therapists . . . phew! I felt exhausted just hearing her list. It soon became clear that – although her focus was now on healing – Cassie was listening to the same harsh, workaholic inner voices that had allowed the cancer to develop. She was still stressing herself out, and not surprisingly, new lumps had developed in her breast. When I asked what she did for fun, she looked at me as if I were crazy. 'I don't have time for fun! I have to heal the cancer!' Her healing journey had become another work project for her, which she must do perfectly like everything else in her life.

In our session, we released some of the trauma from Cassie's past, and installed new beliefs into her subconscious, such as 'Doing nothing is healing', and 'The more I relax, the more I heal'. Then she met a penguin as her new power animal, which told her to lighten up, have fun and stop worrying what others think of her. Cassie realised it was time to stop heeding the critical voices from her past – and that her life might depend upon listening to that playful penguin.

How do you know whether a voice comes from your lizard brain or from your higher self? *By how it makes you feel!* If a voice makes you feel warm, loving, joyful, clear-headed, playful, fun-loving, liberated, passionate, inspired, visionary, excited or expansive, listen to it! That is a phoenix voice. If it makes you feel heavy, restricted, guilty, burdened, resentful, flawed, insecure, anxious, doubtful, resigned, bored, unappreciated, despairing, small, confused, hard done by, stuck, limited or trapped – or creates a knot in your solar plexus – that is a lizard voice. It is the voice of fear, in myriad different disguises. It feels unsafe or unloved. Lizard voices are designed for when you are in immediate physical danger. Otherwise, show them the door.

Exercise
SPOTTING YOUR LIZARDS

Complete the following sentences, as fully as you can. Don't edit or censor what comes out. Just let it flow. As you become more aware of your stress patterns, and of the fear-based messages from your lizard voices, you can remain conscious when the stress response is triggered. Instead of going into fight-flight-freeze and running on autopilot, you can calm and soothe yourself. Then you can make more mature choices.

❖ I feel unsafe when . . .

❖ I feel unloved when . . .

❖ The way I cope when I feel anxious is . . .

❖ The way I cope when I feel unloved is . . .

❖ A better way of coping would be . . .

❖ What my lizard voices tell me about myself is . . .

❖ What my lizard voices tell me about other people is . . .

❖ What my lizard voices tell me about life is . . .

❖ What I want to say to my lizard voices, from the wise and loving parts of me, is . . .

THOUGHTS AND VIBRATIONS

The stress response is not all or none. Some lizard voices can throw you into a blind panic, while others just make you a little tense. Some of the cells in our body can be switched into protection (fear) mode, while others remain in growth (love) mode. You might be slightly wary because a dog growls at you from a distance; or you might be terrified as it runs towards you baring its teeth. You might be mildly disappointed when you are not offered that new job, or you might be devastated because you had set your heart on it and see it as a door that is forever closing, and perhaps because it triggers childhood rejection or insecurity. Or you might shrug over the lost job, and tell yourself, 'It's all working out. Something even better is just around the corner . . .', without even going into the stress response.

Every thought has a vibrational frequency. How do we know this? Well, everything is energy. Energy moves in waves. Waves have both amplitude (intensity) and frequency (speed). Everything in physical reality is vibrational in nature – from sound, light and temperature to thoughts and emotions. As we saw in Chapter 3, thoughts are energy fields that carry information, sending signals via the cellular membrane to the DNA, turning genes on and off.

The higher the frequency of our thoughts, the slower our brainwaves, and the more expanded our awareness. Slower brainwaves such as alpha and theta seem to be linked with inspiration and creativity, deep meditation, mystical awareness, extrasensory perception, and accelerated or instant healing. (Crucially, the crossover state between alpha and theta is also linked with the resolution of traumatic memories.) These slower brainwaves give us access to the further reaches of human potential.[127]

Why do we need to know that every thought has a vibrational frequency? Because the stress response lowers the frequency of our thoughts – and emotions are indicators of our vibrational frequency. That is their job. When we feel good, we are thinking at a high vibrational frequency. We are aligned with our higher self. We are in the wave response. This allows the body to go into its natural default mode in which growth, healing and maintenance take place. Which inner voices you listen to determines whether you remain healthy, or what kind of dis-eases you become vulnerable to – and also whether you express your loving, joyful and creative potential.

THE EMOTIONAL LADDER

Abraham has provided a scale that shows how our emotions are related to our current vibrational frequency. I call this the emotional ladder[128] – and it can be seen as a stairway to happiness and health. As you release the stress response and move up the stairway, lizard voices fade into the background, and the voice of your higher self predominates. You feel better and better, and your physical health improves more and more.

If you could hold yourself consistently at the top of the emotional ladder for just a few days – though this is far from easy – any disease in your body could heal itself. Tumours or kidney stones or arthritis might vanish overnight, and occasionally this does happen. Towards the top of the emotional ladder you become more wave-like and less particle-like, which means that energy can flow more easily into different forms and your body realigns itself with health.

Instant healing is unusual, because it is difficult to *hold* yourself at the top of the emotional ladder if your habits of thought usually bring you tumbling towards the bottom, or even the mid-range. Most of us have an 'emotional set point', which is a habitual vibrational frequency where we most often hang out. This might be (at best) around joy, love and enthusiasm; or (in the mid-range) around over-whelm, worry or frustration; or (at worst) around guilt, insecurity, fear or even despair. We gravitate back towards thoughts within our usual vibrational range. It is *easiest* to think those thoughts. After all, we have lots of well-established neural pathways that allow us to keep thinking those thoughts.

What is more, every emotion has its own chemical signature, and if we are not 'feeding' our body with thoughts that

The Emotional Ladder

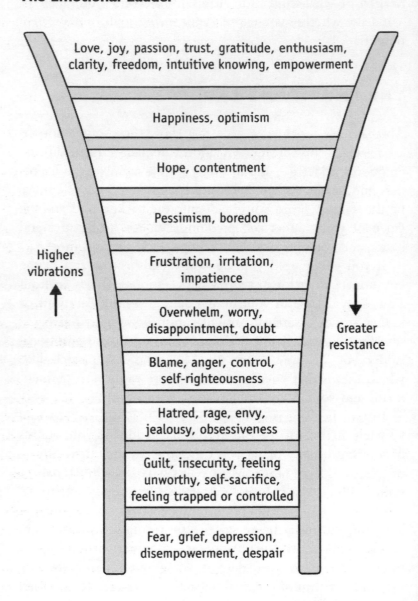

Love, joy, passion, trust, gratitude, enthusiasm, clarity, freedom, intuitive knowing, empowerment

Happiness, optimism

Hope, contentment

Pessimism, boredom

Frustration, irritation, impatience

Overwhelm, worry, disappointment, doubt

Blame, anger, control, self-righteousness

Hatred, rage, envy, jealousy, obsessiveness

Guilt, insecurity, feeling unworthy, self-sacrifice, feeling trapped or controlled

Fear, grief, depression, disempowerment, despair

Higher vibrations ↑

↓ Greater resistance

support our habitual neurochemistry, we begin to feel uneasy. Change always feels uncomfortable at first. Our protein receptors come to crave those familiar emotions from those familiar thoughts. As Joe Dispenza puts it, 'If we are not getting the chemicals we have become accustomed to, a voice from the past begins to fire in our brain.'[129] A lizard voice.

This might sound as if we are designed to avoid change and growth – but the opposite is true. We are designed to grow and evolve, which is why we have emotions that *feel bad* when we are listening to lizard voices, and why we get sick if we cling to our old habits of thought and behaviour. After all, those lizard voices are only intended to keep us alive while we are vulnerable – when we are very young, or facing a hungry tiger. Those fearful voices make us contract and hold back. They keep us safe when we are in danger.

Most of the time, we are meant to listen to the voice of our higher self – which calls us in positive directions. Phoenix voices help us make choices based on our future rather than our past – so they often take us out of our comfort zone. They challenge our old identity and family-ar patterns. They call us towards expansion, towards fulfilling our dreams, and fulfilling our potential. They lead us to see the best in everyone, to love and appreciate life, and to love and honour ourselves. They help us relax and chill out. They make us reach out and connect. They give us faith in a loving universe, and help us trust that everything is working out. When we listen to a phoenix voice, we *feel good*.

The trouble is, unless you are using your emotions as *guidance*, your ego might believe that a lizard voice is telling you the truth. You might believe that you really do not deserve love, or you're not allowed to make your own decisions, or that someone else has the right to control you, or that you cannot trust people, or there isn't enough time, or you must please others, or you're not achieving enough, or that you are bad and unworthy – or whatever your own lizard voices tend to say. Do those voices make you feel good? Of course not – but they sound familiar, and have become old friends.

You get accustomed to feeling anxious or guilty or frustrated or overwhelmed, and it feels 'normal' to you.

Some spiritual teachers see the ego, or conscious self, as a bad thing – but without an ego, you would be psychotic, and have no sense of personal identity or boundaries. Having an ego is essential. It only becomes a problem when it is dominated by fear-based voices from the past. What you need is a *healthy* ego – one that is attuned to your higher self, rather than to lizard voices. When your particle self becomes aware of its wave-like qualities, it expands its creative potential. Then all your selves can work together in harmony – and there are no limits to what is then possible.

CLIMBING THE LADDER

Let's see how the stress response relates to the emotional ladder. The initial response to stress is usually fight mode, which is the highest frequency of the three stress responses. This relates to rage or revenge at worst, and frustration or irritation at best. When you feel angry or self-righteous, or determined to fight something, it can feel pretty good – especially if you had been feeling helpless or insecure before. As I often joke, this means that if you have a choice between blaming someone else or blaming yourself, you should always blame someone else! Anger feels better than guilt.

However, if you waver over whether you can win a battle, and self-doubt sets in, then you go into flight mode – which doesn't feel so good. The resistance in your energy system has increased. You might then withdraw, feel guilty, become submissive, deny anything is wrong, or do anything to keep the peace. At worst, you go into the freeze response – which is the lowest point you can reach on the emotional ladder. You are now blocking your own energy flow in an extreme way. This feels about as bad as life gets, and many people have suicidal thoughts when they are in a chronic freeze response, since they know that death would feel a whole lot better.

Let's head in the other direction. As you go above fight mode on the emotional ladder, you begin to leave the stress response behind. From anger, if you released some resistance, you might move up the ladder towards irritation, or disappointment, or seeing what happened as not such a big deal. More and more of your cells are flipping into the healing response – which releases happy hormones into your bloodstream – as you listen more and more to the voice of your higher self, and less and less to the fearful lizard voices.

Your consciousness now expands, and you begin to see a bigger picture. Perhaps you can see how you invited their behaviour, or how you had some responsibility for it. Or perhaps you can understand why they behaved as they did, given their background or their way of thinking. Perhaps you just feel slightly frustrated by now. You might even be moving towards forgiveness – or beyond.

Once those negative lizard voices are out of hearing range, you feel unconditional love, joy, trust, appreciation, passion, enthusiasm, freedom and empowerment. Now you think clearly, and have accurate intuitive hunches. You become visionary about the future. Everything looks wonderful. Anything feels possible. You are in a state of pure bliss. This is about as good as life gets. From the top of the ladder, life is a bowl of cherries.

What lies at the heart of emotional intelligence is learning how to calm and soothe your own emotions. When you feel bad, it is crucial to recognise that no-one and nothing 'out there' needs to change even if it seems obvious that the problem is 'out there'. The problem lies within. Your higher self never feels negative emotion, so you are listening to lizard voices that are not aligned with your higher self.

Whenever you feel negative emotion, turn the spotlight on your resistant habits of thought – such as complaining, criticising, blaming, justifying, defending, over-analysing, being a victim, being a rescuer, worrying, over-caring, feeling guilty, seeking approval, avoiding risks, driving yourself too hard or expecting the worst – and deliberately choose more positive and life-affirming thoughts which *feel good*.

You can slowly retrain your neurochemistry to stabilise in a higher range of frequencies. You can also learn energy tools and make lifestyle changes that help you stay relaxed and heart-centred. Once you know that you can be happy, trusting and optimistic in any situation, regardless of what is happening or how anyone else behaves, you have found true freedom. This is the key to unconditional love. It allows your body to heal itself – and it makes you much more pleasant to be around!

FOCUSING ON YOUR DESIRES

One way of climbing the emotional ladder towards health and happiness is to focus upon what you appreciate and what you desire – rather than on what you see as bad, wrong or missing. Whenever you focus upon a problem or concern, or what someone else is doing wrong ('I don't have enough money to pay the bills.' 'The doctor tells me I have diabetes, and it is incurable.' 'My son never does his homework.') that will make you feel bad. If you focus upon what you desire in the same situation, it always makes you feel good, or at least brings a feeling of relief. ('I want to have plenty of money.' 'My body is designed to be well, so I'm sure there is a way of healing diabetes.' 'I can trust my son to make his own choices.') *A feeling of relief is a sure sign that you are releasing resistance.*

Once you have found relief, you have to *hold* your thoughts there, instead of leaping in with negative thoughts which contradict your desire – doubts about whether you can have what you want, whether you are being realistic, whether it might upset someone else, whether you deserve it . . . It is easier to carry on thinking the same thoughts that you usually think, but then nothing changes. If you are sick, you will stay sick. If you feel poor, you will stay poor. If you feel stuck, you will stay stuck. Somehow you have to find a way of shifting your habits of thought.

You cannot leap up the emotional ladder. You cannot shift your vibrations abruptly – or if you do, it tends to be an uncomfortable and bumpy ride, or docs not last. It is wisest to take it step by step. This is why positive affirmations sometimes do not work, since they are outside your frequency range. You might be mouthing the words, but they are not shifting how you *feel* (which is what really matters). You cannot leap from despair to optimism – if you try, it feels empty and inauthentic – but you can move from despair to anger, or from frustration to hope, or from optimism to belief. The trick is simply to fish around for possible thoughts until you find one that brings a sense of relief.

A useful tool I learnt from Abraham is to say, 'Wouldn't it be nice if . . .' This can often bring a smile to your face! You are not saying (yet) that you believe this will happen. You are just playing with the possibility of a positive outcome, and seeing the universe as your friend. ('Wouldn't it be nice if some money came to me unexpectedly?' 'Wouldn't it be nice if I found a natural way of healing diabetes on the internet?') Instead of focusing on the problem, you are now opening up to possible solutions. Your consciousness expands, you relax – and your body shifts into healing mode.

THE LAW OF ATTRACTION: LIKE ATTRACTS LIKE

We have looked at how our emotions operate rather like satellite navigation, guiding us towards thoughts that are aligned with our higher self, and with what we desire – and giving us a warning to 'turn around' in response to negative thinking. However, our thoughts not only affect our mental and physical health, and how we deal with life. They also determine what events and circumstances we attract into our lives. Within the Divine Matrix, or universal energy field, everything is interconnected like a vast cosmic tapestry.

The law of attraction says that like attracts like. We are like magnets, pulling towards us whatever we hold in our consciousness. The more you think like a wave – feeling loving and connected, looking at what is good and positive, and all that you appreciate in life, and focusing on where you are going and what you desire – the more you attract events and circumstances that mirror that positive focus. If you focus upon sickness and problems, you get more of those. If you focus on health and solutions, that is what you attract.

In a psycho-energetic universe, it is consciousness that collapses the quantum wave function, and this determines which of many possible realities come into physical existence – whether in your body, or in the outside world. More simply, we create our own reality. This takes us into woo-woo land as far as materialists are concerned, but it fits with new paradigm science – and countless authors, scientists and healers are coming to this same conclusion.[130]

Your conscious mind is designed to focus and set intentions. Since you get what you focus upon, the more you think like a particle – feeling separate and fearful, or looking at what is bad, wrong or missing in self, others or the world – the more you attract events and circumstances which mirror your negativity. If you focus upon the positive, that is what you get.

The ego gap

It is the *gap* between your ego and your future self that sets up disease. The drawback of this is that enthusiastic people with big dreams who are mostly positive thinkers can become seriously ill, whereas mere complainers and grumblers who expect life to be mundane might just have minor aches and pains! If you fervently want to change the world, for example, you can become seriously ill if you remain focused on what you see as 'bad and wrong', instead of being a visionary and focusing on what you desire. You can also become ill if you strive to make your dreams come true simply by *taking action*, without first bringing your thoughts into alignment with what you want. Taking action is remarkably ineffective (and exhausting) in comparison with shifting your vibrations. When you raise your vibrations, your ego and higher self work together in harmony. You *know* that miracles happen, so you can sit back and watch while the Red Sea parts to fulfil your desire!

If you desperately want anything – personal or global – while also telling yourself it is impossible or unlikely, you create huge conflict in your energy system. After all, your higher self holds no limitations. It knows you can create anything. Feeling desperate is a sign of heavy resistance, since your higher self takes it for granted that you can have anything you want. *Ask and it is given.* But unless you come into alignment with your dreams, they come to inhabit your bodymind as symptoms and disease. This means that you have to look at subconscious beliefs and patterns that are getting in your way.

Let's suppose that you want a soulmate in your life – yet you associate love with shame, guilt and disapproval, because of emotional traumas in childhood. Your neural pathways – the hard-wiring of thoughts in your brain – will link together *love-shame-guilt-disapproval*, forming a 'neural net'. This neural net then becomes an attractor field for relationships that fit that pattern. You will perceive relationships through this childhood filter, attract those who match your patterns, distort whatever you experience to fit your neural net, or (energetically) push others to comply with your expectations. It becomes a self-fulfilling prophecy – and the loving relationship you long for cannot happen until you shift your beliefs.

NEW THOUGHTS, NEW BODY

The neurological rule is that 'neurons that fire together, wire together'. If you keep associating two or more things together, your neurochemistry comes to reflect that. Perhaps, as a woman, your brain's neural network links these conditions: menopause-weight gain-insomnia-uncomfortable flushes. If so, this will serve as an attractor field within your body for those symptoms once you reach the menopause. Or perhaps you were told as a child, 'You're just like your Aunt Jane' who is overweight and arthritic. So you form a neural net that links Aunt Jane-me-overweight-arthritis. And guess what eventually happens?

The new biology shows how the law of attraction applies to the physical body. The mind hard-wires the body, building neural pathways and (more complex) neural nets that make it easier to think familiar thoughts, which release a familiar pattern of neurochemicals. We feel 'at home' with these thoughts, and they attract thoughts (and circumstances) of a similar frequency. If we try to shift our thoughts, it feels uncomfortable at first, since we are 'addicted' to our usual thoughts. This has become our personality, like a well-worn shoe.

As we have seen, the stress response puts your bodymind into defensive mode – with huge knock-on effects for your biochemistry and physiology. Stress hormones pour into your bloodstream, the immune system shuts down, the digestive system is suppressed, unhealthy genes are activated, the frontal lobes are drained of blood and so on. This sets up patterns of dis-ease. Your body mirrors your habitual thoughts and vibrational frequency. The law of attraction brings you whatever you focus upon. If you keep thinking the same thoughts, you keep re-creating the same body. New thoughts, new body.

You dream your body into being, day after day. If you expect to wake up with hands crippled with arthritis, because that is what you experienced when you woke up yesterday, then that is what will happen today and tomorrow. But what if you began to imagine something new and different? What if you aligned with your higher self – which has healthy hands – and imagined your hands to be healthy, and kept feeling it and visualising and dreaming it until those healthy hands felt as real as your physical body? Then your physical hands would begin to morph to fit your consciousness.

That is the way our conscious universe works. The path towards your dreams and desires is always laid out for you, if only you pay attention to your emotional guidance, and reach towards joy and trust and intuitive knowing – instead of listening to lizards.

Your body can do whatever you can imagine. And you have the constant feedback system of your emotions to tell you whether your thoughts are aligned with your health and happiness. Those lizard voices can be *so* convincing and *so* familiar that we tend to believe they speak the truth – even if those voices don't make us *feel good*. But your emotions reflect, moment to moment, whether you are using the law of attraction to your advantage. Your emotions are a gift from your higher self.

HEALTH IS ALL VIBRATIONAL

If you linger chronically on the lower rungs of the emotional ladder, this can eventually show up as symptoms or disease. The lower you are on the ladder, the more serious the disease. This does not mean you create a malignant tumour by constantly worrying about getting cancer (although that can happen). More often, it simply means that you have been holding vibrational frequencies that 'match' that of cancer.

According to Abraham, any life-threatening disease means that you have been holding yourself near the bottom of the emotional ladder – perhaps in fear, guilt, disempowerment and despair. Conditions such as hypertension and heart disorders might match chronic vibrations in the vicinity of anger, blame and criticism. Less serious disease such as ulcers or migraines might match stuck vibrations around worry, overwhelm and self-doubt. And so on. (In the next chapter, we will look at the 'body language' of dis-ease, and how to translate its messages.) However, as we shall see, it is crucial to realise that you are not to 'blame' if you become ill. Guilt and self-blame turns you into your own enemy. It comes from your lizard voices – so it will keep you in the stress response, and therefore block healing.

After getting a diagnosis, people often see their body as the 'enemy', then focus the same negative or driven thinking which *created* the disease on their symptoms. Battling against disease is always a self-defeating approach. Whenever I hear that someone has 'lost their battle with cancer', I always think, 'Well, yes, they would if they saw themselves as being at war.' Several studies have found that those who have a 'fighting spirit' towards cancer do much better than those who give in to despair – which is hardly surprising. (One study found a ten-year survival rate of 75 per cent for those with a 'fighting spirit', compared with only 22 per cent for those who felt helpless, hopeless or stoical.[131]) However, 'fighting' a disease is different from having a positive and relaxed expectation of being well again. The fight response is slightly higher on the emotional ladder than the freeze response, but it is still part of the stress response.

What about those who embrace the experience of serious disease, raise their vibrations and commit themselves to a positive healing journey? Surgeon and oncologist Bernie Siegel said that 15–20 per cent of the cancer patients he saw were 'exceptional'. They did not passively do as they were told, and instead took responsibility for their own journey – and they were the ones who showed exceptionally good results.[132] I assume that the same applies to any other disease.

Trying too hard to heal almost always fails. It means that you do not really trust your body to heal itself. The solution becomes part of the problem. You cannot create what you want while focusing on its opposite – while seeing your body as sick or faulty. Creating health means you have to relax, and focus on *wellness*. Mother Teresa wisely said that she would never join an anti-war rally, but she would join a peace parade. She knew about the law of attraction, and was able to focus positively despite the poverty and suffering all around her in Calcutta. Whatever is happening 'out there', we can choose to focus in a positive or negative way – and this is reflected back to us, both in our physical body and in the outside world.

Blame and responsibility

I can almost hear a barrage of voices screaming that this is 'blaming the victim', and it is terrible to suggest that people create their own disease. (I have even been accused of this while speaking at a holistic health centre!) Yet there is no blame within conscious medicine – only responsibility. Blame and guilt belong firmly to the old paradigm, and to the duality of the stress response. I have no hesitation in saying that I created my diagnosis of breast cancer. I see all the emotional stuckness and childhood patterns, and how I kept myself in prolonged inner conflict. But I do not *blame* myself for the cancer, nor do I feel guilty about it; nor do I blame anyone else for it.

Remember that our emotions signal our vibrations. Guilt and blame feel bad, so such thoughts are not aligned with your higher self. On the other hand, responsibility for oneself tends to feel liberating and empowering, so it *is* aligned with your higher self. If you beat yourself up for having an illness, you are blaming yourself – rather than taking responsibility for it. You haven't done anything 'wrong' if you become ill, or create other unwanted experiences. You have simply given yourself a learning experience that can help launch you into a new future. Good for you!

The only alternative to saying that you create your own illness is seeing yourself as a victim of it. Then you separate your mind from your body, feel helpless, and will hand your body over to an 'expert' to sort it out. It is OK to consult a conventional doctor, but if that is *all* you do, you might lose the potential for growth and change that the illness is offering you. In addition, you could say, 'How interesting that I have created this. Let me assume that this illness has a positive role to play in my life. It has come as a helpful messenger. There is something within me that needs to be explored, so that I can grow and evolve – chronic habits of thought, inner conflicts, stuck patterns, or blocked dreams and desires – and this illness is pointing me in the right direction.' Then you take back your own power. You are no longer a victim, but a powerful creator. And the illness becomes your guide and teacher.

HOPE (OR ABOVE) ALLOWS HEALING

The rule is that when you feel negative emotion, you are currently attracting what you do *not* want. When you feel positive emotion, you are attracting what you do want. If you can think about any diagnosis or disease you have, and feel at least hopeful about it (on the emotional ladder), then you are in the healing response. Your body will then naturally begin to heal itself. Alternatively, if you could forget about the diagnosis completely, and just focus on anything else that makes you feel positive – at least hopeful, and preferably even better – that would likewise take you into the healing response. The higher your vibrations, the faster you heal.

Positive thinking is a waste of time unless you are tuned into your emotions. It is how you *feel* that matters, not the words you are spouting. I recently heard someone angrily denouncing positive thinking for health on the radio. She was a 'cancer survivor' (her term), and furious that anyone would suggest that thoughts had any role to play in cancer, after all she had been through with surgery, chemotherapy and radiation! She saw herself as having had no choice in this harsh treatment process. This woman was a long way from being able to use joyful affirmations – but was presumably escaping from her painful feelings of victimhood and disempowerment by moving up to rage on the emotional ladder.

Like a radio tuned to a low frequency, you cannot hear higher frequencies until you are within range of them. Once you come closer they might be quiet or slightly scrambled at first, but as you tune in more, they become louder and clearer. Stay tuned to that frequency, and your health improves. Your vibrations move to a new emotional set point. You have climbed up the emotional ladder. And since the universe responds to your vibrations, just as your body does, your life will also change for the better – which brings even more positive thoughts. From hope or above, you are in a virtuous cycle. *Health, happiness – and life itself – is all about your vibrational state.*

Positive thinking and health is our default mode – as long as we are not focused on negative thoughts and limitations, blocked desires or habitual patterns from the past. Just as a cork bobs to the surface unless we hold it beneath the water, the higher self speaks to us unless we drown it out with lizard voices from the past. If we are not listening, it sends us negative emotions as a helpful warning sign. And if we do not pay attention to our emotions, the bodymind begins to send up distress flares as a wake-up call. Isn't this doubly helpful, once we know how this well-designed guidance system works?

Just to clarify: our emotions signal the gap between our ego and our higher self. Feeling good means you are feeling God. All you have to do is listen to the voice of love and joy, rather than the voice of fear and judgement. You have to love and accept whatever is right now, while focusing on the positive future you are moving towards. Relax – and trust in a loving universe. Follow your bliss. Then you climb that stairway to happiness – and to health.

So we have established that the body mirrors our chronic thoughts, and that illness is a helpful messenger which signals inner conflict – warning us that we have slipped down the emotional ladder and need to change direction. In the next two chapters, we explore the ways in which the body 'speaks' to us through symptoms and disease, and how to decipher its language. It's time to discover what your body is telling you.

Chapter Eight

BODY LANGUAGE

The body is always talking to us, if we will only take the time to listen.

Louise L Hay[133]

Why does one person become diabetic or arthritic in response to chronic stress, while someone else develops an ulcer or kidney stones? And how do you know what it *means* if you break a leg, or have constipation? We have seen that when the stress response is activated by negative thoughts, we feel negative emotion – and if this becomes chronic, emotional or physical dis-ease is eventually set up. But what determines what *form* a dis-ease will take? How can we understand the language of the body?

Conventional medicine would simply point towards genes, exposure to viruses and toxins, and other physical factors to explain illness. Conscious medicine is more poetic and dream-like. Just as quantum physics restored consciousness to science, conscious medicine restores meaning to illness and dis-ease. We live in a universe in which everything is energy-consciousness, and everything communicates in meaningful ways. Illness and the body are no exceptions.

Whether we develop a toothache, a headache or stomach pain – or any other symptom or disease – depends upon the links between the human energy field (also known as the aura, or biofield) and consciousness. It is the nature of our thoughts, emotional expression and defences that determine how energy flows within our biofield, and this creates either vibrant health or various forms of emotional and physical dis-ease. (We will look more at the human energy field in Chapter 9.)

DREAM DICTIONARY

Many people first learnt about the mental and emotional causes of physical disease through the pioneering work of Louise Hay. Louise herself was diagnosed as having cancer of the vagina, and realised this stemmed from being raped at the age of five, and being battered as a child. She reasoned that there was little point in having the cancer removed surgically unless she first healed the deep-seated resentment and lack of self-love that dated back to her childhood. Over the next six months, she detoxified her mind and body – using affirmations, visualisations and a healthy diet – and, as Louise says, the cancer healed itself.[134]

Over the years that followed, Louise Hay observed people with various disorders, noted the emotional patterns that were associated with each dis-ease, and developed specific affirmations for healing. She gradually developed a 'dream dictionary' of illness.[135] Of course, individuals vary and she does say that her list only offers a starting point for exploration – but she also suggests it is accurate, in her experience, 90–95 per cent of the time.

For example, a friend of mine had a son who was suddenly having nosebleeds, and asked me what this might symbolise. The 'dream dictionary' answer is that nosebleeds are about feeling overlooked and wanting recognition, or crying for love. The boy's sister had been getting a lot of attention because she was being bullied at school, and at the same time his mother had started a demanding new job. This is when the nosebleeds had begun.

Over the past thirty years, like Louise Hay and many other practitioners, I've seen common patterns in symptoms and dis-ease, as if the body does have a language of its own. The body speaks to us through the symbolism of symptoms and organs. It also speaks to us through disturbances in the meridians and chakras, the body's energy channels (see Chapter 9). And sometimes it speaks to us by mirroring our own words, or producing symptoms that symbolise what we are doing to ourselves, what we need or what we are avoiding. Learning to speak this particular 'body language' – that is, how the body communicates through illness – can help in tracking down the vibrational causes of dis-ease.

What can ailments mean?

For example, constipation is generally a sign that you are holding on, and refusing to let go of the past. I see it as similar to getting a parking ticket; it means you have stayed in the same place for too long. So the question is, 'What are you clinging to that needs to be released?' It might be a suppressed emotion, a relationship, a job or unresolved situation, or beliefs and attitudes that are no longer serving you. Diarrhoea, on the other hand, is more akin to getting a speeding ticket. If you have diarrhoea, what are you running away from, or trying to release that is toxic? Or do you feel that life is running away from you, and you have lost control? What are you pushing away out of fear, or unable to process?

Skin disorders are often about self-esteem and identity, since the skin is the meeting point between you and the outside world. If someone describes a skin problem, they often use words such as weepy, irritated or angry – which reveals the primary emotion that underlies the disorder.

A young woman came to see me recently about chronic eczema. In her childhood, Maya felt she was not listened to and respected. Her parents came to England from Sri Lanka, and were very fearful about the new culture, and overprotective of her. As well as feeling different because of her skin colour, Maya felt in conflict at home because of the culture clash between her school friends and her family. She did not fully belong anywhere.

As an adult, Maya became a social worker, drawn to helping underdogs and the disempowered because she identified with them – a work environment that replicated her childhood. She was bullied at work as she had been as a child; and by dealing with crisis all day long, she was constantly thrown into the stress response. For many years, her skin showed signs of her inner conflict. She noticed that her skin burnt up whenever her boss was controlling or critical, or she did not feel listened to and respected. A family-ar old pattern. Maya realised that she didn't love and respect *herself* enough, and this was the message she was 'broadcasting' to others. As we released some of the trauma from her childhood, she became much more positive, self-nurturing and joyful – even at work. Her skin steadily improved, and she found that she could eat foods that previously had caused flare-ups of eczema.

Back pain tends to come from feeling unsupported. The upper back is linked with whether you feel emotionally supported, and whether you freely give and receive love. A frozen shoulder is often a sign of feeling burdened by responsibility (and secretly angry about it). The mid-back is connected with guilt and lack of self-forgiveness, and being caught up in the past. The lower back is likely to become tense or painful when you are concerned about money and security.

Last year, Glenda consulted me over longstanding back pain that had been triggered by an accident several years earlier. She had seen a variety of physiotherapists, chiropractors, osteopaths and other health practitioners, but the pain remained. When someone has been trying to heal for a long time like this, there are always subconscious blockages to getting better. (See Chapter 11.) We looked at the circumstances of Glenda's original 'accident'. (After all, there are no 'accidents' in a conscious universe! Everything is meaningful, and everything that comes to you matches your vibrations.) At that time, she had recently ended her marriage after discovering that her husband had had several affairs. He moved several hundred miles away, and she felt alone and unsupported with the children – then she fell down the stairs at home. The chronic back pain was both a way of asking for help and support, and a way of saying angrily to her ex-husband, 'Look what you did to me! Look how much I have suffered!' She laughed when she realised that she had been punishing *herself* for years in an attempt to get back at him.

As we worked on releasing her anger and resentment, Glenda recognised that the marriage had not been good for her either. She saw that she had pushed her husband away for a long time before he left. It felt easier to blame him and see herself as a victim, yet secretly she felt guilty. (Pain often involves unresolved guilt and self-punishment.) With energy psychology, she quickly moved beyond blame and guilt from the past, and became focused on a positive future. Soon after this, she saw a new healing practitioner who quickly relieved her back pain. She credited him with the 'cure', but I also felt pretty sure that our session allowed her to find him – and to let go of her pain at last.

Problems with eyesight can relate to what you saw that you didn't want to see, or what you don't want to look at right now. Some practitioners of energy psychology are finding they can often correct eyesight by releasing past trauma. It makes sense that the eye muscles might chronic-ally tighten or distort in response to seeing something traumatic, or wanting to 'turn a blind eye' to what is going on. When children develop eyesight problems, they usually don't want to see what is going on in the family.

A woman who attended one of my workshops told me that she became more and more long-sighted while married to a man who was alcoholic. When she finally left him her eyesight returned to normal. (Conventional medicine often relates eyesight problems to ageing, but conscious medicine refutes this.) Long-sightedness can be about fear of the present, or of seeing what is in front of us. Short-sightedness suggests lack of trust in the future, and not wanting to see ahead.

Astigmatism might mean you are distorting yourself or your views to fit in with others. And cataracts often grow when you cannot look at the future with any joy – which is why they are common in elderly people who are drifting aimlessly towards death, rather than joyfully planning the rest of their lives.

Problems with the ears raise similar questions about what painful things you have heard, or what you don't want to hear. I heard of a woman who had recurrent ear infections whose abuser used to whisper in her ear before each episode of abuse. Children often get earaches because they are told things they do not want to hear, or because they hear their parents arguing, or because of the tension of 'polite' conversations or little gibes when parents are avoiding issues.

Which side of the body is affected is also significant. The right side of the body is typically connected with your masculine energy, will and action, the outer world, your father and relationships with men. The left side is connected more with your feminine energy, the inner world, your mother and relationships with women. The right side (linked with the left brain) is about actively giving, while the left side (right brain) is about openness to receiving.

I do have reservations about a 'dream dictionary' approach to illness, since it can become a self-fulfilling prophecy. You see whatever you are looking for, or squeeze it to fit your preconceptions. It also becomes limiting and prescriptive if you say, 'Ah yes, a cough means resistance to change' – because it might mean something else for *this* person. So I use these common patterns as a doorway to explore, while keeping an open mind as to how a symptom or disease might have been triggered in this unique person, and what it might mean for them.

For a given person, the dynamics of disease are often complex and multi-layered, and a dream dictionary can over-simplify. However, I have often found such dictionaries to be helpful pointers – so here is a selection of common patterns:

Common patterns of illness and underlying meaning

Allergies – Feeling unsafe. Not owning your power. Suppressed weeping.

Anaemia – Feeling under-nourished or unloved. Feeling drained by someone or something. Lack of inner strength to face family issues.

Ankle injury – Feeling your support system is collapsing. Pulled in different directions.

Arthritis – Criticism of self and others. Perfectionism. Feeling burdened or victimised. Being inflexible in attitudes/choices.

Asthma – Suppressed grief and sorrow. Feeling suffocated (by a relationship or situation). Feeling unworthy to live – 'not even allowed to breathe'.

Autoimmune disorders (e.g. rheumatoid arthritis, diabetes, lupus) – Despair, giving up, feeling powerless. Lack of self-love. Self-criticism and self-attack.

Back pain – Upper back equates to feeling emotionally unsupported. The mid-back is associated with guilt and lack of self-forgiveness and the lower back is associated with worries about money and security.

Blood disorders (e.g. anaemia, leukemia, lymphoma, DVT) – Often relate to family conflicts (blood ties), or need for own identity/freedom.

Breast – Being over-protective or over-caring. Not feeling nurtured. Lack of self-nurturing.

Cancer – Lack of self-love. Feeling hopeless and helpless. Longstanding resentment. Hurtful situation that 'eats away' at you. (See also Chapter 9.)

Carpal tunnel syndrome – Feelings of injustice. Not owning your power.

Chronic fatigue – Helpless, despairing, lonely. Tired of giving too much. Tired of trying to prove self worthy. Needing to head in a new direction.

Cold sores – Anger and resentment. Feeling burdened or pressurised.

Common cold – Confusion or overwhelm. Feeling hurt. A minor transition point in life – letting go of what has been.

Concussion – Not wanting to know something you need to hear. Blocking fresh insights.

Conjunctivitis – Frustration and anger. Not seeing the best in others.

Constipation – Holding on to the past. Anxiety about change. Refusal to let go of old ideas or situations. Not trusting in the flow of life.

Cough – Resistance to change. Holding back.

Crohn's disease – Chronic fear and anxiety. Feeling not good enough.

Cystitis – 'Pissed off' with someone, often sexual partner. Fear of intimacy. Feeling uncomfortable with change.

Dementia – Feeling hopeless and helpless. Not wanting to struggle on with life. Not wanting to face reality. Unresolved anger. Wanting to die, yet afraid to die.

Diabetes – Chronic shock. Keeping the 'sweetness of life' at bay. Suppressed anger. Deep sorrow. Longing for what might have been. Obsessed with being in control.

Diarrhoea – Feeling out of control. Too much to take in. Trying to release something toxic.

Dizziness – Feeling overloaded. Scattered energy. Confused about which direction to take.

Ears – What don't you want to hear? Or what did you hear that traumatised you?

Eczema – Feeling irritated or frustrated. Deep feelings of hurt. Giving power away.

Epilepsy – Wanting to run away. Fear and struggle. Feeling persecuted.

Eyes – What don't you want to see? Or what did you see that traumatised you?

Feet – Fear of taking a step forward or 'putting your foot in it.'

Fungal infections (e.g. athlete's foot, thrush) – Refusal to let go of the past. Not willing to move on. (Location of infection in body reveals more about what the issue is.)

Gallstones – Bitterness, resentment, criticism. Longstanding anger and blame.

Headache – Inner conflict, often between head and heart. Avoiding something.

Heart – Broken-hearted. Joylessness. Feeling trapped in a situation that breaks the heart. Blockages around giving/receiving love. Driven to achieve.

Herpes – Guilt and shame. Suppressed anger.

Hodgkin's Disease – Desperate need for approval.

Huntington's Chorea – Helplessness, hopelessness and grief (passed down family chain).

Hypertension (high blood pressure) – Needing to be in control. Anger. Not trusting in life. Longstanding unresolved issue.

Hypotension (low blood pressure) – Loss of enthusiasm for life. Defeatist attitude. Avoiding responsibility. Lack of love in childhood.

Incontinence – Emotions that feel out of control. Tired of holding back.

Inflammation – Anger and/or anxiety.

Influenza – Expecting the worst.

Injury – Guilt and need for self-punishment.

Irritable bowel syndrome – Holding back your feelings. Insecurity. Unable to let go of control.

Kidney disorders – Fear and shame. Not feeling safe in the world. 'Yes, but' thinking.

Knee problems – Self-righteousness. Stubbornness. Not willing to be flexible.

Laryngitis – Too angry to speak. Afraid of speaking your truth. Or self-judgement over what you have said.

Ligaments – Control issues.

Liver disease – Suppressed anger. Critical attitudes.

Lung problems – Feeling undeserving of life. Life-denying attitudes. Deep grief and sorrow.

Lupus – Fear of standing up for yourself. Giving up in despair. Suppressed grief and sadness.

Migraine – Feeling driven. A perfectionist and hard on self. Resisting the flow of life.

Multiple sclerosis – Hardened, critical attitudes. Inflexibility. Fear. Lack of forgiveness. Wanting to be dependent.

Neck pain – Stiff and inflexible. Self-righteous. Not seeing other points of view.

Pain – Guilt. Lack of self-forgiveness. Self-judgement.

Premenstrual syndrome – Negative thoughts about being a woman. Giving power away.

Prostate – Feeling powerless or unworthy. Conflicts over sexuality.

Shingles – Lack of self-nurturing. Inner cry for love and attention.

Sinus problems – Irritation with someone close. Suppressed tears and grief.

Spine – Not standing up for yourself. Feelings of inferiority, perhaps masked by pride.

Stroke – Resistance to change. Negative thinking. Not enough joy in life.

Throat, sore – Suppressed anger. Not being true to self.

Thyroid problems – Frustrated creativity. Seeking approval instead of expressing your needs.

Tinnitus – Refusing to hear your inner voice.

TMJ (jaw) – Unexpressed rage and desire for revenge.

Ulcers – Feeling not good enough. Pressurised anxiety. Over-concerned with details.

Varicose veins – Feeling unsupported, or emotionally overwhelmed.

I cannot cover every common disease and body part here, since that would require a book in itself. If you would like a more complete 'dream dictionary' of illness and the body, some of my favourite books which offer this are: Louise Hay, *Heal Your Body A–Z*; Deb Shapiro, *Your Body Speaks Your Mind*; Karol K. Truman, *Feelings Buried Alive Never Die*; and Vianna Stibal, *Theta Healing: Disease and Disorder*.

Once you have insight into what a symptom or disease is about, you can explore the underlying traumas, unresolved conflicts or negative beliefs – using the tools offered in this book, or in the reading and resource list at the end. Your body is giving you clues as to what is blocking you from being in the wave response, and once you pay careful attention, the symptoms will often subside. Sometimes this means being ruthlessly honest with yourself and facing issues you might have been avoiding. Often it means breaking through the old defensive strategies you set up in childhood as a way of feeling safe, taking the risk of making new choices and reaching towards a more positive and joyful future. The bigger the symptoms, the bigger the change that is being called for.

BODY LANGUAGE

Since the body does speak to us in a dream-like way, it often uses our language. It is worth listening out for any repeated phrases you use that refer to the body, since this can weaken that area and set up dis-ease when you are under stress. Our magic word 'Abracadabra' comes from the Aramaic for 'I create as I speak' — so speak with care!

Some common examples are:

✧ He's a pain in the neck

✧ I cannot stomach this

✧ This will be the death of me

✧ I cannot 'stand' this any longer

✧ It is getting under my skin

✧ Turning a blind eye

✧ I put my foot in it

✧ This makes me sick

✧ Get off my back

✧ It is breaking my heart

You can also observe someone's body language as they talk about a condition, which can be revealing. Dan Benor, a medical doctor and author on healing, reports on a woman with rheumatoid arthritis in her hands, who sat with her fists clenched as she talked about her condition. He asked, 'What do you think your hands might be saying?' She claimed not to understand what he meant, and it was only when he repeated the question twice more that she said, in a hostile tone, 'Are you saying I'm angry?' The very obvious anger made them both laugh. This opened the door to exploring and releasing her pent-up anger over several months. A year later, she was free from arthritis.[136]

Asking how someone felt in response to their diagnosis can also be revealing. The emotional response is often a clue to the emotional cause. It is the same stuck vibration. For example, a man with a rare degenerative disorder told me that the diagnosis made him feel 'trapped' in his body. I asked him what else made him feel trapped, and he admitted that he felt trapped in a cold and distant marriage he had outgrown twenty years earlier. His 'inflexibility' in insisting that he would not let go of his marriage vows, no matter how miserable and limited he felt, was reflected in the growing inflexibility and pain in his body.

Similarly, a woman told me that she found having osteoporosis 'irritating and frustrating', and 'as if my body isn't supporting me properly'. I asked what else made her feel this way, and she told me about a longstanding problem at work that had begun just before the condition first flared up. Her boss kept overruling her decisions in favour of a new male colleague. This led us back to similar feelings from childhood because her younger brother 'always came first, in a hundred little ways', and she felt second-best, frustrated and unsupported. Feeling unsupported is a common pattern underlying osteoporosis.

Another clue to body language is that a symptom can reveal what you are doing to yourself, or what step you are avoiding. If a condition leaves you immobilised or paralysed, the question is: 'Why are you stopping yourself moving?' or 'What are you avoiding?' A doctor friend told me of a patient with multiple sclerosis who was suddenly wheelchair-bound. When they talked, the man admitted that he 'did not ever want to walk up those prison steps' to visit his incarcerated son again. The situation was too troubling for him. After seeing this link and acknowledging his painful feelings, he was quickly able to walk again.

If you have broken a leg, the same question applies. 'Why are you immobilising yourself?' Bones represent the strength or foundation of our lives, and in my experience represent issues of inner strength and trust – trust in self, others or the universe.

I have lost count of how many people have told me they desperately 'needed a *break*' – using those very words – before breaking a bone! A mature student who was terrified of exams told me that she foolishly found herself thinking, 'I can't *face* these exams' just before falling off her bicycle, badly grazing her face and breaking her writing arm, two days before her finals began. A distant relative of mine desperately wanted a year off work – but told himself that he could not possibly do so – before mangling himself in a road accident, causing multiple broken bones and other injuries. Be mindful of what you say. Your ever-helpful body is listening to every word!

TALKING TO THE BODY

Even if you cannot figure out what a symptom or disease means by interpreting the body language, you can talk to your body – or to the condition – directly. After all, everything is conscious. Your body has its own intelligence, and is responding to your thoughts moment by moment, so it seems reasonable to suggest that it can hear and communicate with us.

The ancient wisdom of shamanism tells us that everything has a voice. We can talk to a roaring river, a rugged mountain, a great oak tree or a fluttering breeze. The new physics suggests that energy is inseparable from consciousness. They are two sides of the same coin – so anything that is energy (that is, everything!) has to be conscious. Its consciousness might not be the same as human consciousness, but it is conscious nevertheless.

The Norwegian storyteller Marit Jarstad had hepatitis B for

twenty-five years, which chronically affected her health and weakened her immune system. Then she heard that almost every cell is renewed after seven years – so she began to wonder how this illness was being perpetuated in her body. She decided to talk to her liver. For three months, she spoke to her liver every morning, saying, 'All is well. There is no danger any more.' (This is a great way of releasing the stress response.) She had to admit that it felt rather strange to be talking to her liver, but after several weeks, she suddenly felt well. A blood test showed that she was free of hepatitis, and she has remained well ever since.[137]

Not only can you talk to your body (or a disease), but it can talk back to you. If it stretches your belief system to imagine this, then see it as tapping into your intuition, or the wisdom of your expanded consciousness. That is just as true, since you have to expand your consciousness in order to 'translate' the answers to a question from non-human sources. You have to align with your higher self, at least to a reasonable extent, in order to receive a message. However, it isn't at all difficult to talk and listen to your body (or a symptom, or even to a cloud or a river). Anyone can do it. Some people are naturally good at it, while others become better with practice.

After I had a cancer diagnosis, I had several conversations with the tumour. It told me that it had come 'in answer to my prayers' – and I quickly saw that it not only offered me a way of resolving the situation that had triggered the cancer, but also gave me a potentially serious condition to heal. This would allow me to deeply explore the world of conscious medicine, which I had wanted to write about for a very long time. The tumour was a personal and professional gift.

A recent client of mine was suffering from chronic fatigue syndrome, and was also searching for her life's work. When I asked her to meet her disease, it was a huge and immovable boulder – so I asked her to find out what positive purpose this boulder was serving for her. It said it was forcing her to become more still and meditative, and simply to 'be' more. Her higher purpose was to help others connect with nature spirits, and it was prodding her towards her true path. It also wanted her to stop pushing herself so much and being so serious – to have more fun and to dance – which would also help her to connect with the unseen forces of nature. She felt excited and inspired by this message, and the boulder then transformed into a small green balloon. If she paid attention to what she had heard, the illness would no longer be needed in her life.

Whatever your symptom or disease, it always has gifts for you. Doctor and healer Darren Weissman refers to symptoms as 'gifts in strange wrapping paper'.[138] You might not welcome them at the time, but they are calling you to expand your consciousness and shift into the wave response – and if you unwrap your gift with care, it will guide you towards a healthier and happier future. (We look more at the hidden gifts of disease in Chapter 12.)

You might choose to speak to your body intelligence as a whole, or to an affected organ, or to the symptom or disease. Just close your eyes and relax – maybe with some soft meditative music playing in the background – and breathe slowly and deeply, pretending that you are breathing through your heart. Or use whatever technique helps you to go into a meditative state. Then imagine that you are tuning a radio until it reaches the frequency labelled 'my body' or 'my kidneys' or 'the pain in my neck' or 'the extra weight on my hips' or 'the tumour in my liver' or whatever. Avoid calling it 'my tumour' or 'my cystitis' since this links a disorder with your identity. It is not what you *are*; it is only what you are temporarily *doing*.

Once you sense that you are on the right frequency (or even if you are unsure) ask the body part or disease, gently and lovingly, for any information that would allow you to heal, or anything you need to know that is blocking you from getting better. It might speak to you in thoughts, feelings, sensations, memories, images, direct intuitive knowing, or even in sounds and colours. It all depends on how you translate the vibrations it is transmitting. Or you can write a letter to your kidney or left ankle or headaches or hepatitis.

Then relax, breathe deeply and write back to yourself from that body part or dis-ease, *using the hand you do not normally use to write*. You might be amazed at what spills out on to the paper.

At one of my workshops, a woman with painful carpal tunnel syndrome spoke to the disorder in an inner journey. It told her that she was uncomfortable with the ethics of the company she was working for, and was not being true to herself. She happened to be working for a pharmaceutical company, and since she was training to be a yoga teacher in her spare time, she was torn apart by the conflicting models – but had told herself that she needed the steady income. (This repeated the patterns of her anxious father when she was a child.) On 'hearing' this from the carpal tunnel syndrome, she made a pact with her body that she would look for another job to pay her mortgage, while she moved towards setting up a professional yoga practice. She imme-diately broke into a sweat, and felt a huge energy surge which moved up her spine and down into her arms. She emailed later to say that the carpal tunnel syndrome had disappeared within a few days – and she had handed in her notice.

It is essential to speak kindly to your body, or even to a disease. I heard about a man with a spleen disorder who went to see an energy healer. She said to him, rather accus-ingly, 'Have you been angry with your spleen?' When she had 'tuned into' his spleen, its energy was curled into a tight and anxious ball, like a child who had been shouted at. He rather shamefacedly admitted that he *had* fired a lot of anger at his spleen!

The body is always our friend. Unless you are getting in its way, your body will remain healthy. However, it will faith-fully mirror back the state of your consciousness. If you have symptoms, the body is helpfully waving a red flag at you. It is asking you to wake up, and make some changes.

Overleaf is an inner journey in which you meet with a symptom or disease, and discover more about its message for you – and also meet with your inner healer. Your inner healer is usually an aspect of your higher self or your body intelligence, though sometimes it takes the form of a guide or teacher from the unseen realms. (A guided version of this inner journey is available on my *Healing Your Dis-ease* CD.)

Exercise
MEETING YOUR DISEASE AND YOUR INNER HEALER

Close your eyes, relax deeply, and imagine breathing in and out through your heart. Then imagine that you are in a sacred garden – the sacred garden of your bodymind. Use all your senses to find yourself there, opening the doorway to a deeper reality. When you are ready, go to the place in your garden that holds the symptom or dis-ease that you wish to heal. What does this place look like? What can you hear or sense? How does it feel to be here?

Now ask the symptom or disease to join you – to take on some form that you can speak to. Allow it to join you – whatever form it takes – and greet it with honour and respect, knowing it has been trying to serve you in some way. Perhaps it has been trying to draw your attention to unhealthy patterns of thought that have been dragging you down, and limiting your potential. Perhaps it has come because you have been blocking your own dreams and desires. Maybe it has been trying to protect you from duties or responsibilities that you do not want – or perhaps it is a way of asking for nurturing and support from others, or an excuse for taking time out for yourself, or slowing down the pace of your life. Perhaps it is drawing your attention to needs that you have been ignoring. Perhaps it has been a way of indirectly punishing or controlling others, or even a way of punishing yourself. Perhaps the illness has come as a way of waking you up spiritually, or to shift you out of stuckness. Or maybe it has come in an attempt to resolve some conflict, or to force you to deal with an issue you've been trying to ignore.

Talk now to this person, creature or being that represents your disease, and ask why it has come into your life. Your body is always your friend – so what is the message it has been trying to give you? What gifts has this symptom or disease come to bring you? And ask your dis-ease: 'What do I have to change – within myself or my life – so that this dis-ease can leave my bodymind, and I can be healthy again? What strengths or qualities do I need to develop? What is the future self that I am trying to give birth to?'

When you are ready, give thanks to the dis-ease, and ask yourself whether it has served its purpose, and you are willing to let it go. If so, watch it being transformed into light, then breaking up into a million fragments of light – and see those tiny beams of light dissolve or melt into the greater Light, and vanish. Feel the relief as you let it go.

Now go to another place in your garden, where you will meet with your inner healer – who might be an angel or archangel, a wise one, healer or shaman from an ancient culture, a being of light or a power animal. This might represent your higher self, a spiritual guide, or your body intelligence. Greet your inner healer – and ask it to heal whatever traumas, thoughts, emotional patterns and neural pathways set up this symptom or dis-ease. Allow this healing to take place – allowing your inner healer to work with your energy.

When the healing is complete, ask your DNA to absorb this healthy new patterning, and to activate a healthy and happy new blueprint for your future – releasing negative thoughts, awakening your higher self, and allowing you to trust in a loving Universe. Allow your inner healer to give you any final guidance that you need to hear. Then give thanks to it – and ask for your healing to continue in the hours, days and weeks to come. When you are ready, bring your awareness fully back into your physical body – knowing that your body is now healing, and that you are now giving birth to a new self.

Even if you are healthy, you can still talk to your body, sending it love and gratitude on a daily basis. This is another form of preventive healthcare! Your body 'hears' everything, and responds to loving and appreciative thoughts with the healing response, just as it responds to fearful or critical thoughts with the stress response. Imagine how you might feel if you were indelibly glued to someone who constantly fretted about aches and pains, worried about ageing, or cringed every time you looked in the mirror. You live with yourself all day, every day — and your body lives with what is going on in your head, whether it is relaxed and loving, or anxious and critical. Whenever you go to the bathroom, take that opportunity to gaze in the mirror, and say, 'I love you. You're amazing/ beautiful/wonderful!' Your body will really appreciate it.

In the next chapter, we will look at other ways in which the body can 'speak' to us, through the language of the meridians and chakras — and how we can heal ourselves by paying attention to these messages.

Chapter Nine

OUR CONSCIOUS BIOFIELD

Your body is a cascading fountain of energy systems, remarkably complex, exquisitely coordinated, and entirely unique.

Donna Eden[139]

Former NASA physicist and healer Barbara Brennan describes the aura as the 'missing link' between biology, medicine and psychotherapy.[140] It is the aura (or biofield – the body's energy system) that connects the invisible realms of consciousness with the visible realms of the physical body. And in case you believe that talking about the aura takes us into woo-woo land, oriental medicine has used this knowledge for thousands of years, and there has been modern scientific evidence for it since the 1970s.

It is distortions in our aura – caused primarily by negative beliefs, unmet needs and blocked emotions – which eventually filter down to the physical body, and show up as physical and mental dis-ease. Changes always take place at an energy level first, before becoming physical, which is why energy healers and clairvoyants can often predict physical disease long before it becomes diagnosable.

In her fascinating book *Infinite Mind*, scientist Valerie Hunt describes her twenty-five years of scientific research into the human energy field, and how ELF (extremely low-frequency) patterns correspond to biological processes, while EHF (extremely high-frequency) waves are linked to our thoughts and awareness. She found that everyone has their own 'energy field signature', rather like a fingerprint, which relates to their dominant patterns of thinking, childhood traumas and other individual factors.

Valerie Hunt found that emotions seem to play a crucial role in *organising* the human energy field – and that our energy is coherent in health, and becomes incoherent in disease. In other words, the aura mirrors our consciousness – and when our mind and emotions are not healthy and harmonious, this gets downloaded into the body via our energy field, expressing itself as disease. As Louise Hay and others have rightly suggested, the body does 'talk' to us about our emotional state through the language of physical dis-ease.

The body can speak to us in different languages – and alongside the 'dream dictionary' and other clues offered in Chapter 8, it is useful to speak the language of the body's energy channels and centres, known as meridians and chakras (described below). Knowing that the lung meridian is linked with grief, for example, can be useful when you are wondering what might have triggered pneumonia, or knowing that the throat chakra is about self-expression might help in finding the root of a thyroid problem. As well as offering insight, there are practical tools that can help to balance our meridians and chakras.

MERIDIANS AND CHAKRAS

The human biofield is a structured energy system, just like the human body. The body has tissues, blood, organs and bones while the biofield includes energy structures known as the meridians, chakras and strange flows. Since meridian tapping therapies like EFT are now becoming so popular, and more and more people are now aware of the chakras through yoga and other spiritual practices, I am devoting most of this chapter to the meridians and chakras.

So what are they? Within the human energy field, there are lines of energy (like flowing rivers) and centres of energy (like spinning whirlpools) – known respectively as meridians and chakras. There is evidence from cave paintings that people knew about the meridians in ancient times, and Chinese medicine has used this knowledge as the basis of acupuncture for 5000 years. Likewise, yogis and mystics have known about the chakras since time immemorial. This energy wisdom is part of our ancient cultural heritage.

Meridians are energy pathways along which energy naturally flows – just as water flows naturally along a riverbed. They allow subtle energy (or chi) to be distributed around our body. Just as our arteries and veins carry blood around the physical body, the meridians carry energy around the subtle body. Every organ and system in the body is fed by at least one meridian, and if the flow of energy in that meridian is blocked or out of balance, it affects the associated body part or system – eventually resulting in disease. The chakras regulate the flow of energy, operating rather like pumps or valves.

Both the meridians and chakras relate to specific bodily parts and systems as well as to psychological functions. Since energy and consciousness are interwoven like a fine tapestry, every thought and emotion affects our meridians and chakras. Likewise, if our energy system is influenced – perhaps using acupuncture or hands-on healing – this in turn affects our consciousness (as well as our physical body).

Modern science has been slow to acknowledge that the meridians and chakras even exist. Subtle energy simply means energy that is vibrating faster than the energy which we perceive as physical matter – just as infra-red and ultra-violet light vibrate at frequencies just beyond what our eye can see. Yet the whole concept of subtle energy has often been pooh-poohed by Western medicine, since we did not have the technology to measure such energy until recently. ('If you cannot see and measure it, it isn't real!')

In 1971, American journalist James Reston underwent an appendectomy in China and was given acupuncture for pain relief, which was rapidly effective. His news report stimulated a flowering of interest in Chinese medicine and the human energy field in the West.[141]

As a form of analgesia, for example, acupuncture works 70–80 per cent of the time, as compared with about 30 per cent for a placebo.[142] Most acupuncture research has focused on pain relief, since that is easy to study – but acupuncture is a complete system of medicine in itself, and is not just used for symptomatic relief. More and more doctors and hospitals now recognise its effectiveness, and are recommending acupuncture, shiatsu, EFT and other meridian therapies.

MERIDIAN TAPPING

Energy psychology began with a woman known as Mary, who had a severe water phobia. Mary could not go out and even had to close her curtains if it was raining. She lived near the ocean, but could not bear to be within sight of it. She could not take a shower, and had to bathe in a tiny amount of water, which she still found acutely stressful. After seeing several other therapists, she went to clinical psychologist Roger Callahan – who tried all his usual approaches without success.

However, Roger was studying Chinese medicine, and following a hunch one day, he asked Mary how she felt when she thought about water. 'Sick to my stomach', said Mary. Roger asked her to tap just under her eye – the start of the stomach meridian – while thinking about her problem. A minute later, Mary said, 'It's gone!' Amazingly, her water phobia was completely cured. To prove it, she dashed to a swimming pool in the complex they were in, and lowered herself into the water. The next day, she waded happily into the ocean – and her phobia never returned.

The stomach meridian is associated with obsessive worry,

and by tapping on the meridian point while focusing on the problem, Mary gave fresh instructions to her energy system: 'Your energy can flow while I'm thinking about water. Water is safe!' Without even knowing the original trauma, her phobia was gone. (Phobias tend to be a cinch to cure with energy psychology, since they are often triggered by a single traumatic event. Other issues can be more complex, and take longer.)

Roger Callahan realised that he had hit on something big, and he went on to develop Thought Field Therapy (TFT). Engineer Gary Craig, who trained in Thought Field Therapy, then distilled it into the simpler process of EFT, the basics of which can be learnt in a few minutes. EFT has now become the most widely used form of energy psychology – used by many thousands of practitioners as well as for self-help.

Here are just a few examples from the vast collection of EFT successes:[143]

❖ A woman who was struggling with infertility had spent a small fortune on what conventional medicine could offer, with no success. A single session of EFT revealed that she was holding guilt from childhood about not caring for her father when he was sick, and later died. Since she felt inadequate as a caregiver, she was subconsciously blocking herself from being a mother. (In my experience, guilt and lack of self-forgiveness is *the* most common emotional trigger for infertility.) Two months after the EFT session, she was pregnant.

❖ A woman with hepatitis C tapped on all her anger about her abusive childhood, and her self-criticism and self-hatred. (Chinese medicine links the liver with anger, and rage turned against the self – which becomes guilt and shame.) After a lot of EFT tapping, she noticed that she was no longer beating herself up. As she healed emotionally, she felt better physically too. She came off disability benefits, went back to work and her blood tests returned to normal. 'EFT literally saved my life,' she says.

❖ A client who had lost an arm was suffering from phantom limb pain – which is notoriously difficult to treat using conventional methods. She was seen after attempting suicide. Two minutes of EFT totally resolved the pain. Instead of obsessing about her lost arm, she began to smile and said, 'There is still a lot more of me left!' As her EFT therapist said, it was nothing short of a miracle.

❖ Another EFT practitioner reports on a woman who had suffered with irritable bowel syndrome for three years, and was struggling to get through the day. Her therapist noticed that the woman often said, 'I don't give a shit,' when the truth is that she did care. She also had issues around feeling unsafe, letting go and feeling controlled. Four brief sessions of EFT – an hour or so in total – brought complete relief from the IBS.

❖ At the age of forty-three, a man was diagnosed with kidney cancer and secondary tumours in the spine. He had been told that nothing could be done medically, and that he did not have long to live. A three-hour session of EFT dealt with the childhood death of his father from cancer, and his anger at his mother for hiding the truth and not letting him say goodbye. After this session, he felt much better and his despair lifted. Within a week he was jogging again. He had another hour of EFT, then continued to 'tap' on his own whenever necessary. Soon after, a scan showed him to be clear of cancer, and two years on, he remained healthy.

❖ A woman had suffered from restless legs syndrome for twenty years, which left her unable to relax and interrupted her sleep. She had two sessions of EFT – which focused on guilt from childhood, and guilt about placing her disabled daughter in a home –

and the problem vanished. She also felt released from the guilt and sadness that had plagued her for so long.

✥ A woman with ovarian cancer and secondary tumours was scheduled for surgery to remove several tumours from her abdomen. Chemotherapy was having little effect, and she was told the cancer was spreading. Then she had a two-hour EFT session that focused on her fear of the cancer, her anger and blame towards an ex-partner, and making positive affirmations about her health. Two weeks later, an abdominal operation was cut short since the surgeon could find no tumours present. Her doctor told her she was a 'medical miracle'.

Let me clarify that these miraculous healings came from people tapping gently on their body while focusing on physical symptoms, stuck emotions or significant events from the past. It is based solely on shifting energy-consciousness. Within conventional medicine, such an approach would seem laughably absurd. Yet it works! And although it is certainly not a panacea, EFT has proven remarkably effective with a vast range of emotional and physical disorders. Since everything is energy, and all energy is interconnected, it has also been used to treat people at a distance, in surrogate healing (where one person stands in for another), in healing animals, and even in 'healing' inanimate objects such as cars and computers!

Even beginners tend to have a success rate of about 70 per cent, while more experienced practitioners report success rates of 80–95 per cent. In thirty years of working in mind–body medicine, I have never found any other single tool that is so powerful and effective. Energy psychology has also radically changed my understanding of health and dis-ease.[144]

One of the wonderful things about EFT is that you can use it for self-help – and the only tool you need is your fingers, which are always at hand! It is also a simple tech-nique anyone can learn. (My son learnt about 'tapping' when he was only four years old.) So how do you *practise* EFT? Here is a simple guide.

Exercise
A BASIC GUIDE TO EFT

EFT can be used for any emotional or physical dis-ease. In the Set-Up phase of EFT, you accept your starting point – that is, that you currently have this emotional or physical symptom. This takes you into a place of non-judgement (or unconditional love), which allows healing to take place. After the Set-Up, you tap through ten specific points on the body while focusing on the problem/memory/symptom, or while saying, 'This anxiety' or 'This back pain', or whatever applies. Tap five to seven times on each point with two or three fingers, sharply but not hard enough to cause any discomfort. The exact number of taps is not important. Points can be tapped on either (or both) sides of the body, and the order does not matter. (If any point is painful or tender, you can hold the point instead, while breathing deeply for a couple of breaths and focusing on the issue.)

Before you begin, assess the severity of the negative emotion or symptom by asking where it lies on a 1–10 scale – where 10 is as bad as it could be. This is known as the SUDS level (Subjective Units of Distress), and helps you track your progress. When dealing with emotional trauma, it is best to guess what it might be if you focused on it, rather than bringing up intense feeling. (If you do ever plunge into negative emotion, just tap on all the tapping points shown while feeling what you are feeling, and it will soon dissipate.)

EFT Tapping Points

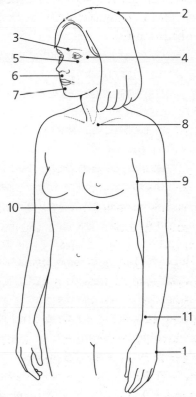

A. The Set-Up: Tap the side of your hand (point 1 above) – the Karate Chop point – while saying: 'Even though I have/feel . . . [this symptom or problem], I totally love and accept myself'. If it feels impossible to say, 'I totally love and accept myself,' you can use 'I really want to love and accept myself.' Say this three times while tapping the side of your hand – with emphasis and conviction. (Experienced EFT practitioners tend to extend this Set-Up phase, often for several minutes, throwing in all the underlying issues, emotions and negative beliefs. A lot of reframing is done at this stage.) If you are using EFT with a young child, you can tap on their points yourself or ask them to copy you – and use the wording, 'Even though I have/feel . . . I'm a really wonderful girl/boy' (or whatever words feel right).

B. The Sequence: Tap the following points while referring to your problem – e.g. 'This anger', 'This headache' or 'Feeling abandoned'. With two or three fingers together, tap these points sharply: Top of Head (2), Eyebrow (3), Side of Eye (4), Under Eye (5), Under Nose (6), Chin Point (below lip) (7), Collar Bone (8), Beneath Arm (9), Beneath Nipple (10) and Inner Wrist (11). Repeat the tapping sequence once or twice more (without the Set-Up), using a reminder phrase each time. You can say something different on each point, which helps you to stay focused. (For example, 'this headache', 'it feels crushing', 'my head is in a vice', 'I am feeling crushed', 'I'm being held in a vice', 'I'm feeling trapped', 'I'm under pressure', 'I'm pressurising myself', 'my head feels so tense'.) Then reassess how the original symptom or emotion feels on a 1–10 scale.

C. Follow-Through: *If there is some improvement,* but part of the problem remains, then reassess your SUDS level on a 1–10 scale. Perhaps your headache has improved from a level 8 headache to a level 4 headache. Then tap the side of your hand: 'Even though I still have some of this [problem] left' or 'Even though I still have this level 4 headache, I totally love and accept myself.' Repeat three times. Then tap the Sequence above, while saying/thinking about 'Remaining [problem]' Or 'This level 4 headache' on each point. Repeat as necessary. Keep tapping until the initial feeling or symptom has diminished to nothing, or at least is much improved. If new symptoms come up or the pain moves to another place, tap on the new symptoms. (This is a good sign that energy is shifting, and is known as 'chasing the pain'.) Sometimes it helps to be more specific – for example, 'this sharp pain in my left temple' rather than 'this headache'. Or tap on whatever new thoughts, issues or memories came up as you were tapping through the points.

If there is no improvement, repeat the Set-Up with more emphasis and conviction. Or you might need to re-phrase the Set-Up to get past any 'psychological reversal' (that is, resistance to getting better). It might help to say, 'Even though I don't want to get better, I totally love and accept myself.' Or 'Even though I'm afraid of getting better, I totally love . . .' Or 'Even though I feel I don't

deserve to get better, I totally love . . .' Then do the tapping. Take a
deep breath. Reassess how you feel – and tap for any new issues,
symptoms or memories that the tapping has brought up. New
insights often come up. Keep tapping until the initial feeling or symptom has diminished to nothing, or at least is very much improved.

D. Positive Choice: Now choose what you want to
feel/believe/create in place of the feeling, symptoms or disease.
For example, tap on the Karate Chop point while saying, 'I now
choose to feel inner peace about this', or 'I now choose for my
ankle to be strong and healthy', or 'I now choose for my blood
pressure to drop to 120/80', or 'I now choose to believe that my
body is healing itself naturally'. Then tap each point while saying a
short reminder phrase such as 'inner peace', or '120 over 80'.
Finish off by saying, 'Thank you, Universe!' or 'Thank you, God'.

Chronic problems: Repeat tapping regularly until the problem is
resolved – perhaps three to five times daily for several days or
even weeks. (Sometimes it helps to tap slowly, breathing deeply as
you do so, and perhaps lingering on a point that feels good. You
can also hold each point while taking a full breath, which can be
useful if a point is painful.) A single session of tapping – doing
perhaps three to four rounds of tapping – will sometimes resolve
an issue completely. However, different aspects of an issue or
trauma might each need their own session of tapping. For example,
'Even though I felt so frightened when my mother walked away
and left me on my first day at school', then 'Even though I felt so
angry when she walked away', then 'Even though I felt so alone in
the world'. You might need to tap on different underlying emotions
or beliefs, or different traumatic aspects of an incident in the past.
Sometimes you will suddenly hit upon the underlying issue or
blocked emotion, and the problem is resolved.

If you are tapping for a negative feeling, or for a physical symptom
or disease, you can address the emotion or symptoms, or you
can address the trauma that triggered the dis-ease. If tapping on a
symptom does not work, you usually need to tap on the underlying emotions or specific events from the past. After working on

whatever seemed to trigger a symptom or emotion, ask yourself what that event reminded you of, or when you felt that way as a child. The earlier the event, the more likely it is to be highly significant. Then use EFT on that memory. ('Even though I felt so ashamed when I wet my pants in nursery school . . .') Keep tapping until the memory has no emotional charge left – until it feels irrelevant, or fades into the background.

(Note: This gives you a basic introduction to EFT. For serious disease or severe trauma, always consult a professional EFT therapist. Most people find it easier to get results with a therapist than working on their own. It is tricky to see our own issues clearly, and a therapist will 'hold' you emotionally while you release problems, help you to make connections and reframe what is going on, as well as having a whole bag of tools and techniques. If you plan to use EFT with clients/patients, you should be trained at least to Level 1 in EFT. For further information, see the Resources for Health and Well-being at the back of this book.)

THE LINK BETWEEN MERIDIANS, EMOTIONS AND TAPPING POINTS

Remember the EFT principle (from Chapter 7): 'Every negative emotion is caused by a disruption in the body's energy system.' Whenever we feel anxious, guilty or resentful, for example, one or more of our meridians is out of whack. There are fourteen major meridians, which correspond with different organs and areas of the body, and different emotional states. The tapping points in EFT relate to these meridians, and as the points are tapped while focusing on a specific issue, it clears and balances that meridian – resulting in more positive emotions, fresh insights and thoughts of a higher vibration. This is why EFT is sometimes called acupuncture without needles.

The table of Meridians, Tapping Points and Emotions shows how we feel when each meridian is either balanced and flowing or blocked and imbalanced. The tapping points indicate where on the body to tap (or hold) while focusing on the negative emotion or thought. Most of these are the points used in EFT.

Meridians, Tapping Points and Emotions

Meridian name	Location of tapping point	Imbalanced	Balanced
BLADDER	Inner eyebrow	Hopelessness, suspicion	Hope, trust
GALL BLADDER	Outer eyebrow	Rage/judgement towards others	Tolerance, kindness
STOMACH	Under eye	Obsessive worry	Trust in big picture
GOVERNING	Under nose	Lacking courage, no backbone	Inner strength, standing tall
CENTRAL	Under lower lip	Feeling vulnerable	Centred and secure
KIDNEY	Under collarbone (K-27s)	Fearful isolation, shame	Moving towards others, gentle on self
SPLEEN	Under arm	Over-compassionate towards others	Compassion for self
SMALL INTESTINE	Side of hand (karate chop point)	Indecision, pulled in more than one direction	Decisiveness, discernment
HEART	Inside of wrist, or thymus gland	Heartache	Love for self/others
LUNG	Inside of wrist	Grief, detachment	Letting go, having faith
CIRCULATION – SEX	Inside of wrist	Bewildered by choices, neglecting heart's needs	Clarity about desires and needs of heart
TRIPLE WARMER	Hold both temples in palms, or tap 'gamut point' on back of hand (see p 228)	Fight or flight, extreme stress	Feeling safe

Cont. over page

Meridian name	Location of tapping point	Imbalanced	Balanced
LARGE INTESTINE	Just below elbow crease on forearm; or outer edge of nostrils	Controlling, holding on	Surrendering, letting go
LIVER	Tap chest below nipples, or hold both temples	Rage turned against self, guilt	Kindness towards self, self-acceptance

Thanks to energy psychology, we now know that tapping with your fingers on the start or end of a meridian or other crucial acupuncture points, while focusing on an issue which short-circuits that meridian – as signalled by negative emotion – is often enough to get that meridian flowing again. Since each meridian is associated with specific emotions, as well as specific body parts or systems, the meridians are another possible expression of 'body language' (as are the chakras).

If someone has a kidney disorder, for example, it points towards fearful isolation and shame as the underlying emotions. This will relate to earlier trauma in which these emotions and the need to protect oneself by withdrawing, pretence or denial first became a pattern. A useful tapping point to remember are the K-27s, at the end of the kidney meridian. Tapping here instructs your energy to go forwards again if it is flowing the wrong way (which makes you feel tired and resistant). It is a great point to tap if you are feeling tired, anxious, ashamed or have an impulse to withdraw from people.

To find the K-27s, put your fingers on your collarbone, and slide them towards the centre where there is a bump. Drop down slightly then slightly outwards, where there is usually a slight indent that a couple of fingers can nestle in. Tap here with two or three fingers of one or (preferably) both hands. Crossing your hands over makes it even more effective, since it helps energy cross over between the left and right side of your body.

The bladder meridian relates to fear too, but in a slightly different way. A disturbed bladder meridian is often associated with feelings of mistrust, suspicion and hopelessness. As most of us have noticed, anxiety often 'goes to the bladder' when we feel anxious and vulnerable.

The large intestine meridian, not surprisingly, is linked with letting go – and constipation is often a warning sign that you are holding on to the past, or refusing to let go of a situation, habit or belief that is not good for you (see also Chapter 8, page 184). People with bowel disorders often have issues around being in control, and others might find them pernickety, obsessive or controlling. The paradox is that the more we try to control things, the more we feel out of control. Learning to let go and trust in others – or trust your body, or surrender to the universe – is the lesson that needs to be learnt, so that your energy can flow freely again. If you find yourself holding on, tapping the large intestine meridian regularly might get your life flowing again.

The liver meridian is associated with guilt, and rage turned against the self. After being separated from the man I fell in love with, I had recurrent pain in my left big toe, which varied from slightly tender to very painful. At times, I could not wear my fell-walking boots because of the pain. After the abrupt separation, I cried endless tears of grief and sorrow, but – typical of those who later get a cancer diagnosis – I felt little anger. I readily empathised with others' behaviour, which often left me repressing anger or turning it against myself, rather than releasing it in a positive way.

A few months after my cancer diagnosis, at an advanced workshop on Advanced Psych-K (a form of energy psychology – see Chapter 1), I eventually addressed this minor physical symptom. As I released 'whatever is stuck in my big toe', I felt a rush of energy move out of me. It felt as if a dark cloud had lifted, and someone across the room noticed that I suddenly shone like a light. The whole process took about five minutes, and − after three years of pain − my toe has never bothered me since. The liver meridian starts at the big toe, and ends at the exact place where the tumour developed.

(For details of the meridian pathways, see Donna Eden's *Energy Medicine* or Cyndi Dale's *The Subtle Body*.)

CHAKRA LANGUAGE

Chakra is a Sanskrit word meaning wheel, disc or vortex. The chakras are centres of spinning energy within the human biofield, which regulate the flow of energy. Knowledge of the chakras probably originated in India, and are part of the ancient tradition of Ayurvedic medicine that dates back more than 4000 years. If the meridians were compared to railway lines, the chakras would be the railway stations. There are seven major chakras within your body, between your tailbone and the crown of your head (plus other chakras above the head and beneath the feet − and over one hundred secondary chakras in your body).

Like the meridians, your chakras reflect the state of your consciousness, and are linked to systems and organs in the physical body. Each of the seven major chakras is associated with an endocrine gland. When you experience stress or tension about an issue in your life, it affects that chakra, which in turn affects that endocrine gland, which releases hormones that change our biochemistry and physical functioning.

Whereas the meridians give clues as to which *emotions* are involved in a dis-ease, I see the chakras as pointing more towards the underlying *issues* or traumas involved. The chakras are said to carry an energetic imprint of all the emotionally significant events in our lives − and a sensitive healer can 'read' a great deal about your past by tuning into your chakras.

The Locations of the Seven Major Chakras

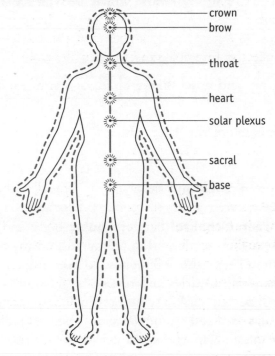

THE SEVEN CHAKRAS AND THEIR MEANINGS

1. The root or base chakra (at the tailbone)

Issues: Survival, security, home, belonging and money. Being grounded and embodied. Also, the relationship with mother and Mother Earth. Emotions of insecurity and fear.

Endocrine gland: Adrenals.

Symptoms: First chakra symptoms include tailbone or lower back pain or injury, sciatica, constipation, piles, colitis and diarrhoea, dairy and wheat allergies; also problems affecting the hands, feet and legs.

When I resigned from the National Health Service to write my first book, *Living Magically*, I drafted much of the first chapter while lying on the floor because of unexplained pain in my tailbone. Giving up my steady salary had triggered primitive 'survival fears', which are typical of first chakra disturbance.

To balance the first chakra:

❖ Jump up and down like a child, or stamp each foot in turn

❖ Walk barefoot on the earth

❖ Go jogging

❖ Get enough rest and sleep

2. The sacral chakra (between pubic bone and navel)
Issues: Sexuality, gender, pleasure, joy and creativity. Appetite for food and sex. Also willingness to feel our emotions.
Endocrine gland: Ovaries and testes.
Symptoms: Second chakra symptoms include prostate disorders in men, all sexual and reproductive dis-ease, and problems with the large intestine, appendix, bladder, hip area, wrists and ankles.

Men with prostate cancer I have seen have often been shamed or blocked around their sexuality, or are uncomfortable with their masculine power and identity. Likewise, women with second chakra problems are often ill at ease with their femininity and womanhood. I remember a woman I saw with endometriosis whose second chakra felt to me like a sewer, filled with smelly brown sludge. As I cleared it, she revealed that she had been sexually abused as a child – though her father had 'preferred' abusing her sister, leaving her with a lot of confusion, self-hatred and insecurity. She felt that having a woman's body was a liability rather than a pleasure.

To balance the second chakra:

❖ Walk from your pelvis (think Marilyn Monroe!)

❖ Swing your pelvis in circles while standing still, knees slightly bent

❖ Try tantric sex

3. The solar plexus chakra (at the solar plexus)
Issues: Worthiness/deserving, freedom, personal power and control. Feeling trapped, or like a victim. Primary emotion is suppressed anger. Connected with the mental body and thinking.
Endocrine gland: Pancreas.
Symptoms: Third chakra disease includes digestive disorders, diabetes, hypoglycaemia, ulcers, irritable bowel syndrome, liver or kidney disease, gallstones and hiatus hernia. All of these involve suppressed anger in one form or another, and not stepping into your power. This chakra also affects the mid-spine, calves and forearms.

I see the third chakra as the Inner Child chakra. People with disorders in this area of the body tend to feel disempowered and unworthy, and often behave like either (weak and helpless) Victims or (critical, angry or cold) Persecutors. They are often poor at expressing anger in constructive ways, or taking responsibility for their own lives. (See also the Drama Triangle, Chapter 6, for more on ego states.)

To balance the third chakra:

✧ Do sit-ups

✧ Try the yoga pose the Bow – lie on your stomach, bend your knees and reach back to hold your ankles. Lift your head, arch your back and balance on your stomach, breathing deeply

✧ Place your feet hip-width apart, with knees slightly bent. Swing from the waist from side to side, letting your arms follow the swing. Imagine breathing in the colour yellow

4. The heart chakra (at the heart)
Issues: Issues around relationships and connectedness; romantic love; 'losing heart'; blockages in giving and receiving love; self-judgement; feeling unloved; grief and loss.
Endocrine gland: Thymus.

Symptoms: The heart chakra relates to coronary heart disease, circulatory disorders, the breasts, ribcage, lungs, diaphragm and knees. The peak time for heart attacks is nine o'clock on Monday morning – presumably because people are returning to work and 'their heart isn't in it'. (The best predictor of a first heart attack is not high blood pressure, smoking or any other physical factor. It is chronic job dissatisfaction.)

To balance the fourth chakra:

✧ Be grateful and appreciative

✧ Try the yoga pose the Cobra – lay on your stomach with your arms bent and palms face down by your shoulders. Slowly lift your head, shoulders and back as far as you comfortably can. Relax and hold, breathing deeply

✧ Stand up, and open your arms expansively as you breathe in, as if opening your heart to the world. Then close your arms to hug yourself, offering love to yourself, as you breathe out. Imagine filling yourself with green light as you continue to do this

Some chakra experts suggest that all forms of cancer are linked with heart chakra disturbance, so let's look briefly here at what cancer is about. The most typical patterns associated with cancer are:

✧ Major unresolved conflict/turmoil

✧ Feeling helpless and disempowered

✧ Unresolved or traumatic grief

✧ Suppressed anger, which alternates with guilt

✧ Holding oneself back

✧ Caring for others at one's own expense

✧ Lack of self-nurturing

✧ Giving but not receiving love

✧ Feeling silenced by others

✧ Being driven by critical, judgemental inner voices

✧ Wanting to escape from a painful situation, and seeing 'no way out'

The site of cancer reveals more about what is going on – so look at the chakra and/or meridian linked with that site, or the symbolism of that part of the body. The tumour usually develops in a place that expresses the emotional conflict. It takes on the 'growth' that is being blocked at other levels. (One woman said, 'I grew a tumour to fill the emptiness inside me.'[145])

The breast, for example, is associated with nurturing and mothering, and breast problems can symbolise not nurturing the self, or feeling conflicted over a loving relationship. As well as the heart chakra, it can be linked with sexual relationships and the second chakra. In her lovely book *Women of Silence*, Grace Gawler describes women with breast cancer as like a 'pot-bound plant'. There is a more expansive future that awaits you, but you will not allow yourself to go there – typically held back by guilt, fear of disapproval, being over-responsible for others, or feeling that you have 'no choice'. She describes beautifully the torturous emotions I went through while setting up breast cancer myself. I heard the siren call of a loving relationship that I desired but was 'not allowed' to move towards, which left me in constant turmoil.

5. The throat chakra
Issues: Self-expression, freedom of speech, creativity.
Endocrine gland: Thyroid.
Symptoms: Throat chakra diseases include thyroid and parathyroid disorders, sore throats, laryngitis and mouth problems; also problems affecting the arms and hands.

If you have a throat chakra condition, the crucial questions to ask are: What are you not saying? Are you expressing what you want, and how you feel? Are you speaking your truth? Are you doing what you love at work? (Throat chakra imbalance can also be linked with saying *too* much, or using harsh words.) One client of mine had repeated throat infections over many years, until she left her high-pressure job in newspaper journalism and became a business workshop facilitator with a lighter schedule and more positive focus. Once she had happily found her career niche, the sore throats did not return.

To balance the fifth chakra:

◆ Try neck rolls (unless you have neck pain). Lift your head upwards, then slowly roll your head in a circular motion, stretching your neck. Pause in tight places until the muscles relax, or massage yourself. Roll in both directions

◆ Imagine breathing sky-blue light into your throat area

6. The brow chakra

Issues: Intuition, extrasensory perception, clarity, and whether we feel in harmony with our spiritual beliefs or practice. Feelings of clarity vs confusion.
Endocrine gland: Pituitary.
Symptoms: Disorders linked with the brow chakra (also known as the third eye chakra) include headaches, migraine, tinnitus, sinusitis, pituitary disease, nervous system disorders, and problems with the eyes, ears and nose.

Some people have brow chakra disorders because they are blocking their intuitive or psychic development – sometimes because of irrational fear passed down the generations. (Did you know that the Church puts a cross on a child's forehead during a christening as a symbolic gesture of closing the third eye?) We have a long history of fear and suppression of 'feminine' intuition and mystical powers.

To balance the sixth chakra:

◆ Palm your eyes – rub your hands together until they are warm, then hold your palms over your eyes, letting your eyes relax into the warmth and darkness. Hold for a few minutes

✧ Open your mouth and stick out your tongue. Move your tongue in random directions, and follow that direction with your eyes. (Weird, but it works!) Imagine breathing in midnight blue as you do this

✧ Do some meditation (see Chapter 3, the 'Breathe!' exercise), focusing on the third eye area

7. The crown chakra

Issues: Spiritual fulfilment, mystical awareness, trust in higher guidance. Relationship with father, authority figures and God. Feelings of empathy and connectedness, or feeling separate and isolated.

Endocrine gland: Pineal.

Symptoms: Crown chakra disorders include depression, dementia, schizophrenia, strokes, multiple sclerosis, Parkinson's disease and epilepsy. Also linked to hair and nails.

In many traditional cultures, such as Native American or Inuit society, epilepsy was seen as a special gift that gave people access to altered states of consciousness, and allowed them to journey into the invisible realms. Those with epilepsy were often chosen as apprentice shamans – the medicine men and women of their culture. I am not suggesting that epilepsy is a good thing – just that conventional medicine tends to see anything unusual as a problem that needs to be corrected so that you can be 'normal' again, instead of looking for the potential gifts. How we see anything depends upon the lens we are looking through.

To balance your seventh chakra:

✧ Crown pull – place your thumbs on your temples and curl your fingers slightly so they rest just above your eyebrows. Slowly, and with some pressure, pull your fingers apart, stretching the skin. Move your fingertips up to your hairline, and repeat. Keep moving your fingers back over the top of your head, repeating the slow stretch – moving down the back of your head

✧ Guided inner journeys to higher realms (e.g. see my CD set, *Living in the Fourth Dimension*)

✧ Circle your hand clockwise over the top of your head, while filling yourself with bright white light

Clearing and balancing all of your chakras – either on your own, or with a partner – will leave you feeling centred, grounded and energised. Here are two of the methods I use:

Exercise
BALANCING THE CHAKRAS

1. This is a method you can use with a partner. (You can also balance your own chakras using step b, without the muscle-testing procedure.)

   a) **Muscle-testing chakras:** The person lies on their back, and raises both arms, putting the backs of their wrists together. Ask them to resist as you briefly try to pull their wrists apart. This should give a strong muscle-test. Next, tap the air just above each chakra twice, then re-do the wrist test. If the muscle-test is now weak, that chakra is out of balance (at least at the level you tapped; the biofield has seven layers which move out from the body).

   b) **To balance chakras:** Rotate one hand anti-clockwise above the chakra, starting with the first or base chakra (tailbone), or with the lowest chakra that is out of balance. Move at whatever speed feels right, and in as large a circle as feels right, to clear the chakra – perhaps varying it as the healing proceeds. After three to five minutes, change to clockwise movements for one to two minutes. Then move up to the next chakra that needs balancing. When the recipient is male, on the crown (seventh) chakra only, start with a clockwise movement, ending with an anti-clockwise movement.

c) **To end:** Re-test each chakra, ensuring that the muscle-test is now strong.
(I was taught this particular method by healer Donna Eden, author of *Energy Medicine*.)

2. Another popular method is to close your eyes, deeply relax, then focus on each chakra in turn, starting with the tailbone and moving up to the crown chakra. While holding your attention on each chakra, visualise it spinning clockwise – that is, picture your body as if a clock is visible on your chest to someone looking at you, and see the chakra turning like the hands of the clock. Do this for two to three minutes per chakra, moving on whenever it feels right, while visualising the colour associated with that chakra. These are the colours of the rainbow: red for the base chakra, orange for sacral chakra, yellow for solar plexus, green for heart chakra, sky blue for throat chakra, indigo blue for the brow, and either violet, gold or sparkling white light for the crown chakra.

The body often uses a combination of these different 'body languages'. For example, the tumour in my own breast was at the end of the liver meridian, and in my heart chakra. The *liver meridian* was short-circuited because I felt I was not allowed to be angry, and had turned the rage against myself, transforming it into guilt. The tumour was directly over the heart, and my *heart chakra* was disturbed because the central issue was about giving and receiving love, and feeling separate from love. The *breast* symbolised the relationship which I wanted to 'love and nurture', but felt blocked from continuing – as well as my own difficulty in nurturing myself. The breast is also a symbol of the divine feminine, which we are reclaiming at a global level, as we become more spiritually and ecologically aware, and more in touch with our emotions and intuition. (See Chapter 12.)

If chakras become disconnected, this is often mirrored by inner conflict within the personality. For example, if the heart chakra is disconnected from the sacral chakra, and the sacral chakra is overcharged, the person might be drawn towards casual sexual encounters, and be unable to make a loving connection with a steady partner. They might also become vulnerable to sexually transmitted disease. When the energy of these chakras is reconnected, their relationships would begin to shift and deepen.

When energy flows freely through your meridians, and your chakras are balanced and connected, this corresponds to being in the wave response. You feel wonderful – and you remain healthy. *If your energy shifts, your consciousness shifts – and vice versa.* When energy is not flowing as it should, the disturbances in your biofield eventually filter down to the physical body – and the emotional root of the problem is then revealed by reading the 'body language' of the disorder.

THE STRANGE FLOWS

The strange flows are less well known than the meridians and chakras, but they are essential to health and healing – and since they also activate joy and intuition, I particularly love working with them. (See my earlier book, *Wild Love*.) Also known as the extraordinary meridians or psychic circuits, the strange flows get their name from the quirky and unpredictable way in which they jump around. Their energy does not follow accustomed pathways like the meridians, but simply goes wherever it is needed.

The strange flows work in partnership with the triple warmer to govern our immune system. The triple warmer is the meridian that governs the fight-flight-freeze response. Whenever it senses danger, the triple warmer goes on red alert, and sends signals to the hypothalamus. It prepares you for the battlefield – perhaps to protect you from a virus or bacteria, or a difficult conversation with your boss. The strange flows, by contrast, work towards harmony and cooperation. They have more of a 'feminine' approach, maintaining health by ensuring peace and calmness within your energy field, and helping all your organs and systems to work together – but the strange flows are overruled when the triple warmer activates the stress response.

In our stress-filled, over-busy and addictive society, the triple warmer tends to be hyperactive and needs to be soothed, whereas our peace-loving strange flows need to be encouraged and activated. Every autoimmune disorder – such as rheumatoid arthritis, lupus, Crohn's disease and multiple sclerosis – involves an over-active triple warmer; while immune deficiency disease means that the triple warmer has headed towards burnout. Allergies and environmental disorders are likewise due to the triple warmer being out of balance, wrongly identifying friends as foes. Whenever we 'lose it', flying into a rage or becoming hysterical – or we feel overwhelmed and frozen – the triple warmer has gone into overkill.

The triple warmer operates very much like our limited ego: fear-ridden, judgemental, over-busy and driven. It sees the world as a dangerous place, strives to avoid risk and is highly resistant to change. It is the voice of conservatism. I see it as a good metaphor for conventional medicine, since it battles against 'enemies' and is hypervigilant and over-responsible. It lives in a fearful world of separate particles – whereas the strange flows occupy a world of loving waves. I see the strange flows as mirroring the world of conscious medicine and the new paradigm – joyful, radiant, intuitive, creative, mystical, unpredictable, spontaneous, self-nurturing, playful, free and alive.

CREATING BALANCE

So how can you calm the triple warmer and encourage the strange flows? When I was a child, I often brushed my long hair over the top of my ears with my fingers – which is an intuitive way of soothing the triple warmer, since it traces the meridian in the opposite direction to its flow.

You can do this more effectively by following the meridian with the fingers of one hand all the way from the outer corner of your eyebrow, over your ears, down your neck and outer arm, and off the tip of your ring finger. Trace the meridian a few times on both sides of your body. It will feel calming. (If you are suffering from immune deficiency disease or feel chronically exhausted, your triple warmer needs to be stimulated. This is a rare occasion when you should trace the meridian in the other direction, starting from the ring finger.)

Another way to soothe the triple warmer is to tap the 'gamut point' while focusing on whatever is bothering you, until your thoughts and feelings shift, or until you sense your body relaxing. The gamut point is on the back of your hand, just behind the knuckles, between your ring finger and little finger (and is another tapping point sometimes used in EFT). Balancing your chakras is another way of bringing the triple warmer into balance, which in turn allows the strange flows to come into operation.

Whatever your state of health, getting the strange flows moving is always a good idea – and it feels wonderful! Here are a few simple ways of activating the strange flows:

❖ Conjure up a happy or loving memory – or daydream about something you want to happen

❖ Focus on gratitude and appreciation – for your body, for your loved ones, for all that is good in your life, or simply for the fact that the sun came up this morning. Imagine the energy of gratitude spreading throughout your body

❖ Stretching or yoga

❖ Wild dancing

❖ Making love

❖ Imagine that you're breathing in coloured light – whatever colour you fancy – seeing it spread into every cell in your body

❖ Do anything wacky and fun. One of my favourites is to bounce on my son's garden trampoline! (A small rebounder will serve the same purpose. Bouncing is also great for your lymphatic system)

❖ Laugh

❖ Hook up your belly button and third eye. Hook a middle finger into your belly button, and place the middle finger of your other hand on your third eye (between and just above your eyebrows). Press both points firmly while also pulling up slightly. Hold for a minute or two. This not only activates your strange flows, but strengthens your whole auric field[146]

(Donna Eden's groundbreaking book, *Energy Medicine*, offers much more about the strange flows and the triple warmer, while Stephanie Mines's lovely book, *We Are All In Shock*, outlines the TARA Approach as a gentle yet powerful way to activate the strange flows.)

❂

So now you have some clues as to what a disease might be about, and have learnt how to translate the various languages the body might use. You know that disease begins with trauma and negative beliefs, which then get downloaded into the biofield – affecting the meridians, chakras and strange flows. And you know that it is crucial to our mental and physical health to deactivate the stress response, and shift into the wave response.

We have focused mostly on the inner work of the healing journey so far. However, most people turn to health professionals, healers and therapists when they are facing emotional or physical dis-ease – if only to help them clarify the inner work they need to do, and to act as guides or cheerleaders along the way. In the next chapter, we look at the role of health practitioners in the healing journey.

Chapter Ten

FINDING A GIANT PENDULUM

*Everything we think, say and do holographically affects
everyone else through the life energy field.*

Barbara Brennan[147]

If healing comes from being in the wave response and
tapping into our higher self, what is the role of healers
and therapists within conscious medicine? Can you affect
someone else's consciousness? The answer is Yes – and we
do so all the time, either inspiring and uplifting others,
or dragging them down. We can also directly affect
others' energy systems through our focused intention,
which is the basis of much energy medicine and hands-
on healing.

In *Healing: A Doctor in Search of a Miracle*, physician
William Nolen suggests that energy healers can heal an
average of 70 per cent of the time – which is dramatically better than the average drug, which has a success rate
only slightly better than a placebo.[148] As I know from my
own experience, energy healing can be very powerful and
effective.

THE ROLE OF THE HEALER

I see a true healer as rather like a giant pendulum. If one hundred small pendulums are swinging in a room, along with one large one, the small ones all gradually entrain to the rhythm of the giant pendulum. They all come into resonance with that one powerful energy. A good healer is one who stands so firmly rooted in the wave response, so firmly connected to happiness and well-being, so strongly believing in your potential as a conscious creator, that they do not really 'see' your sickness. They have total faith in your bodymind's ability to heal itself – or perhaps in their own ability to be a catalyst for that – and soak you in unconditional love, until you are bathing in that timeless ocean of freedom, trust and intuitive knowing.

A healer might be handing out a prescription or herbs, sticking needles into you, giving energy healing, massaging you, muscle-testing or talking to you – but *what* they do is not the point. Healing is much more about *who they are*. It is all about their state of awareness, and entraining you into a healthy state. *They make you feel safe and loved – since they are bathing in the ocean of the wave response themselves.* The greatest gift that any healer can offer is their state of consciousness – which is why it is so crucial for healers and therapists to work on their own issues, keep their lives in balance, live with joy and be true to themselves.

I am not suggesting that healers need to be perfect, or to have fully resolved their own issues. Neither is possible! On the contrary, we are all 'wounded healers' and we need to be real and authentic about that. All too often, doctors and healers have been placed on pedestals and seen as all-knowing and wise – which is not a comfortable position for anyone, and denies our humanity. It can be helpful to acknowledge our own issues, and to sit easily and happily with the messiness of being human. However, we can aim to stay in the wave response, as far as possible which allows us to stay fully present to ourselves and our clients, without 'running away' into tools or prescriptions or role-playing.

Good healers have a knack for releasing resistance and helping you become more wave-like. They soothe and reassure you. They help you shift from fear to love. They see solutions rather than problems. They listen carefully and with compassion, but are not so empathic that they get sucked into your 'story'. They pay little attention to lizard voices. Instead they keep a firm eye on who you *really* are – the wave self beyond the story, beyond the victimhood, beyond the symptoms, beyond the medical prognosis. They see your higher potential, and help your energy to flow in that direction.

When Jesus healed the woman who touched his robe, he said to her, 'Your faith has made you whole'. This acknowledged that she had *allowed* herself to be healed. (Jesus also told the woman to 'Go home and tell no-one'. Why? Because others might question her faith and pull her out of the wave response.) As most good healers acknowledge, they cannot heal anyone; they can only help people to heal themselves. Ultimately, it is Source energy – call it God, if you prefer – that heals. Jesus didn't 'heal' anyone. He simply stood as a giant pendulum, a symbol of unconditional love and higher consciousness, and helped people resonate with that wave-like state within themselves. Once you are firmly there, no illness is possible.

One study found that patients with minor ailments who saw a doctor who was positive and reassuring were nearly twice as likely to report being better two weeks later, compared to those who saw doctors who said they were unsure what was wrong.[149] Studies have also found that an enthusiastic doctor can heal 70–90 per cent of patients using dummy pills, whereas a sceptic will only heal 30–40 per cent with the same pills.[150] A good doctor-healer is an optimist who expects the best to happen.

Conscious medicine assures us that it is our emotional state that allows us to heal. A steady diet of hope, optimism, humour and love allows us to heal. In a negative state such as fear, guilt, doubt or despair, we cannot allow healing in. A good doctor is, first and foremost, a good psychologist. A true healer helps us to *feel good*. Then whatever treatment we choose is likely to work.

THE NOCEBO RESPONSE

Almost everyone has heard about the placebo response. On average, around 30 per cent of people get better when offered a sugar pill or other procedure that has no physiological effect, but which they *believe* is going to heal, but in some cases the placebo response can be as high as 90 per cent.[151] (Those who don't respond to placebos have inner blockages to getting well, such as secondary gain or unresolved conflict.) Placebos can work even when people are *told* they are just taking sugar pills. How weird is that?! And they tend to work better if they are given an impressive-sounding name, smell medicinal or have unpleasant side effects. Pills of different colours have differing effectiveness as placebos; for example, blue dummy pills 'work' better as sedatives than red dummy pills.[152]

Without the placebo response, the pharmaceutical industry would have perished by now, since most drugs are only slightly better than placebos, as the industry itself admits. The placebo response is seen as a nuisance by medical researchers, yet it is the basis of all healing. Drugs mostly help because they give us hope − and at hope or above, the bodymind begins to *heal itself.*

The nocebo response is less well known. This is what happens when harmful suggestions and negative beliefs are implanted, or when people react badly to placebo treatments. For example, people who are given placebos instead of active chemotherapy will often experience nausea and other side effects, and even have their hair fall out. About one-third of people who take dummy pills report side effects − including headaches, mild dizziness, drowsiness, difficulty in concentrating, and stomach upsets.

In one study, people with asthma were given drugs that should have made their symptoms worse, but were told they were bronchodilators, which would normally help. The 'wrong' drug reduced their symptoms by 50 per cent. Another group was told that the drug was a bronchoconstrictor, which should worsen their symptoms, when it was actually a 'helpful' bronchodilator. The nocebo information reduced the drug's effectiveness by 50 per cent.[153]

DIAGNOSIS – KILL OR CURE?

Most doctors would deny giving harmful suggestions, and insist they are just being honest with their patients or doing what is required of them. Yet whenever they warn patients about possible side effects of prescribed drugs, they are likely to trigger the nocebo response. Whenever they say that diabetes is chronic and incurable, or that Parkinson's disease is progressive, or that a chronic back problem is unlikely to improve, or that someone probably has only three months to live with lung cancer, they might sincerely believe this to be the truth – but what they are doing is setting up the potentially dangerous nocebo response.

Research has shown that doctors and nurses can speed up death simply by giving a patient a terminal diagnosis.[154] Although there is no intent to harm, this is pure voodoo, disguised as scientific medicine! Likewise, much of what passes for health education and preventive healthcare is simply a way of spreading fear, and increases the likelihood of disease.[155]

Conscious medicine would suggest that a diagnosis is a mixed blessing. It can kill or cure, depending upon how it is delivered, and how the patient perceives it through their own filters. A doctor's job should be to diagnose (if at all) in a way that brings relief, and gives hope and optimism. Instead of focusing on what goes 'wrong' in our bodies, doctors and healers should be deliberately collecting miraculous stories of healing from all over the planet, and filling their patients with genuine optimism that they can and will get better – if only they are willing to let go of old habits of thought, and are open to change.

One client of mine feels cheerful and positive and has minimal symptoms until she goes for her three-monthly hospital appointment. Her consultant then 'reminds' her that she has a chronic degenerative disorder with a poor prognosis, does a couple of tests, tut-tuts and shakes his head – and leaves her anxious and distraught. Her symptoms rapidly worsen, she loses faith in her ability to heal herself, then contacts me to repair the damage and get back on track. At a recent meeting the consultant told her, 'You will *not* recover from this disease.' Though I'm sure he believed he was simply telling her the truth, this is shockingly bad medicine. It is unconscious medicine. It is the nocebo response at work – and no medic who understands the role of beliefs and the stress response in disease would talk like this.

This woman's diagnosis is myasthenia gravis, which conventional medicine sees as progressive and incurable. Daniel Block is a naturopathic doctor who was given this diagnosis fifteen years ago, at the age of twenty-two, when he already had severe symptoms. Instead of using conventional medicine, he used alternative approaches – and healed himself. He has taken no medication and had no surgery. He plays soccer, hockey and golf, and also competes in karate at an international level. Like so many others, he sees the root of illness as negative and stressful thinking – and has found that myasthenia gravis is often linked with self-loathing, perfectionism and other forms of self-attack. Homoeopath Louis Klein has also cured several cases of myasthenia gravis.[156]

One of the doctors in our Conscious Medicine Circle (see the Foreword) insists that 'diagnosis is sorcery' (which leaves him none too popular with some of his colleagues!). When patients arrive with a diagnosis, he dismisses it and asks what they are actually feeling or experiencing – then explores healing from there. Unfortunately, most doctors are still bound up in a materialist model that tells them that the mind has little impact on the body, and that disease is real and separate from the person who 'has' it, and are often unaware of the potential impact of their words. As a result, many practitioners of energy psychology are now treating diagnosis as a trauma. If badly handled, diagnosis (and medical procedures) can throw us into the freeze response, leaving us dissociated and in chronic stress – which is a serious health risk in itself, and makes healing almost impossible.

Jon Kabat-Zinn, founder of the well-known Stress Reduction Clinic in Massachusetts, reports on a middle-aged librarian with chronic congestive heart failure.[157] She had been monitored in a heart clinic for a decade, was still going to work and doing her household chores, and was not in any immediate danger. She was in the clinic with a group of medical trainees when a well-known heart specialist arrived. He greeted the woman, turned to the trainees and said 'This woman has TS,' then abruptly left. The woman started to sweat profusely and panic. Her pulse rose to 150 beats per minute, and her lungs – which had been clear a few minutes earlier – began to fill with fluid. When asked what was wrong, she explained to a doctor that the specialist said she had TS. She had guessed this to mean 'Terminal Situation'. The doctor, amused at first, quickly reassured her that it meant 'tricuspid stenosis', which described the state of her heart valve. However, the woman was now convinced that she was dying. Her lungs continued to fill with fluid, she lost consciousness – and died of heart failure later that day.

Author Grace Gawler compares a cancer diagnosis with the Aboriginal tradition of bone-pointing.[158] If an Aboriginal medicine man pointed a bone at you because of some serious transgression, you were as good as dead. You would be shunned by your community, your health would rapidly decline, and the tribe would only gather around you again at death to say goodbye. In modern society, many people see cancer as a similar death sentence – and if that is how they see it, it becomes a self-fulfilling prophecy. Before they married, Grace's husband had bone cancer that led to a leg amputation. Several months later, Ian was told that he now had secondary cancer, and was given only a few months to live. Instead he pioneered his own healing journey based on stress control, diet and meditation, and made a full recovery. The couple later set up a cancer support centre in Australia.

In *Your Body Believes Every Word You Say*, author Barbara Levine talks of someone having a 'bout of cancer' as if it were just a passing bout of flu.[159] This phrase is far less likely to trigger a major stress response. When I had a cancer diagnosis,

I told my young son that I had a 'tiny bit of cancer' (which was entirely true – the rest of my body was just fine). Within conscious medicine, any symptom or dis ease is just an indicator of stuck vibrations – so it isn't a big deal unless you make it into one. And perhaps the best use of diagnosis is simply as a helpful pointer towards the underlying emotional issues.

The more you make a big deal out of any diagnosis, or turn it into a drama, the more likely you are to be thinking like a helpless victim rather than a conscious creator. Once you are in the wave response, nothing seems like such a big deal. This is not the same as being in denial about an illness, and vaguely hoping it will go away – while being secretly afraid that it will not. It is a state of relaxed and intuitive knowing that assures you that all is well, that you are being held in the arms of love, and are being constantly guided towards health, happiness and well-being.

SICK OR HEALTHY BELIEFS

Health is all vibrational, so how you *think* and *feel* about any diagnosis is crucial. Even if your health practitioner fills you with doom and gloom, you do not have to believe it. If a doctor pronounces a condition to be terminal, incurable or progressive, they are only talking about the limitations of conventional medicine. If what they say makes you feel bad, that is your emotional guidance telling you that your higher self does not agree with them. Look for stories of people who have healed themselves of whatever disease you have, and remind yourself of them daily. Send copies to your doctor – or give them a copy of this book – and if he or she is not interested and grateful, find yourself a new doctor.

However, do remember that health practitioners are always doing the best they can, within the limitations of their own beliefs, training and background. No one is *intending* to be harmful or obstructive; they simply do not know how to be a giant pendulum. You might want to inspire them to see things differently, or open them up to new possibilities –

but don't push against anyone, criticise them or expect them to change. This only keeps you in the stress response. As always, the one who really needs to change their mind is you!

Your body will mirror back your beliefs, so it is well worth ensuring that you are holding positive beliefs that support health and healing – regardless of what your health practitioners might believe. Even if you do not have a 'giant pendulum' around you, you can become one for yourself.

Exercise
HEALING YOUR 'SICK' BELIEFS

1. If you have a current dis-ease or diagnosis, write down all your thoughts and beliefs about it – including what you have read about or heard from health professionals and other 'experts', or from family and friends. Also, write down what you believe in general about health, sickness and the body, including what you learnt as a child. Which of these thoughts and beliefs make you feel expansive, powerful and free? Which thoughts bring you a sense of relief? Those are the thoughts that are aligned with your higher self. If a thought makes you feel bad, it is not because the truth is harsh – it is because you are thinking an untruth.

   To practise conscious medicine, you need to choose thoughts that feel good, regardless of what the reality seems to be. Then reality morphs itself to fit your belief. It might sound wacky, but it is how our psycho-energetic universe works. There is a buffer of time, so reality does not change instantly – but it simply has to come to match your vibrations.

   Change your vibrations, and you change your reality. To do this, choose some new beliefs about your illness – or about health and the body in general – that make you feel good, and hold those thoughts consistently. Remind yourself of these new thoughts until you build new neural pathways that will make those thoughts easier and easier to think. Then your body will begin to morph to match your new beliefs.

2. You can also use EFT (see the EFT guide in Chapter 9) to let go of your old beliefs, and tap in new ones. Or you can use the tools at the end of Chapter 4 to program new beliefs into your bodymind (Changing Your Core Beliefs, p. 97).

THE INFLUENCE OF FAMILY AND FRIENDS

Doctors and nurses are not the only possible source of the nocebo response. Family and friends can be just as dangerous. A friend of mine was healed of a supposedly terminal illness using alternative approaches and discharged herself from the hospital. Instead of celebrating her miraculous return to health, her family put her under daily pressure. 'You should have carried on seeing the doctors', 'Don't get too hopeful', and, 'You should be going for regular treatment.' Worry and concern, even when they are well intentioned, are a form of black magic. Her family's negativity and pressure caused her so much daily stress and angst that it became a self-fulfilling prophecy, and within a few months, her symptoms began to return. However, she had learnt her lesson and spotted the lizard voices. She saw an energy healer and a therapist to heal the disease again – and this time, she learnt to keep clear boundaries and be more assertive with her family.

Of course, outer voices are always a mirror of inner voices. Others can influence us, for better or worse, but only if we are open to that influence. So if your health practitioners or family are less than optimistic and reassuring, this has to be a vibrational match to something in you. Instead of complaining about them or letting them rattle you – or even worse, believing them – take it as a sign that you have some inner work to do. After all, if it didn't match some thoughts of yours, their words would slide off you as if you were Teflon. There would be nothing to stick to. (My client with myasthenia gravis said her consultant reminded her of her father, who used to say, 'Your dad is always right'.)

If someone rattles your cage, ask yourself: 'Who does this person remind me of?' Look at how you respond to what they say and use it as a helpful message about a stuck vibration within you. How you react to their negativity might well be the same stuckness that has triggered the disease. If you feel angry, ask what else you are angry about – and how you handle anger. If you feel hopeless or despairing, look at how you disempower yourself in other ways. If you are thrown into self-doubt, look at whether you have negative beliefs that need to be uprooted from your subconscious, and replace them with positive new beliefs.

Everything is your friend and teacher. As you change your own beliefs and shift your vibrations, those around you will change too. You might now attract health practitioners who are more positive and supportive, or find that they (or your family) are suddenly hearing about new approaches to health, and having a more open mind. Instead of being surrounded by gloomy Eeyores, you will find irrepressible Tiggers everywhere!

DISTANT HEALING

Since all energy is interconnected, a healer does not have to be physically present. In a conscious universe, we can transcend any limitations of space and time. One of the doctors in our Conscious Medicine Circle recently had a friend with kidney stones. She sent distant healing[160] to her, and 'saw' the kidney stones explode into a thousand pieces. When her friend went for surgery as scheduled, the operation took far longer than expected. The kidney stones had disintegrated into so many tiny pieces that the surgeon had a hard job removing them all.

In 2002, Ronnie Hawkins – a Canadian rock and roll star – found that he had pancreatic cancer, and was given only three or four months to live. His doctors and family were resigned to losing him. Then a teenage healer known as Adam,[161] who had been achieving some remarkable results, offered to send him distant healing. Ronnie felt the impact immediately, and asked for the healing sessions to continue – and six months later, he was pronounced well again. Eight years on, he remains free of cancer.

The healer Adam says that he alters his own frequencies until he is attuned to the frequency of his healee, picks up the information he needs from them, then – using his intention – he transmits the informational frequencies they need to become well again. He already has a degree in molecular biology and is now training in medicine – which bodes well for the future of medicine!

Within the new paradigm, consciousness operates like a quantum field – which means it does not exist in space-time, like a magnetic or gravitational field, but is non-local. This allows for consciousness to have an impact at a distance without any direct contact, beyond the speed of light and without any exchange of energy. Distant healing does not work every time, since no one can *impose* healing on another – but we can *influence* someone towards health if they are open to healing, as long as we are firmly in the wave response.

In a well-known study of the healing impact of prayer, nearly 400 patients admitted to a coronary care unit in San Francisco were randomly assigned to two groups. One group was prayed for by Christian prayer groups at a distance – though neither the patients nor the hospital staff knew who was being prayed for. The results were dramatic. Those who received prayer were far less likely to develop congestive heart failure, five times less likely to need antibiotics, none of them needed mechanical support for breathing, far fewer developed pneumonia or required resuscitation, and none of that group died. Prayer seemed to work better than any 'miracle drug'.[162]

Distant and surrogate healing show that insight into the trigger or underlying cause of a disease is not essential. All that is necessary is to release patterns of energetic resistance, or help love to flow. Insight is helpful only if it releases resistance – if it helps us look through the eyes of love, or make sense of disease, or gives a sense of hope and empowerment, or helps us see beyond a problem to a solution. Sometimes insights expand our consciousness in amazing ways. We see connections and have Aha! moments – and like an overstretched rubber band we never go back to where we were before.

However, if the search for insight keeps reminding us of past trauma or old habits of thought, or focused on 'being ill' or 'being depressed', without shifting those stuck vibrations, it can be unhelpful and can even re-traumatise us. This is one reason why talk therapies work so slowly, if at all, especially when someone has been deeply traumatised. Talk therapy is *so* twentieth century!

MAKING INSPIRED CHOICES

Who or what can help us to heal? From the perspective of conscious medicine, it's all in our vibrations, rather than in our actions. *Which* healthcare approach you choose matters far less than how you *feel* about it – which is one reason why I am not 'against' conventional medicine, nor am I 'for' alternative approaches. It all depends upon the individual, their background, their beliefs, intentions and state of consciousness. Everyone's path is unique. What matters most is your own emotional guidance, rather than trusting in what 'experts' say or listening to fearful lizard voices from the past.

Unfortunately when someone faces a health issue, they often make decisions about how to tackle it from the stress response. This means you are responding from a fearful and childlike state, which is not a good way to make crucial decisions. It makes for easy, compliant patients who go along with whatever a doctor suggests – but you might want to pause before taking action that could harm your body. If you have gallstones, for example, you might well feel relief at the thought of having them surgically removed – and the surgeon might make you feel calm, reassured and optimistic (a sign that they are connected to the Source) – in which case, that is probably a good choice for you. On the other hand, if surgery makes you feel anxious or doubtful, you might want to explore other options and put a decision on hold for a while.

If you are unsure about a decision, it is wise to postpone it until you shift your energy if at all possible. Once you are in the wave response, you are clear-thinking and decisive – and you will make life-affirming choices. At hope or above on the emotional ladder (see Chapter 7, page 168), your energy becomes more coherent. You will then intuitively know what to do, who to see or what approach to take, and you can begin to trust your decisions and impulses.

Making a decision based on fear is less likely to have a positive outcome, and might leave the underlying cause untouched. So you might be motivated to get a short-term 'fix' which sets up more serious health issues in the long term. Positive emotion tells you that you are aligning with your higher self, and receiving intuitive guidance from a source that you can trust – from Source energy itself.

How can you tell the difference between inspiration and motivation? Inspiration pulls you towards what you want, while motivation is based on avoidance. Motivation leads you to avoid possible negative consequences and arises from fear, doubt and insecurity. It is likely to bring you health practitioners who are coming from the stress response. Inspiration moves you towards what feels joyful and light and expansive. It will lead you towards a giant pendulum.

WHICH APPROACH?

The practitioner is more important than the tool. Many alternative and complementary therapists operate in a similar way to conventional medicine – seeing the healer-practitioner as the one with the power to heal, creating dependency, using their tools to 'fix' problems, and ignoring the underlying emotional issues. I have met some alternative therapists who are cold and impersonal, and many conventional doctors who are loving, warm-hearted healers. If I had to choose, I would probably prefer to see the latter. Perhaps this is why so many people ditch their paper prescriptions after seeing a doctor – and still get better. The drugs are mostly irrelevant, as even the drug companies admit. What matters most is how a health practitioner makes you *feel*.

Having said that, conscious medicine would favour approaches based upon shifting energy-consciousness – since you are then tackling the *root* of the problem. And there is now a plethora of tools and therapies available which do just this. Gary Craig, creator of EFT, often said that EFT was 'the ground floor of the new healing high-rise' – and already there are developments from EFT that take energy psychology into a new dimension, such as Matrix Reimprinting.[163]

Countless other healing techniques which are based upon shifting our energy-consciousness are now being introduced, such as Matrix Energetics, Theta Healing, the Lifeline Technique, Reconnective Healing, Quantum Shiatsu, Zero Balancing, the Yuen Method, BodyTalk, ZPoint, Quantum Touch, Nutri-Energetics System (NES), Holoenergetic Healing, the Body Code and Eden Energy Medicine. (See Resources for Health and Well-being, page 325.) All of these lie within the field of conscious medicine – along with more well-established approaches such as acupuncture, homoeopathy, flower essence therapy and craniosacral therapy. There are also approaches that are building firm bridges between conventional medicine and conscious medicine, such as 'mindfulness in medicine' (which uses meditation and self-awareness to reduce the stress response, in both patients and practitioners).[164]

Practitioners of conscious medicine usually integrate both energy and consciousness into their practice. The best energy healers I know are also insightful about the underlying emotional issues, and emphasise the need to tackle personal issues alongside energy work. And the best psychotherapists I know are those who integrate energy-based tools into talk therapy. Energy and consciousness are the yin and yang of healing, and we need both. But above all, good healer-practitioners help you come out of the stress response – and support your vision of a healthy and happy new future.

A crucial factor in choosing a health practitioner is that

they see you as working *together* – rather than seeing themselves as the (parental) 'expert' who tells you what to do. You
are the expert on yourself! Any practitioner of conscious
medicine will help you to feel empowered, rather than taking
your power away – and ideally will offer tools or approaches
with which you can help yourself, or help you clarify what
needs to change in your life. It also needs to be someone
with whom you feel *safe*. Someone who seems relaxed, and
smiles and laughs readily is also a good sign.

Don't fall into the trap of telling yourself that you 'should'
be able to fix your body with the power of your consciousness, and all by yourself. Don't put yourself under that kind
of pressure. It could leave you feeling isolated or not good
enough, which will throw you into the particle response. By
the time you have become ill, the chances are that you have
habits of thought which you have become blind to, have tied
yourself in knots of unresolved conflict, and your energy
system is blocked and out of balance – so seeking outside
help is often essential. Others can see us more clearly than
we can see ourselves. It also feels self-nurturing to see a good
health practitioner, and can at least kick-start the healing
process.

INTEGRATIVE MEDICINE

Many people choose to have surgery or take drugs, then seek
out more conscious approaches to healing or therapy to
explore what is going on at deeper levels. We are straddling
two paradigms in healthcare at the moment, and integrative
medicine allows you to have a foot in both worlds. It might
be easiest for you to believe that surgery will fix a problem
at the physical level – and if the operation is low-risk and
feels positive, or your condition is life-threatening, that could
be a good choice for you. Or it might feel reassuring and
supportive for you to take prescribed drugs. Alongside that,
you might also choose more holistic or conscious approaches.

If you do choose conventional medicine – or you find

yourself in an emergency situation, where this approach is often the best option – you can 'talk' to the drugs and ask them to minimise any side effects, or talk to your body with the same request. Everything is conscious – yes, even a tablet! (It might sound weird, but try it!) Or you can connect with the Source and pray that the surgeon's hands are well guided by higher forces. Reach out for help in whatever way feels right to you. Be gentle on yourself, and enjoy the journey.

Whatever you choose to do, it is important to talk yourself into having made the right decision, so that you are not creating inner conflict. (Just as you need to be happy with what you eat, rather than telling yourself you 'should' be eating different foods.) There is no right or wrong decision about healthcare – and your higher self would never see you as making the 'wrong' choice. Second-guessing yourself can tear you apart and block your healing response. Whatever you choose right now, and whatever choices you have made in the past, come to peace with yourself. Relax – you are doing just fine!

MIRACLES OF HEALING

Doctor and healer Richard Bartlett suggests that all our current models of healing are probably wrong, or at least incomplete, since we are only just beginning to grasp the unlimited potential of our consciousness.[165] It is pretty clear to me that healing usually occurs in step-by-step ways as we move out of the stress response, release resistance due to trauma and negative beliefs, become more coherent, and connect more and more with our wave self. On the whole, we raise our vibrations in a slow and steady way – with lots of ups and downs along the way – and as we stabilise in a higher state of consciousness, health follows. For most minor symptoms, this is a simple and natural process.

When healing from dis-ease seems to occur in a quantum shift, it tends to follow countless mini-shifts in awareness over a period, or trying many approaches that appear not to work, before this apparently sudden tipping point of change. Perhaps we *can* sometimes shift our awareness into a wave-like reality in which 'solid stuff' is highly mutable and flexible, and new connections are made – jumping through a magic portal into a parallel world – but in my experience, 'spontaneous remission' is usually far from spontaneous! It tends to be the outcome of a long, intensive process of inner work and energy healing, which gives birth to a new and healthier self.

Calling anything a 'miracle' simply means that our current scientific model is inadequate, and needs to expand. Some believe that chaos theory and strange attractors offer a scientific framework for healing and miracles. Others point towards superstring theory and the holographic universe. Richard Bartlett suggests that the theory of scalar electromagnetics offers a science of miracles – including stepping into parallel universes, time travel and instant healing. And since I have watched him heal scoliosis (curvature of the spine) live on stage – a party trick which he repeats almost routinely, amidst much fun and laughter, without even touching the person – I know that he is aware of a thing or two about miracles!

However, don't wait for science to catch up before allowing yourself to heal. After all, conventional science says that bumblebees 'cannot' fly – but happily, bumblebees know better!

So now you know what causes illness, how to unwrap the gifts that come disguised as symptoms, and what allows us to heal. You also know how best to choose a healer and a healing approach – and what might allow a 'healing miracle' to unfold. However, the healing journey is not always simple and straightforward. In the next chapter, we look at some of the stumbling blocks you might come across – and how to move beyond them.

Chapter Eleven

JOURNEY TO ITHACA

You need chaos in your soul to give birth to a
dancing star.

Friedrich Nietzsche[166]

Let's suppose that you are now listening to your body language, and you have worked out what a symptom or dis-ease means. Perhaps you have also tracked down the original trauma or underlying negative beliefs, honoured your emotions and moved into a more positive frame of mind. Often this is enough to allow the bodymind to get well again. But what if the symptoms persist? What if you try many approaches to healing and nothing seems to work? What if you feel trapped in disappointment, frustration or even hopelessness? What else might be blocking your healing?

Within the model of conscious medicine, we either heal or remain healthy *unless we are getting in our own way* – that is, unless we are in resistance. Resistance means there is in-coherence (conflict) between our inner selves. One part of us wants to heal, but another part wants to be sick. Or one part is clinging to an unresolved conflict or toxic situation that a healthier part wants to release. In energy psychology, this is called psychological reversal. It is like being a cart attached to two horses that are dragging it in opposite directions. It is not very comfortable, and you cannot move. From the outside, you look stuck; and from the inside, you feel frustrated at best and despairing at worst.

Remember that everything is a friend, and that any blockage holds the potential for change and evolution. Resistance is not a problem, but an opportunity for self-awareness and growth. When you combine the sunlight of consciousness with the rain of resistance, it produces a beautiful rainbow. Even minor symptoms can offer helpful nudges about inner conflict that can help us align with our higher self – and the more serious the disease, the greater the potential hidden within it. A serious diagnosis can throw our lives into chaos, which helpfully shakes up whatever is negative or stuck within our lifestyle, thoughts and energy patterns, so that we can open up to transformation.

It's important to know that you are not somehow 'getting it wrong' if you become seriously ill, seem unable to heal from a disease, or recovery is slow. I had to struggle with this one myself, since it took two or three years for me to heal from breast cancer and resolve the underlying issues. I heard of others who healed tumours overnight, or in days and weeks, and I sometimes beat myself up and felt like a failure! (Yes, despite knowing all that I know!) Eventually I realised – like Arielle Essex with her brain tumour (see Chapter 6, page 128) – that a faster healing journey is not necessarily a better one. There is no right or wrong path.

Instant healing is wonderful, but a longer journey has its own benefits. It can allow much deeper personal changes and insights that have to be slowly integrated, and which cannot happen overnight. I have met people who have been on a healing journey for twenty or thirty years, and who would not have missed that journey for all the tea in China. A serious diagnosis or prolonged healing journey simply means that you are dealing with big issues – issues that might date back over many past lifetimes, or back through many generations of your family – which have the potential to transform your life.

The Greek poet Cavafy wrote a beautiful poem about

the mythical journey to the island of Ithaca, the hero's journey in search of the soul.[167] The poem reminds us that when we finally reach our destination, it might not hold the riches we expected – and that the richness of the journey *is* our destination. Holding on to the dream of Ithaca merely prompted us to set sail. Hope that your journey is a long one, says Cavafy – full of adventure, full of instruction. And I would add: know that there will always be another Ithaca, and another, and another. In an evolving universe, our journey is an eternal one – a never-ending adventure in consciousness. Learning to enjoy the journey, rather than impatiently waiting to reach our destination, is one of the keys to health and happiness.

Sometimes it might take weeks, months or even years to work through our past traumas and negative beliefs, to recognise our patterns and learn how to stay in the wave response. It is all part of the journey. But there can also be unexpected stumbling blocks along the path to wellness. Here are five hidden factors that can block healing or even make you sicker, and which might need to be addressed before you can restore health and well-being:

◇ Secondary gain

◇ Death wishes

◇ The family soul

◇ Diet, toxins and physical factors

◇ Victim mentality

SECONDARY GAIN

We often *assume* that sick people want to be well, but there can be many side benefits of illness, injury and disease. It can bring positive changes or serve hidden functions we might not even be aware of – functions known as 'secondary gain'. It can take a lot of ruthless self-honesty (and self-forgiveness) to track down any secondary gain that might block you from getting well. Here are the crucial questions to ask: What advantages has this dis-ease brought into your life? What might be the downside to getting well again? And how can you meet these needs in more direct ways?

Common forms of secondary gain are:

✧ Getting love, care and support from others (including health professionals)

✧ Avoiding work pressures; getting time off work

✧ Avoiding other unwanted responsibilities

✧ Using the illness as an excuse to say no, avoid taking risks, or to remain childlike

✧ Slowing down the pace of life; having time to relax, or 'find yourself'

✧ Giving you permission to nurture yourself, or be more assertive

✧ Expressing distress and unmet needs

✧ Controlling others

✧ Punishing others (even if they are dead)

✧ Punishing yourself (due to unresolved guilt)

✧ Giving you something to focus upon

✧ Distracting attention from other issues, unresolved conflicts or traumas

✧ Giving you an identity ('I'm a diabetic')

✧ Making you feel special ('I'm highly sensitive to gluten')

✧ A way of feeling connected to family members who had the same disease, or who had similar 'accidents' (see The Family Soul, below)

✧ Resolving a conflict (e.g. avoiding the question of whether to leave a job; or bringing together feuding family members through a common concern for the illness)

✧ Seeing your issues more clearly

✧ 'Waking up' to your spiritual journey

Some families even 'teach' children to be sick by being over-solicitous and giving them treats when they are ill, then withdrawing attention as soon as they become well again. In one family of three children, a five-year-old boy was over-heard saying to his younger sister, 'If you want to grab Mummy's attention, you just have to be sick. That's what I do!' He had already worked out a crucial family dynamic, and how to operate it![168] Sadly, this might have marked the start of a lifetime of chronic illness and game-playing for them both – and perhaps flip-flopping between over-caring for others, or being weak and dependent.

I spoke recently to a woman who had been financially supporting her sick sister for ten years – 'I had the money and she didn't, so what else could I have done?' She was bemused that her sister was furious with her, and they were no longer speaking. She had been unwittingly supporting her sister's illness and dependency – playing Rescuer to her, while seeing her as a weak and helpless Victim (for more on ego states, see Chapter 6, the Drama Triangle). At last, her sister was finding her own power and had turned Persecutor; not surprisingly, she was also starting to recover. Families often play such well-meaning but toxic games as this, seeing them as expressions of love and caring.

In some cases, the reward for disease or disability is obvious. When legal compensation for an accident or injury is being pursued, or early retirement on health grounds, healing is unlikely until the court case or tribunal is over. Even then, guilt about receiving compensation or a pension can some-times prevent a full recovery.

Any serious emotional or physical dis-ease is likely to be

over-determined, with many different dynamics holding it in place. While I worked in the National Health Service, I saw many women who were anorexic (having faced this problem myself in my late teens, which gave me insight into the underlying issues). With one of these young women, we compiled a list of over thirty different functions that her eating disorder was serving for her – such as staying in control, expressing anger, focusing on something she could do well (being thin) to raise her self-esteem, distracting herself from more scary issues about growing up and choosing a career, remaining non-sexual, and fulfilling family injunctions to both 'be perfect' *and* 'be invisible'. It was clear that she was not going to start eating again until she could face those issues and meet her needs in healthier ways. Although it threatened her physical well-being, anorexia was a desperate attempt to survive emotionally.

Likewise if someone is overweight, there are always subconscious reasons for this – such as protecting oneself from sexual advances (which is common in women who have been abused), indirectly expressing anger, mirroring low self-esteem, distracting oneself from other life issues, identifying with an overweight relative, or rebelling against the pervasive attitude that thin is beautiful.

Food often becomes a way of stuffing negative feelings such as anger, shame, hurt and loneliness – and a symbol of 'feeding' one's unmet needs. Some women even learn to binge and vomit as they stuff down their feelings and needs with food, then reject them again by being sick. Addictions are part of the fight-flight response, and show that we are lost in particle thinking. This is why dieting is a waste of time and energy – and exacerbates the unhealthy beliefs that the body (or food) is an enemy, or needs to be controlled. I believe that the body is exactly the weight we have programmed it to be.

Sometimes a dis-ease is an attempt to resolve the problem that triggered it. For example, if a workaholic gets a serious diagnosis and takes time off, the illness can help them take stock and re-balance their lives – *unless* they simply pour their workaholism into the healing journey! Illness can also be a way of getting caring and attention from a distant or distracted partner or family – or of getting someone to stay if you suspect they want to leave. I know of many cases where one partner in an unhappy marriage has become seriously ill or disabled when the children come close to leaving home, where the marriage has been tenuously held together by the children.

Similarly, a child might become sick in an attempt to pull together their parents' disintegrating marriage, or to distract attention from it – or to express hidden feelings or secrets within the family. Generally speaking, in conscious medicine, very sick children are seen as either expressing or trying to heal family dynamics, sometimes from past generations. Or they might have a soul contract – that is, an agreement made before entering this lifetime – to leave early. (We cannot know what another soul's intent is, and being here for a short time might have served their higher purpose.)

Another form of secondary gain from illness is avoiding something you consciously want, but subconsciously fear. Sarah is an 'infertile' woman I saw two years ago, whose mother repeatedly told her she had nearly died while giving birth to her. As a young child, Sarah had obviously translated this into the belief that 'Childbirth is life-threatening' – so it was little wonder that her body resisted pregnancy. It was trying to keep her alive! After we re-programmed her subconscious with a new belief, she was pregnant within a few months.

It is also common for an illness to become so merged with your identity that it feels scary to imagine giving it up. Who would you be without your disease? Or who would you be if you were not on this healing journey? If a disease – or trying to heal yourself – fills a large portion of your time, then it is likely to have become part of your identity. You need to start seeing yourself as someone who is well, and begin to fill your life and thoughts with positive new projects – to begin to think like your healthy future self.

Illness can even become a way of filling someone's social

diary with doctor and hospital appointments – or having a ready topic for conversation – which is one reason why retired people often become hypochondriacal if they do not have caring, supportive relationships and positive projects. The conscious mind needs something to focus upon, so in the absence of anything more positive and creative, it might choose to obsess about symptoms and disease.

Secondary gain is sometimes seen as manipulation, but it is rarely conscious and deliberate. On the positive side, it can give you clues as to what is missing in your life, what you are avoiding, what needs are not being met, or how your life needs to change in order to get well. I often ask clients who are ill: 'How would your life change if you were 100 per cent healthy? Could you change it that way right now?' If there is any anxiety in the response, then their illness is being used as an avoidance strategy or has become an identity. If there is frustration or longing in the reply, there is a dream or desire that they are blocking. And if their answer seems rather flat, I might wonder whether they have enough positive reasons to live.

DEATH WISHES

An extreme form of secondary gain from illness is wanting to die. Clearly, if someone *wants* to die – whether consciously or not – this can prevent healing from a potentially fatal disease. Author and doctor Bernie Siegel reckons that about 15–20 per cent of those with life-threatening disease consciously want to die. I have certainly met many people who died in their forties and fifties who had felt trapped in an emotional or financial mess – some who wanted to escape an unhappy marriage but could not 'justify' getting divorced, some who were workaholic and exhausted, and others who were in so much debt that they could not imagine becoming solvent again. For those who can see 'no way out' of an intolerable situation, the body will often helpfully offer a solution. Death can become an escape route.

More often, there are *subconscious* reasons for setting up a life-threatening disease. I have a young friend who developed ovarian cancer with multiple secondaries at the tender age of twenty-three. The tumours were growing fast, her doctors had given her a grim prognosis, and she was preparing herself for an early death. I muscle-tested her (see Chapter 4, Changing Your Core Beliefs, page 97) and she tested strong (Yes) on the statement: 'I want to die', and weak (No) on 'I want to live'. She was shocked, since this was the opposite of what she consciously wanted, and she was fervently looking for ways to heal the cancer.

I asked her to hold the Whole Brain Posture (see Chapter 4, page 99) while holding the positive statement: 'I want to live'. While doing this, she remembered that in early childhood she had attended a Hare Krishna school, where they taught that the physical world was a 'fallen' place, and being in heaven was where she would find joy and peace. She had been programmed at infant school to look forward to death, rather than life! (Not surprisingly, she then went through traumas in her childhood and early adult life, which confirmed that life was full of suffering – and which triggered the cancer.) It took only a few minutes in the Whole Brain Posture, then she muscle-tested strong on wanting to live, and weak on wanting to die. Her conscious and subconscious mind were now aligned with healing. Shortly after, she had powerful healing sessions with energy healer Tjitze de Jong in which Jesus and Francis of Assisi came to her in visions. When she went back to hospital for another scan soon after, they could find no trace of the tumours.

Almost everyone with a life-threatening diagnosis whom I have ever muscle-tested has been reversed on 'I want to live' and 'I want to die' – even those who have done a lot of inner work and self-healing. In other words, their body-mind has been programmed for death. Sometimes this can be traced back to being an unwanted child, or their mother trying to abort the pregnancy. Sometimes it is because of a belief that life is full of pain and struggle, and death will be better. Sometimes it is because a problem feels unresolvable, and they feel trapped or have given up on a dream.

It might be tough to face up to this, but I believe it is not possible to create a life-threatening disease unless part of you has decided it would be preferable to die – so it is essential to address this if you want to recover. Life feels wonderful from the wave response, so a death wish almost always means you are stuck in the particle response.

Another common reason for death wishes is unresolved guilt – either judging yourself as having done something wrong, or not doing what you 'should' have done. I remember seeing a woman with cancer who was contorted with guilt because her elderly mother had died alone, and she had not visited her for three weeks before. The post-mortem showed her mother was riddled with cancer. Two years later, Theresa was still beating herself up – even though she had had a difficult relationship with her hypercritical and martyr-like mother, who had a strict Catholic background. It was clear that Theresa was holding a lot of repressed anger, but (like many Catholics) felt more comfortable feeling guilty. Although she was now free from having to care for her difficult mother, her guilt and self-hatred had become a malignant prison.

Once she honoured and released this anger that dated back to early childhood, Theresa's guilt over her mother's death disappeared. She saw that her mother had been the best mother she knew how to be, given her strict and oppressive childhood. She also remembered that her mother had been terrified of dying in hospital, and realised that she had probably created the quiet death she wanted at home. Theresa no longer needed to punish herself with cancer, and was able to let go and move on with her life.

Guilt can be a real killer (and is often a cover-up for resentment). A good way to discover whether unresolved guilt might be blocking health is to muscle-test for 'I deserve to live' and 'I deserve to heal' (see Chapter 4, Changing Your Core Beliefs, page 97). Unless these both test strong – and the muscle-test is weak for 'I deserve to be sick' – there is unresolved guilt that needs to be released. Remember that our higher self never judges us, so it is only when seeing through the eyes of your particle self that you feel shame or guilt. When connected with your wave self, you know that you are good and worthy and deserving of everything that is wonderful. Your wave self loves you, everyone and life unconditionally – which is why it is totally free of resistance.

My understanding is that, at a spiritual level, every death can be considered a suicide. This is a planet of free will, and we can, in theory, choose whether to live or to die. No one dies unless they are ready to leave, even if their conscious mind is resisting it. (If this sounds hard to take, remember that death is not a tragedy for our higher self, which knows that we are eternal beings.) With the exception of children who die young, who often have a soul contract to stay for a short while, our time of death is not fixed or pre-ordained. However, we can be *influenced* into leaving early by negative diagnoses from doctors and others who see people as helpless victims of what is happening in their own body.

It is not necessary to become ill in order to die. Some people slip away in their sleep, apparently healthy and well until the end. Others might have fatal 'accidents' as a way of leaving. You do not have to become sick in order to die – but if you *believe* you do, that is likely to be what happens!

Death is not a failure or tragedy. It is simply a choice to move on, to evolve in a new way. It is a cosmic form of recycling. If someone dies, they have not 'failed' to heal themselves, nor have the doctors and nurses failed. I often compare death to choosing to emigrate. Others might feel sad because they will miss seeing you, but it is not a tragic mistake – it is just a choice.

From the old materialist paradigm, death is a taboo subject that brings up a lot of anxiety. If you believe that physical reality is all there is, then death is the end of our existence. When you live in the conscious universe of the new paradigm, you know that we are pure consciousness which freely comes and goes from physical bodies – so death is not such a big issue. The separation of death is just an illusion – albeit a convincing one! One friend of mine even wrote a book with a close friend *after* her friend's death.[169] Countless people have found that they can connect with loved ones after death, as long as they are not lost in grief and sadness. You have to be in the vibrational range of those who have died in order to sense or hear them – which means it is easiest to do so when you are happy. You have to be fully in the wave response, in a state of unconditional love. Since there is no resistance after we die, our so-called 'dead' friends are always in a delightful state of bliss.

If you are faced with a serious or life-threatening diagnosis, your old self is no longer viable. Like a caterpillar that has spun a cocoon, you are being called to evolve. There are two ways for a caterpillar to evolve – by dying in the cocoon, or by becoming a butterfly. And there is no right or wrong choice. It is up to you. Either way, you will be fluttering and dancing into the light.

The family soul

Sometimes the influences that make people become ill – or even die – come from outside the self. In tribal and shamanic cultures, people have long believed that we are affected by the souls of our ancestors – for good or ill – and that this influence can sometimes result in illness and disease. Modern family therapy likewise sees us as embedded in family systems that can pass dysfunction down and across the generations.

Bert Hellinger is a modern pioneer of this systemic view of emotional and physical dis-ease, who introduced the healing approach known as family constellations. As a Catholic priest, Hellinger worked as a missionary in Africa and witnessed the traditional Zulu approach to healing, in which a sick person is seen as revealing disturbed relationships within the wider family or community, including dead ancestors. When he returned to Europe, he trained as a family therapist – and developed the idea of the 'family soul'.

The family soul is a conscious energy field that spans three or four generations, and which holds the disturbed patterns and unresolved issues of our ancestors, dead or alive. Very often, the problem is that love has been withheld or not allowed to flow freely – that is, there has been resistance or trauma stuck in the family energy field – perhaps leading to family feuds, exclusion, addiction, abuse, unhealthy relationships, illness or accidents. The chain of pain tends to be passed down the generations, and is repeated in acts of 'misguided loyalty'. It is well known in family therapy that the most sensitive and vulnerable family member is the one who becomes symptomatic. Yet rather than being in a certain person, the problem is *between* people. The patterns quite often skip one generation and affect the grandchildren, or great-nieces and nephews.

Suicidal feelings or life-threatening disease, for example, might be traced back to an ancestor who was excluded from the family, or whose early death was covered up or forgotten, perhaps because it was too painful. Or unresolved guilt might be passed down the family line, leading to self-destructive patterns such as addiction, workaholism, extreme sports, 'accidents' or suicide. Such patterns are known as systemic entanglement. As their family soul is healed, people often find a stronger sense of identity. Relationships flow into healthier forms, life-affirming choices are made or people feel at peace at last – and physical symptoms and disease are often healed.[170]

In one example, a woman with chronic asthma was named after her sister who died in infancy. Her parents never talked of the dead child, and after hearing about Bert Hellinger's work, she realised that she had to honour her dead sister. She visited her sister's grave, took her flowers, and told her that *she* was the first-born child – which broke her identification with her sister. At last, she had permission to live. She no longer had to take the place of her dead sister. After this, she could breathe freely again.[171]

What happens in a family constellation?

Taking part in a family constellation can be a remarkable experience. It is rather like stepping on stage in a theatre.

Different people play the role of family members and ancestors – or you might play the role of an illness, for example – and as you step into that role, you take on emotions or act out dynamics in strange and moving ways, as if someone had mysteriously written a script for you. Energy moves through you, and you might feel compelled to turn your back on others, to reach out to them, to lie on the ground, to rage or to silently weep.

In my first-ever constellation, I took on the role of a young man I knew nothing about – the brother of a boy who had been sexually abused by a priest. I could immediately feel a strong muscular body and emotional hardness. My eyes darted around, looking out for 'enemies'. I said (as the young man) that I felt the world was divided into goodies and baddies – black or white, with no shades of grey. As the constellation progressed, I felt 'him' soften and begin to open his heart. The lad's mother later told me that he was in the army, and that I had described him perfectly.

The concept of the family soul – and how patterns can be passed on or healed in apparently mysterious ways – is consistent with biologist Rupert Sheldrake's well-known theory of morphic fields.[172] While most biologists were still staring down microscopes, he was considering the history of science and formulating a new framework for biology – a framework that includes the invisible world of energy-consciousness, and the information-carrying fields that animate and organise life, and allow for growth and evolution.[173] I bumped into Rupert Sheldrake on a workshop with Bert Hellinger several years ago – and he sees the family soul as one of these organising energy fields, or morphic fields, which holds memories from the past and 'searches' for resolution and wholeness.

Since the cellular membrane can receive signals from energy fields, disturbances in the family soul can influence our DNA, affecting our feelings, thoughts and even our health. Our energy can get entangled with the energy of our dead ancestors, so that they inhabit us like ghosts. Echoes from the past reverberate down the generations. Scientist Valerie

Hunt likewise suggests that powerful thought-forms can be passed down the generations via fields – and can also be left behind in an environment.[174]

Shamanic cultures would call this 'possession' or 'attached entities' (the second most common cause of dis-ease, after soul loss due to trauma). In modern psycho-energetic terms, we would see 'possession' as a disturbance in the energy field due to taking on others' vibrations – often from the family soul.

Any early death or serious disease before the age of forty-five can be a sign of a disturbed family soul, in which unfinished business is being passed down the generations. Wherever there is a long history of disturbed family patterns such as abuse, alcoholism, suicide, serious illness or early deaths – and an individual approach to healing does not seem to be working – it is worth delving into your family history and exploring what old beliefs or unresolved issues have been passed down the line. Family constellations are one way of healing these entanglements.[175] (I also have a self-help CD available, *Healing Your Family Tree*.)

Bert Hellinger says that we 'unconsciously aspire to equal our parents in suffering' – as if it somehow justifies their choices if we repeat their dysfunctional patterns – and that there is no transformation without guilt. When we break family patterns and follow our own path, we always tend to feel guilty, since guilt is how the old system controls us and holds us in check. Guilt makes us loyal to the family-ar patterns, suppressing our individuality and often making us withhold love from ourselves or others.

The journey to Ithaca almost always involves breaking family-ar patterns, even though it will feel risky or uncomfortable. If we keep our frontal lobes awake (see Chapter 5, Waking up Your Frontal Lobes, page 108), we can begin to ask ourselves questions that our lizard voices would never dare to ask, such as: 'Why would I feel guilty about this?', 'Who says I am not allowed to do what I want?', 'Is this a healthy and life-affirming choice?', 'Am I doing what feels joyful and expansive, or just doing what is expected?', 'Am I expressing love freely, or holding back?' Once you understand how your emotional guidance works, you recognise that guilt is a sign that you are not listening to your higher self. Then you begin to release the family chains that bind you. You listen to the voice of the phoenix – and can fly free.

DIET, TOXINS AND PHYSICAL FACTORS

What about diet, environmental toxins and other physical factors? Isn't there plenty of research that suggests that these affect our health? Perhaps – but we need to be very careful about the difference between correlation and causation. Just because studies find a link between diet and disease, this does not necessarily mean there is a causal connection between the two.

For example, diabetes is fast becoming a pandemic disease that conventional medicine sees as chronic, incurable and dangerous. In Arizona, however, a study of six people with diabetes found that they reversed their diabetes in less than thirty days by shifting to a healthy raw diet and making changes in their lifestyle, including emotional shifts towards positive beliefs, empowerment and self-care.[176] They came off insulin and up to eighteen other medications, their blood sugar returned to normal, excess weight dropped off and they felt more joyful and alive. (Two of these subjects had type 1 diabetes, in which the body does not produce any insulin.)

Does this mean that a raw food diet can cure diabetes? When I watched a DVD about this study, I saw the six subjects making *psychological* shifts associated with self-love and self-nurturing, being freed from their usual daily stressors, given emotional support and bonding, and finding a new sense of self-empowerment over a disease that they had seen as incurable – not to mention the impact of being filmed for thirty days, and the researchers' expectations that the diabetes would be healed. We cannot disentangle the physical and psychological factors here. What the study does (crucially) show is that diabetes is easily curable.

We already know that a hyperactive HPA axis can lead to cells not taking up glucose in response to insulin – so the link between the stress response and diabetes is clear.[177] And the new biology tells us that our *emotional* state is the primary factor that correlates with health or disease, along with our beliefs about health.

In a conscious universe, physical factors such as diet and toxins are always secondary to how we think and feel. We cannot change our diet, start exercising, practise yoga or make any other shift towards a healthier lifestyle without making psychological changes *first*. We are making new choices. A junk food diet is quick, easy and cheap – so it fits with being in the stress response, which often makes us feel that time and money are limited. Stress also makes us dissociate from our body, so that we do not listen to its needs. When we relax into the wave response, we are more likely to devote time to preparing food and want to nurture ourselves well. My point is not to ignore the benefits of good nutrition; rather, to note that both a new choice of diet *and* a new state of health might begin with a shift in emotional state: a shift towards self-love and higher consciousness.

Likewise, there is plenty of evidence that exercise relieves depression – and there are good physiological reasons for this. A doctor friend told me about a patient of hers whose chronic depression vanished after she took up jogging, and began training for a marathon. But what nudges someone to make the *decision* to start running, or cycling, or dancing, or going to the gym? Such a decision must come from listening to a phoenix voice that is self-loving and future-oriented.

In support of this, one study found that the benefits of exercise depend upon your emotional state. When a group of actors worked themselves up into an angry state before taking light exercise, they showed none of the physiological benefits normally associated with exercise. A second group of actors was asked to remain calm, peaceful and stable – and when this group exercised, there was a positive impact on their heart rate, respiration, blood pressure and other measures.[178] It is our emotional state that is primarily in charge of our physiology.

Epigenetic research – which studies how the environment affects how genes are expressed – suggests that our thoughts and beliefs are vastly more powerful than physical factors such as diet or exercise. Channelled wisdom from sources such as Abraham[179] support this view. The body mirrors our *consciousness*. If you munch through a healthy salad while watching doom and gloom on the nine o'clock news, that salad is not going to do your body much good! Much better to eat steak and chips, if that is what you fancy, while relaxing with your loved one, or listening to your favourite music – *unless* you tell yourself that the food you are eating is 'bad' for you, in which case you throw yourself into conflict and trigger the stress response. Our negative thoughts about food can be far more dangerous than the food itself!

The new biology suggests that diet only becomes a significant factor in health when you are under chronic stress, or have already become ill, which is when you most need to 'eat well'.[180] (For this reason, hospitals should serve highly nutritious food – which is rarely the case!) The irony is that when we are stressed we make bad choices, and tend to choose processed foods, caffeine and sugary snacks which give us a quick lift, throw our blood sugar out of balance and exacerbate the stress response. Food then becomes a drug we use to ignore our body's messages, and to energise or anaesthetise ourselves.

At the highest levels of consciousness, food becomes irrelevant. Some individuals have eaten dangerous toxins without harming themselves. What does this tell us about the body? Higher states of consciousness seem to make us far more resilient than usual. And the opposite is also true: when we are in a low state emotionally, we are more vulnerable to physical and environmental toxins.

As I see it, when we feel more like a separate particle, we descend (vibrationally) into a Newtonian universe in which other billiard balls really *can* bash into us – such as pesticides, air pollution or food additives. When we are more wave-like, any toxic energies simply wash through us, since we have moved out of their frequency range. It is also true that you will make healthier choices when your vibrations are high – but even those dietary and environmental toxins you cannot avoid will have far less negative impact.

For this reason, I do not see nutritional medicine as coming under the umbrella of conscious medicine, since its focus is on the physical realms. Diet is secondary to our state of consciousness. (Holistic medicine is not necessarily conscious medicine.) Within the new paradigm, consciousness is the primary factor in health. This doesn't mean there are no physical rules, just that consciousness can bend those rules.

For example, there are dozens of people who have apparently lived without food for long periods – mostly pious and holy men and women. Michael Werner, a Swiss biochemist, stopped eating food in his early fifties, largely out of curiosity.[181] He claimed that his health improved when he stopped eating, he needed far less sleep, his weight remained stable, and he continued his work and family life as normal. He reported feeling better mentally and physically. He sometimes went for ten days without even drinking, which is supposedly impossible. Like others who have 'lived on light', he believes that his body learnt to convert prana, chi or Source energy into nourishment – and that anyone can learn to do this (though a few reportedly died in the attempt to follow the original protocol that Werner based his own personal experiment on, and I would not advise trying it).

An altered state of consciousness can also allow people to walk on fire, have metal hooks pierce their skin without pain, or withstand freezing temperatures without harm. There are stories of naked yogis in the snow who have been draped in freezing wet towels, which soon begin to steam with heat. And what about the well-publicised cases of people lifting cars when a child or loved one had become trapped beneath the vehicle? The physical body is capable of far more than we realise, and is probably limited mostly by our *beliefs* about what is possible.

However, if you are already ill, the rules about diet and

toxins are somewhat different. By the time physical symptoms appear, you have probably been subjecting yourself to emotional toxins for a long time, and these will have translated themselves into physical toxins in your body. You will have become toxic at many different energetic levels of your being. So it is probably wise to detoxify physically as well as emotionally – and a healthy diet and exercise can help with this.

Naturopath Andreas Moritz, author of *Cancer Is Not a Disease*, suggests that a tumour is the body's way of concentrating toxicity in one place, thereby enabling you to stay alive. In other words, cancer is a helpful and protective friend when the body has been overloaded with emotional and/or physical toxins. 'Cancer is more a healing response than it is a disease', he says.[182] Although I think he over-emphasises the role of *physical* toxins, I certainly agree with his positive approach to cancer. If he is right, then pouring further toxins into the body in the form of chemotherapy and radiation cannot be wise – and it makes sense to try natural approaches first. After all, there is nothing inherently dangerous about cancer cells. Cancer only becomes a risk to life when a tumour obstructs the bile duct or other vital pathways. However, the *fear* that can be generated by a cancer diagnosis is hugely toxic to the body.

On my own journey through cancer, I chose to eat an organic wholefood diet that was mostly vegan – which I still generally prefer – but I promised myself that I wouldn't deny myself any food I really wanted. Choosing healthy and wholesome foods is an act of self-love which, in itself, will help to deactivate the stress response and raise your vibrations.

However, if eating a healthy diet feels restrictive and self-denying, then it can become another source of stress – and if you believe that you have to limit yourself to certain foods in order to stay healthy, you have lost faith in your body's natural state of well-being. Likewise, if you tell yourself that a slice of chocolate cake is 'bad' for you but still go ahead and eat it, *that* will activate stress! So it can be a delicate balancing act. Naturopath Darren Weissman[183] suggests eating healthily at least 80 per cent of the time, which allows you to choose an 'unhealthy' meal sometimes without getting stressed over it.

Whatever your diagnosis, an organic wholefood diet packed with green vegetables, fresh juices and plenty of raw food is likely to help you to detoxify – and you might be drawn to avoid red meat, sugar and dairy products, and keep alcohol and caffeine to a minimum while your health is being restored. Omega 3 oils – found in oily fish, flaxseed oil, hemp and pumpkin seeds and walnuts – seem to be a pretty good idea. And naturopathic doctors suggest that drinking six glasses of water a day is essential to stay well hydrated and flush out toxins.

You might also choose to detoxify your environment in other ways by avoiding pollution and chemicals and using natural and eco-friendly products. However, such measures must come from a self-nurturing and positive attitude of supporting your health, rather than avoiding danger or fending off the 'enemy' of disease! If you are anxious and obsessive about diet and toxins, you are supporting the idea that your body is sick or vulnerable, that food is an enemy or that the world is a dangerous place. You are coming from fear rather than love. The body is hugely resilient and naturally self-healing, as long as you keep your vibrations high.

Nutritionists can be very dogmatic about what is the right diet for everyone, what supplements you need, or eating according to your body type or blood group and so on – but 'expert' advice is ever-changing and often confusing. My advice is to listen to your body, since it will be unique. The energy healer Donna Eden, for example, finds that if she cannot lose weight, eating a hot fudge sundae helps to kick-start her metabolism – whereas fruit and vegetables make her gain weight![184] Trust your intuition about what is right for you.[185] Conscious medicine would advocate trusting in what *feels* best to eat.

We only eat three times a day, whereas it is estimated that we have 60,000 thoughts in an average day. Every one of those thoughts can trigger the stress response or the healing response. What is more, the vast majority of our thoughts are found to be habitual and negative. So which do you imagine has more impact on our health? Food or thoughts?

Rather like the family soul, 'unhealthy' food and toxins only become a risk when you are ignoring your emotional guidance and are lost in the stress response. As we de-stress or focus on personal and spiritual growth, we become more conscious – and are then usually drawn towards more whole-some foods, yoga, meditation, exercise and other healthy habits that help the body stay in balance.

From the wave response, we make loving and self-nurturing choices that lead us to feel even better – whereas from the stress response, we make self-destructive choices and get trapped in vicious circles. (We 'cannot find the time' to medi-tate or to prepare a nutritious meal, or it seems pointless. Or we become fearful and obsessive about health.) At its simplest, healing is about getting happy, relaxed and positive in any which way you can – so that your biofield becomes strong and healthy, and your body can heal itself.

VICTIM MENTALITY

The final hidden factor that can prevent healing is having a victim mentality. In a materialist universe, people are often seen as hapless victims of bad luck, chance, coincidence, acci-dents, faulty genes or renegade bacteria and viruses. Many of us learnt to see ourselves as victims from early childhood, and our society and the media encourages this. A victim mentality is so endemic in our culture that we are often blind to it, and accept it as how things are. I have met many deeply spiritual people who know that we create our own reality, yet still see others as 'treating them badly'. (Duh!) Whenever you see yourself as a victim, you give away your power – and you block your ability to heal.

In *Why People Don't Heal and How They Can*, medical intuitive Caroline Myss talks about hiding behind our 'woundology', and how people can create an identity from their wounds and victimhood. I have met many people who cling to their identity as an incest victim, betrayed wife or helpless alcoholic for years and even decades, harbouring toxic emotions that are poisoning their bodymind, and often wrecking their health and relationships. Self-pity, blame and lack of forgiveness can block the healing process. So it is worth asking yourself whether you see yourself as a victim of anything or anyone – whether it is an abusive childhood, a drunk driver, a medical mistake, difficult colleagues, troublesome ex-partner or a faulty set of genes.

In a conscious universe, there are no victims. We create our own lives through the law of attraction (see Chapter 7) and, at a soul level, we chose the circumstances of our birth. One of the most powerful shifts you can make is from seeing yourself as a victim to seeing yourself as a creator. This is central to shifting into the new paradigm as a way of life.

If you wrote your current illness or other challenge into your life-script, why might you have done this? If you removed the strange wrapping paper, what might the hidden gifts be? This shifts you from the particle response to the wave response, and reconnects you with your higher self. It sets you free to tell yourself a new story – a story in which you are the hero and innovator, moving through challenges in a positive and creative way.

Exercise
TELLING A NEW STORY

Look at a current or recent challenge in your life – such as a diagnosis or dis-ease, or any situation that left you feeling disempowered, stuck or wounded. What is your current story about this? Do you see yourself as a victim of faulty genes, or a wandering virus, or medical mistakes, or baggage from your childhood, or recent stress? Do you see yourself as a helpless victim of others' behaviour, or the economy, or anything else? Or even as a helpless victim of your own neurosis? Or do you assume that this challenge has come as a friend and teacher? Are you telling yourself a positive and empowering story? What stories are others telling you about this situation?

Re-write the story as if it were a play, in which you are the triumphant hero. The higher truth is that you are the playwright and director of your own show. You really are writing the script for this situation. You are dreaming it all into reality. You get to choose the storyline. So are you writing a comedy or a tragedy? Why would you write this illness or challenge into your life-script? What positive reason might you have for doing this? And what do you want the outcome to be?

How does the hero deal with this situation? What does he or she learn from it? What is the positive outcome? Which new characters might you pull in as guides or helpers? Why was this a pivotal time in the hero's life — marking the birth of a new self who was more . . . what? More loving, strong, assertive, passionate, spiritual, visionary, self-aware, trusting, at peace, sensitive, empowered, happy, spontaneous, creative, uninhibited, adventurous?

How did the hero start thinking in a new way as they dealt with this challenge? How did this prompt them to let go of their old patterns, or honour their dreams, or give birth to a new future? How did their hero's journey to Ithaca have a positive impact on others?

Tell a new story about this illness or challenge — a story that makes you feel inspired and positive. Feel your way into this new story until this is how you see the situation. Take charge of your own script — and the universe will begin to reflect your new story.

We are nearly at the end of our journey into conscious medicine — though as with any journey, the end is just another beginning. As we approach our destination, a new door always opens and a new horizon beckons. There is a new Ithaca to sail towards, and another hero's journey to begin. In an evolving universe, life can never be perfect. Our adventure in consciousness is an eternal one.

In the final chapter, I summarise twelve steps that turn

the theory of conscious medicine into practice. We also look further at the gifts of dis-ease, and how conscious medicine can help us to evolve into our future self – and even help to heal our world.

Chapter Twelve

FROM COCOON TO BUTTERFLY

*When you move toward that which is most fulfilling and
life-enhancing – with joy and pleasure – healing follows.*

Christiane Northrup[186]

Let's suppose that you have an emotional or physical dis-ease.
If you want to tackle it using conscious medicine, how can you
turn all this theory into practice? What are the practical steps
that can help you transform illness – to move through it with
grace, embrace it as a friend and teacher, and gather its gifts?

Here are twelve steps to help you move from dis-ease to
wellness. There are no guarantees, of course, but each of these
steps is likely to be helpful. Some or all of these steps might
be appropriate, depending on the nature of the problem.

Exercise
TWELVE STEPS TOWARDS WELLNESS

1. Deal with any trauma or unresolved conflict underlying this
   dis-ease. (Clues: When did it start? What was going on then?

What is bothering you on a frequent or daily basis? It might be one big thing, or a hundred little things that mirror habits of thought such as worry, self-doubt, criticism, approval-seeking or guilt.) Does this situation or event mirror earlier traumas, negative beliefs or childhood patterns?

2. What do you need to release – either currently, or from the past? Is there a decision you need to make? (For example, letting go of a job, relationship or situation that no longer serves you, or an old family-ar pattern.) What part of you needs to die so that you can give birth to a new self? Where have you seen yourself as a victim – perhaps feeling trapped, helpless, hard done by, stuck, undervalued, unworthy or disempowered? Who have you criticised or blamed for your unhappiness? Or who have you been trying to protect or rescue? And whom do you need to forgive, including yourself?

3. What negative beliefs are you holding about yourself, others or the world? Where have you tried to please others, or conform to expectations, instead of honouring yourself? What dreams, desires, needs or feelings have you pushed aside? What parts of yourself have been squashed or denied? In what ways are you not loving yourself enough?

4. How can you bring more joy, fun and laughter into your life? If you followed your bliss, how would you change your lifestyle or relationships? What is missing in your life? How can you move away from toxins in your life, and towards nutrients?

5. How can you best support your physical body while you work out what is going on? (For example, drinking plenty of water, healthy nutrition, exercise, daily sunshine, time in nature and lots of rest, relaxation and sleep.) Stretch and move your body. Give yourself sensual delights. Get out of your head, and into your body.

6. If an issue is manifesting as a physical symptom or disease, what is your body trying to point towards? What

body language is it using? What does your body – or the body part or symptom itself – have to say about this dis-ease?

7. What advantages has this dis-ease brought into your life? What is the secondary gain? How is it serving you? Likewise, what are the downsides to getting well? And how can you meet your needs in healthy ways? How would your life change if you were 100 per cent healthy? Can you change it now? Can you feel any resistance to this? If the disease is serious or life-threatening, list all your reasons for wanting to live or be healthy. Do you really want to live – or to be healthy? If so, why?

8. What beliefs are you holding about the illness or disease – or what have you heard from others about it? What are your beliefs about health and the body? What healthy new beliefs do you wish to hold?

9. What kind of healing would be the right path for you? This might involve energy psychology, homoeopathy, life coaching, acupuncture, massage or bodywork, hypnosis, neurolinguistic programming (NLP), flower essences, cranial osteopathy, shaking medicine, nutrition and supplements, psychotherapy, energy healing, shamanic healing – or whatever makes sense to you and feels good. (See Resources for Health and Well-being, page 325.) It might also include drugs, surgery or other forms of conventional medicine.

10. What new projects or higher purpose can you focus on to channel your thoughts in a positive direction? (This is sometimes enough for healing, if only you can focus on it enough to stop thinking about the illness.)

11. How can you become a vibrational match to the future self who is already well? How does your future self think, feel, act and live? What new choices has it made? How can you become this joyful and radiantly healthy self?

12. What are the hidden gifts in this disease? Where is it leading you? How might you help others as you heal this? How can it help you evolve, to move beyond the old habits

and family-ar patterns of the past, and to live your dreams – to move beyond your limiting cocoon, and become a butterfly?

YOUR FUTURE SELF

In an evolving universe, we are designed to grow and change – to move towards our goals and dreams, to keep learning, to face new challenges, to become more self-aware and fulfil our potential – rather than remaining fixed and stagnant. This means there is always a gap between who you are and who you want to become – which brings up negative emotion. That warning signal is trying to guide you towards your dreams and desires. It is urging you to close the gap between your ego and your higher self. As we have seen, if you don't listen to this 'whisper' of negative emotions, then your body helpfully begins to talk to you and eventually 'shout' at you. And so will your life.

Transformation comes from setting yourself free from the lizard voices of the past, with their warnings and threats and limitations – and reaching for your dreams. Your higher self is not a perfect being who is fixed and immutable. It is constantly changing and evolving in response to your well-spring of dreams and desires. As soon as a dream becomes a reality, and the gap closes between your ego and higher self, a new dream or desire inevitably beckons – and the gap opens up again. This is the eternal journey of life. Without this gap, we would never grow and evolve.

Your higher self is your future self. It holds all your potential, based upon what you have lived so far, and what dreams you have launched into the Universe. As long as you remain focused on where you are going, and on all that is good and right in life, you move towards those dreams – and towards health and happiness. If you turn around, like Lot's wife, and look back where you came from (or even at where you are) with any fear, criticism or self-doubt – if you listen to lizard voices – you might turn into a pillar of salt. Your higher self never looks back. It holds itself, shining and radiant as an angel, in the future of your dreams.

One way of releasing resistance and marking a transition point between your past and future selves is to use ritual. Fire ceremonies have long been one of my favourite rituals – but you could also walk slowly across a long bridge, releasing your former self with each step and stepping into a new life; or bury something symbolic of the past; or plant a young shrub or tree to represent your new future. Rituals are a simple but powerful way of letting go of negative beliefs and old ways of being – and bringing every part of yourself into harmony with your dreams for the future.

Exercise
FIRE CEREMONY

You need a fireproof pot, matches, a candle or night light, a pen and two pieces of paper. Set up a clutter-free ceremonial space – perhaps with gentle music, extra candles and incense – or choose a special place in nature. Decide upon an old pattern, habit of thought or lifestyle you feel ready to release, and a new pattern with which to replace it.

On one piece of paper, write 'I release . . .' and on the other, write 'I give birth to . . .' For example: I release a poverty mentality and I give birth to prosperity thinking. I release anger and give birth to compassion. I release worry and give birth to trust. I release neediness and give birth to self-reliance. I release over-analysing and give birth to being heart-centred. I release seeking approval and give birth to self-love and authenticity. I release my hectic lifestyle and give birth to more stillness and relaxation. I release being single and give birth to a loving, co-creative partnership. I release victimhood and give birth to self-empowerment. I release sickness and give birth to health.

When you are ready, light the candle. You might wish to call in guides, angels or helpers from the unseen realms, sensing or imagining them joining you. Then sit quietly with the first piece of paper and reflect on how this pattern has played out in your life, and why you wish to release it. Then light it and place it in the pot. Now sit with your second piece of paper, and reflect on how this new quality or habit will change your life. Imagine becoming this new self. Then light the paper, and place it in the pot. Watch the paper burning until the fire is completely extinguished. Ask your unseen helpers to support you in changing these old habits of thought or behaviour, and giving birth to the new.

In the weeks and months that follow, the universe will offer you many opportunities to practise your new habit and become this new self. Remind yourself of your new commitment, and step into your future self.

FROM HEALING TO EVOLVING

As Albert Einstein said, we cannot solve a problem from the same level of mind that created it. We cannot resolve the world's ecological challenges from the same particle thinking that created them. But we can solve those problems. We cannot resolve chronic and degenerative diseases from the same particle thinking that sets them up. But we can heal those diseases. We simply have to expand our consciousness – to think outside the box of materialism, which sets up beliefs in scarcity, beliefs in victimhood and beliefs that the body is a clockwork machine that can become faulty and needs to be fixed. Particle thinking is no longer working for us.

Where there are problems, your higher self already has the solutions. Where there is pain and suffering, your higher self already knows the path to relief. Where there is illness and disease, your future self is now healthier than ever. All it takes is for you to focus on what you *desire*, and imagine it has already happened, then you are led step by step towards that future.

A conscious universe is one of boundless potential. A world that responds imaginatively to our dreams and desires. A world that morphs itself to fit our intentions. The universe is not evolving towards perfection, since that would mean stagnation. It is evolving towards whatever we can envision. We are dreaming our world into being.

As I see it, *the higher purpose of dis-ease is to help us become our future self.* Its purpose is to create its own solution – to push us into conscious evolution. To truly heal (while remaining in the physical body) we must expand our consciousness: that is, create a new level of mind with more positive beliefs, bigger dreams, new thoughts and choices, different neural nets and pathways and more stress-free neuro-chemistry – which in turn creates a new body and a new life.

In this loving universe, nothing is bad or wrong, and everything has meaning and purpose. Illness and disease are meant to be a catalyst for our conscious evolution. They force us to become our wave self – moving beyond fear and struggle into unconditional love and oneness. This is crucial to an evolving universe.

Illness and disease nudge you – with gentle whispers or with loud shouts – to become your future self. Rather than *healing*, which can imply returning to a former state, you are *evolving* into a new self. The caterpillar has to face the darkness and confinement of the chrysalis before finding the freedom and beauty of a new state of being. Likewise, you might need to pass through the dark cocoon of illness before you can emerge into the sunlit garden, and find that you now have wings. You have become a butterfly.

THE GIFTS OF DIS-EASE

Some authors suggest that illness comes to teach us 'lessons', but this implies there is something wrong with us, which higher forces are trying to correct – as if the earth were a training ground for wayward souls. This is not the way I see it. I believe that we are meant to be happy – but when anything is less than enjoyable, this loving universe is designed in such a way that there will always be hidden gifts from this pain, like the rainbow that follows the storm. These gifts will help us expand and grow. So gifts can be seen as 'lessons', but only in the sense that we are forever evolving – not evolving towards some mythical perfection, but towards becoming more fully and authentically *ourselves*.

So what are the hidden gifts of dis-ease? Some of the most common gifts are:

✧ Getting in touch with your emotions

✧ Shifting your priorities

✧ Becoming more honest and authentic

✧ Finding personal identity and freedom

✧ Learning to love and nurture yourself

✧ Creating more balance in your life

✧ Releasing past trauma and negative beliefs

✧ Letting go of addictions and codependency

✧ Learning to say 'no'

✧ Integrating 'lost' parts of yourself

✧ Reclaiming your sexuality and sensuality

✧ Letting go of toxic relationships or family patterns

✧ Getting in touch with your body

✧ Balancing your masculine/feminine energy (or left/right brain)

✧ Learning to focus more positively

✧ Finding a new direction or a new sense of purpose

✧ Deepening your spiritual awareness

✧ Lightening up and having more fun

✧ Learning to honour your own feelings and needs

✧ Reaching for your dreams

✧ Learning to be true to yourself

In short, the gifts lie in letting go of lizard voices and attuning to your higher self – that is, shifting into the wave response. Any illness or disease is nudging you to be more true to yourself, and to set yourself free.

My own journey through 'cancering' transformed me in so many ways. I learnt to be fully present with myself – which in turn allowed me to be more heart-centred and authentic with others. I was no longer controlled by guilt, and by trying to be good and perfect. I became more self-nurturing and self-accepting. I learnt so much about my patterns from the past, what triggered the stress response in me, and how and why I had blocked myself from having a loving and intimate relationship. My relationships became deeper and richer, and a much higher priority in my life. I also became more appreciative of simple pleasures like watching the sun rise, sinking my toes into warm grass or feeling soft rain upon my face.

Above all, I learnt how to be happy without condition. I found that I can be happy (and healthy) whatever is happening, simply by choosing the direction of my thoughts, while using my emotions as guidance. This allows me to live with unconditional love – which is true freedom. These were all 'lessons' I had been spiralling around for many years, but they finally came home to roost through the cancer. For that, I was truly grateful. And today, I feel fitter and healthier than ever.

Of course, we can learn and grow *without* needing to become ill, or face crisis and drama in our lives. But sometimes this seems to be the best way to do it. Sometimes the need for change builds and builds until it explodes into our lives, and fully grabs our attention – then real transformation is possible. Never judge your own path, or anyone else's. Illness is not a mistake or failure. Whatever happens, all is well. Within the bigger picture, everything is always unfolding perfectly.

Exercise
BECOMING YOUR FUTURE SELF

Close your eyes, relax deeply, and imagine that you are in a meadow in springtime. The sun is high in the sky, and you are sitting in the long grass, with a soft breeze caressing your face. Use all your senses to make this scene come alive. Then notice that there is a bridge nearby – and make your way across the bridge to the other side, towards your future – the highest possible future that awaits you. It is a future in which you are vibrantly healthy and radiantly happy, a future as unlimited and expansive as you can imagine. Make your way to a meeting place, a sacred place – and in this place, call your future self to come and join you, looking much like you, yet more joyful, more at peace, more filled with light.

Notice how it feels to be in the presence of your future self. Know that this future self does already exist, at an energy level. It exists in the quantum field of all possibilities, and your consciousness can bring it into physical reality – by letting go of fear and guilt and blame, and connecting with who you really are, which is unconditional love, and trust, and deep wisdom. What does this future self wish to tell you – whether in words or thoughts, or in images, or intuitive knowing? How has your life changed in this potential future? Allow your future self to tell you how to step into that future – how to create that beautiful future for yourself. What did you change so that you shifted your old patterns and created a new future for yourself?

Now receive a gift from your future self, a gift that might symbolise strengths or qualities that you need to invite in, a step you need to take, an experience you need to have or a mystery you need to unravel. Accept this gift and take it into your heart. Then allow yourself to merge with this future self, stepping into it, or allowing it to step into you, then feeling it within you – allowing it to merge into your mental body, changing your thoughts and beliefs, then into your emotional body, shifting your feelings and releasing the past, and into your physical body and DNA, changing the genetic blueprint for your future at an energy level.

Feel your energy changing as you merge more and more completely with this future self . . . taking in as much of its energy as you can . . . letting go of old patterns, old habits of thought, old ways of being . . . and raising your vibrations to as high a level as you can comfortably handle right now . . .

If you have a specific health issue, give yourself advice from this future self. What do you need to hear – about what needs to be released from the past, new beliefs that you need to hold, new visions for the future, practical steps to take, or a creative way of approaching this? How do you see it differently, looking through the eyes of this future self? Know that all the wisdom you ever need is inside you. You have access to Infinite Intelligence, or the Source. You can tap into limitless help from the unseen realms – and you can create anything that you can imagine, if only you love and appreciate 'what is' right now, and trust that even better is to come.

When you are ready, bring your consciousness fully back into your physical body, bringing the energy-consciousness of your future self with you – feeling at peace with yourself, and full of joyful anticipation for what lies ahead.

(A fuller version of this inner journey is available on my CD, *Your Future Self*.)

HEALING THE WORLD

Since we are all connected, our personal issues are also global issues – and as we heal ourselves, we help to heal our world. In my view, much of our personal distress can be traced back to the loss of the divine feminine (or loss of connection with the Source), and the imbalances reflected by patriarchal religion. Many of the widespread issues we are now healing at a personal level – such as child abuse, codependency, anxiety, depression, addictions and workaholism (as well as ecological challenges) – mirror this global issue. Patriarchal religion separated us from the Source energy by setting up a distant God – thus making us vulnerable to the particle response. When we reconnect with the divine feminine, we shift into the wave response (and vice versa). Reclaiming the power of the divine feminine is therefore at the heart of the healing journey.

Our emotional and physical dis-ease often centres around the need to reclaim our emotions and intuition; to become more authentic and heart-centred; to spend more time being and relating and less time doing and achieving; to create healthy relationships that support our growth, freedom and creativity; and to ground and embody ourselves, which are all aspects of the divine feminine. There is an overwhelming need to own our dark and light Shadow, rather than project our disowned qualities on to others, or give our power away to others. Many of us need to give up trying to fix or 'rescue' others or the world, and shift from compulsive caretaking, or feeling like victims, to an equal and empowering *partnership* with others (including our own body). Likewise we also need to reclaim a healthy spirituality – one which is free from fear, guilt and dogma, and which sees us as *co-creators* with the Source rather than seeing us as childlike and powerless in relation to God/the Source. So many of our problems simply cannot be resolved until we expand our consciousness and reconnect with the invisible realms.

In my own case, my bodily disease mirrored feeling *separate from love*, and distanced from a man I loved. This not only reflected my childhood issues, but also the global issue of healing our patriarchal belief in a distant and judgemental father God in the sky, and needing to reconnect with unconditional love and oneness: reclaiming the divine feminine. The fact that a feminine part of my body was affected symbolised this 'wounded feminine'. The core of my healing journey was to heal within myself the fear and judgement that separated me from love. This paved the way for the sacred alchemy of a co-creative partnership in the future: a relationship based upon unconditional love, in which you bring out each other's highest potential. And it helped me to remain more and more stable in the wave response, whatever happens.

Sometimes it helps to recognise that we are not alone with our issues, but share them with countless others. Our childhood mirrors global issues, not just family issues. Our personal challenges are much more meaningful and significant than they appear on the surface, and can be seen as part of a mythic journey through our collective consciousness – or what mythologist Joseph Campbell called 'the hero's journey'.

Our personal healing – our own journey to Ithaca – is part of the current evolution in human consciousness. Emotional or physical dis-ease is a nudge from our higher self towards becoming *homo spiritus*. It is an epic voyage towards bringing mind, body and soul into greater harmony, rather like playing notes from higher octaves that we could not even hear before. Seeing symptoms within this larger context can help us tell an inspiring new story, and shift into the wave response.

LOVE SETS US FREE

What really heals us, and helps us become our future self? The simple answer is: unconditional love. It is unconditional love that allows Source, or Universal, energy to flow. Love allows us to feel safe, and come out of the stress response. Love dissolves the defences that stand between the ego and our authentic self. Love turns us into giant pendulums, and the best health practitioners simply ooze it from every pore of their being. The poet Rumi said, 'Love is for vanishing into the sky' – a wonderful description of the wave response, which breaks down all barriers so that energy can flow freely.

Love is that which affirms, values and honours everything.

Love is the force that connects all which seems to be separate. Love dissolves fear. Love finds no place in the heart for criticism or blame or guilt – or even for forgiveness, since love is beyond judgement. And love shines its light in *every* direction – towards self, others and the world. When love fails to shine its light towards the self, it is not love but insecurity. When we do not live with *self-respecting* love – when we put others first, seek approval, exhaust ourselves, squash our feelings, ignore our own needs, settle for second best, blame others, abandon our dreams or give in to others – we are listening to lizard voices, and are out of alignment with our higher self. And sooner or later, our bodymind waves its red flag with mental or physical health problems.

As we shift towards living in a conscious universe, we realise that it is the invisible forces of love and consciousness that shape the visible world of 'solid stuff'. Consciousness shapes energy shapes matter. The material world is not quite what it seems. It is far more malleable and responsive to our thoughts than Descartes and Newton would ever have imagined. As we shift from thinking like a particle to becoming more like a wave, we align with our higher self – and know that love is the key to creating whatever we want in life. Love shapes the dust that forms our physical bodies – and it is love that allows the body to shift into optimal health and well-being.

The body is a mirror of our consciousness – like everything else in our lives. As you shift from the particle response to the wave response, your consciousness expands and you see a bigger picture. You move towards love and freedom and joy. You are no longer a helpless victim, desperately trying to control life, or scrabbling to be good and perfect. Instead you have become a powerful, loving co-creator with the unseen forces of the universe. You are aware of the cosmic dance between the visible and invisible realms, and you know how to be a dreamer and visionary.

Your soul slips laughing through the old prison bars of guilt and blame. From here, there are no enemies, for everything is seen as a friend. You embrace everything that life offers, with all its ups and downs. There is no 'me' and 'not-me', for everything is seen as a mirror. You listen to the whispers – and give thanks. Loneliness is a distant memory. Fear lies in another galaxy. Every day is full of delight and wonder.

From the wave response, there is only love and oneness. You are aware of your individuality, and value your own uniqueness, while being aware that you are a drop within a greater ocean, forever connected. Fun and laughter abound. You breathe deeply into your belly. The world comes alive to you. The rocks, clouds and dragonflies speak to you. Time expands into the endless opportunities of a hazy summer day. You are living your wildest dreams – free at last. You choose whatever makes your heart sing and your spirit dance. You are bathed in an ocean of unconditional love. And your body shimmers with health, vitality and radiance.

References

[1] Bruce Lipton, *The Biology of Belief*, Hay House, 2008, p. 121.

[2] Gill Edwards, 'The Psychology of Cancer', *Changes: Journal of the Psychology and Psychotherapy Association*, 1986 April, pp. 193–195.

[3] As described in my first book, *Living Magically*, Piatkus, 1991.

[4] For an alternative view and research on cancer, see Andreas Moritz, *Cancer Is Not a Disease: It's a Survival Mechanism*, Cygnus Books, 2009. Moritz suggests that untreated cancer has a four times higher remission rate than medically treated cancer, and that chemotherapy is only helpful in about 2 per cent of cases. Also see Ty Bollinger, *Step Outside the Box*, Infinity 510 Partners, 2006/2009, who suggests that alternative approaches to cancer are vastly more effective than profit-driven conventional medicine. Also see Jonathan Chamberlain, *The Cancer Recovery Guide: 15 Alternative and Complementary Strategies for Restoring Health*, Clairview, 2008.

[5] Quote on front cover of Norman Shealy and Dawson Church, *Soul Medicine*, Elite Books, 2006.

[6] Lewis Carroll, *Alice's Adventures in Wonderland*. (First published in 1865.)

[7] For example, Marc Ian Barasch and Caryle Hirshberg, *Remarkable Recovery*, Headline Books, 1995, pp. 159–161; Michael Talbot, *Holographic Universe*, HarperCollins, 2006, p. 99; Larry Dossey, *Healing Breakthroughs*, Piatkus, 1993, pp. 41–47;

Candace Pert, *Your Body Is Your Subconscious Mind* CD, Sounds True, 2000. Clairvoyant healer Donna Eden notes that the auric fields of alters look different in ways that are almost impossible to fake.

[8] Reported by Yu Lin, Chinese medicine practitioner. See www.pureinsight.org/node/1499.

[9] J. Bruce Moseley et al., 'A Controlled Trial of Arthroscopic Surgery for Osteoarthritis of the Knee', *New England Journal of Medicine*, 2002 July, vol. 347, pp. 81–88.

[10] Bruce Lipton, *The Biology of Belief*, Hay House, 2008, pp. 139-40.

[11] Alexandra Kirkley et al., 'A Randomised Trial of Arthroscopic Surgery for Osteoarthritis of the Knee', *New England Journal of Medicine*, 2008 September, vol 359, pp. 1097–1107.

[12] Henry K. Beecher, 'Surgery as Placebo: A Quantitative Study of Bias', *Journal of American Medical Association*, 1961, vol. 176, no. 13, pp. 1102-1107.

[13] Holy Bible, Mark 5: 21–24. (Also Matthew 9:18–26; Luke 8:40–56.)

[14] Martin Brofman, 'The Body Reflects Consciousness', talk given at College of Psychic Studies, London. See also his book *Anything Can Be Healed*, Findhorn, 2003. His website can be viewed at www.healer.ch.

[15] Joe Dispenza, *Evolve Your Brain*, Health Communications, 2007.

[16] Donna Eden, *Energy Medicine*, Tarcher/Putnam, 1998. Website: www.innersource.net.

[17] Richard Moss, *Black Butterfly*, Celestial Arts, 1987.

[18] The story is told in Richard Bartlett, *The Physics of Miracles*, Simon & Schuster, 2009, pp. 16-18.

[19] Richard Bartlett, *Matrix Energetics*, Beyond Words, 2007, p. 183.

[20] For example, Gary Groesbeck and Donna Bach. See www.EFTuniverse.com for details.

[21] See www.tatlife.com (Tapas Acupressure Technique) and www.psych-k.com (Psych-K).

[22] TAT newsletter, report from Bronia Fuchs-Willig, 2007. Website: www.tatlife.com.

[23] TAT newsletter, December 2007. Website: www.tatlife.com.

[24] Psych-K newsletter from Larry Valmore, January 2008. Website: www.psych-k.com.

[25] Quoted in Marilyn Ferguson, *The Aquarian Conspiracy*, Paladin, 1982, p. 215.

[26] Norman Shealy, *Soul Medicine*, Elite Books, 2006.

[27] Lynne McTaggart, *What Doctors Don't Tell You*, Thorsons, 1996, pp. 7–8.

[28] For example, Lynne McTaggart, *What Doctors Don't Tell You*, Thorsons, 1996; John Abramson, *Overdosed America*, HarperPerennial, 2005; and Michael T. Murray, *What the Drug Companies Won't Tell You and Your Doctor Doesn't Know*, Simon & Schuster, 2009.

[29] G. Greenberg, 2003, referred to in Bruce Lipton, *The Biology of Belief*, Hay House, 2008, p. 138.

[30] Allen Roses, worldwide Vice-President of Genetics at GlaxoSmithKline quoted in Norman Shealy and Dawson Church, *Soul Medicine*, Elite Books, 2006, p. 138. For original news report, see Steve Connor (Science Editor), 'Glaxo chief: Our drugs do not work on most patients', *Independent*, 3 December 2003.

[31] For example, John Abramson, *Overdosed America*, Harper Perennial, 2005; Michael T. Murray, *What the Drug Companies Won't Tell You and Your Doctor Doesn't Know*, Simon & Schuster, 2009, pp. 133–153.

[32] Dr C. G. G. Nittinger, *The Evils of Vaccination by C. C. Shieferdecker MD*, 1856.

[33] For example, Walene James, *Immunization: The Reality Behind the Myth*, Greenwood Press, 1989; Lynne McTaggart, *What Doctors Don't Tell You*, Thorsons, 1996, Chapter 6; Leon Chaitow, *Vaccination and Immunisation: Dangers, Delusions and Alternatives*, C.W. Daniel, 2009.

[34] WHO statistics on the use of CAM (complementary and alternative medicine) – see www.independentliving.co.uk/tradmed.html.

[35] Amit Goswami, *The Quantum Doctor*, Hampton Roads, 2004.

[36] Rudolph Ballentine, *Radical Healing*, Harmony Books, 1999, p. 33.

[37] For example, some studies have found a 40 per cent increase in spirituality in those recently diagnosed with HIV/AIDS – see Dawson Church, *The Genie in Your Genes*, Elite Books, 2007, p. 61.

[38] Norman Shealy and Dawson Church, *Soul Medicine*, Elite Books, 2006, p. 20.

[39] For example, see Lynne McTaggart, *What Doctors Don't Tell You*, Thorsons, 1996, pp. 210–212; and Michael T. Murray, *What the Drug Companies Won't Tell You and Your Doctor Doesn't Know*, Simon & Schuster, 2009, pp. 195–205 on the risks of drugs for hypertension and natural alternatives; also John Abramson, *Overdosed America*, HarperPerennial, 2005.

[40] Rupert Sheldrake, *The Rebirth of Nature*, Rider, 1991, p. 32.

[41] Quoted in Michael T. Murray, *What the Drug Companies Won't Tell You and Your Doctor Doesn't Know*, Simon & Schuster, 2009, p. 77.

[42] Story told by Lewis Mehl-Madrona at a workshop – see Recommended Reading.

[43] For example, see Dean Radin, *The Conscious Universe*, HarperCollins, 1997; Michael Talbot, *The Holographic Universe*, HarperCollins, 2006; Larry Dossey, *Healing Words*, Harper Collins, 1993; David Hamilton, *How Your Mind Can Heal Your Body*, Hay House, 2008, and countless other books. See Recommended Reading for further information.

[44] Dean Radin, *The Conscious Universe*, HarperCollins, 1997, p. 140.

[45] Books by Matthew Manning include *Your Mind Can Heal Your Body*, Piatkus, 2007. See also www.matthewmanning.com.

[46] Thomas Kuhn, *The Structure of Scientific Revolutions*, University of Chicago Press, 1962.

[47] James Jeans, *The Mysterious Universe*, Cambridge University Press, 1937, p. 122.

[48] *101 Miracles of Natural Healing* video. Shown at my

workshops by permission of the director, Luke Chan. Website: www.chilel.com

[49] For example, Amit Goswami, *The Self-Aware Universe*, Tarcher/Putnam, 1995.

[50] David Bohm, *Wholeness and the Implicate Order*, Routledge & Kegan Paul, 1980.

[51] See my earlier book, *Wild Love*, Piatkus, 2006, which includes the chapter: 'Does God Need Therapy?'.

[52] The 'law of attraction' was popularised by the Abraham material, created by Esther and Jerry Hicks. See www.abraham-hicks.com.

[53] Norman C. Shealy and Caroline M. Myss, *The Creation of Health* (Stillpoint, 1998).

[54] For example, Sonia J. Lupien, Alexandra Fiocco et al., 'Stress hormones and human memory function across the lifespan', *Psychoneuroendocrinology*, 2005 April, vol. 30, issue 3, pp. 225–242.

[55] Jill Bolte-Taylor, *My Stroke of Insight*, Hodder & Stoughton, 2009, pp. 68–69.

[56] For example, see Doc Childre and Howard Martin, *The HeartMath Solution*, Piatkus, 1999.

[57] For example, see Daniel Goleman, *Emotional Intelligence*, Bloomsbury, 1996; and Doc Childre and Howard Martin, *The HeartMath Solution*, Piatkus, 1999.

[58] See website www.heartmath.com – or Doc Childre and Howard Martin, *The HeartMath Solution*, Piatkus, 1999.

[59] Claire Sylvia, *A Change of Heart*, Little, Brown & Co., 1997.

[60] Max von Pettenkofer (1818–1901) famously swallowed a flask of cholera bacilli, without serious consequences, to make this point. He pioneered a public health approach to the prevention of disease in Germany.

[61] Cecil Helman, *Suburban Shaman*, Hammersmith, 2006, p. 63.

[62] Developed by Silvia Hartmann – see www.emotrance.com.

[63] Dawson Church, *The Genie in Your Genes*, Elite Books, 2007, p. 149.

[64] For a popular account, see Robert M. Sapolsky, *Why Zebras Don't Get Ulcers*, First Owl, 2004. A more recent textbook is Kathleen A. Kendall-Tackett, *The Psychoneuroimmunology of*

Chronic Disease: Exploring the Links Between Inflammation, Stress, and Illness, American Psychological Association, 2009. Many of the books on the Recommended Reading list also cover this topic.

[65] Reported in Dawson Church, *The Genie in Your Genes*, Elite Books, 2007, p. 38.

[66] Rollin McCraty, 'The physiological and psychological effects of compassion and anger', *Journal of Advancement in Medicine*, 1995, vol. 8, no. 2, pp. 87–105.

[67] Masaru Emoto has produced three beautiful volumes of photographs with text about his work: *Messages from Water, Vols I and II*, Hado Kyoikusha Co. Also *Love Thyself: The Message from Water III*, Hay House, 2004.

[68] For example, Paul Grossman et al., 'Mindfulness-based stress reduction and health benefits: A meta-analysis', *Journal of Psychosomatic Research*, 2004, vol. 57, pp. 35–43. Jon Kabat-Zinn has conducted several studies on meditation – e.g. see his book *Coming to Our Senses*, Piatkus, 2005, pp. 368–375.

[69] Jack Kornfield, *Meditation for Beginners*, Bantam, 2005 – a Buddhist approach. Wayne Dyer, *Getting in the Gap*, Hay House, 2003.

[70] Adapted from Stella Weller, *The Breath Book*, HarperCollins, 1999, p. 70. See also Swami Saradananda, *The Power of Breath*, Duncan Baird, 2009.

[71] Bruce Lipton, *The Biology of Belief*, Hay House, 2008.

[72] 'Local and Non-local Effects of Coherent Heart Frequencies on Conformational Changes of DNA' – see www.heartmath.org.

[73] Candace Pert, *Molecules of Emotion*, Simon & Schuster, 1998.

[74] See Larry Dossey, *Healing Breakthroughs*, Piatkus, 1993, pp. 151–2.

[75] For example, see Deepak Chopra, *Ageless Body, Timeless Mind*, Rider and Co., 2008.

[76] Joe Dispenza, *Evolve Your Brain*, Health Communications, 2007. Quote from DVD 'What the Bleep Do We Know?'

[77] Ryke Geerd Hamer, 'The Five Biological Laws of the New Medicine', paper presented at First International Congress on Complementary and Alternative Medical Cancer Treatment,

Madrid, May 2005. See www.whale.to/cancer/hamer2.pdf.

[78] For example, see Richard Flook, *Why Am I Sick?* , MPG Books, 2009. Also see Meta-Medicine in the Resources for Health and Well-being, p. 328.

[79] See video on TAT and Allergy – www.tatlife.com.

[80] Peter Levine, *Waking the Tiger*, North Atlantic Books, 1997. Peter Levine developed the method of Somatic Experiencing for releasing trauma.

[81] Some ancient and indigenous cultures do make use of shaking to release trauma – e.g. see Bradford Keeney, *Shaking Medicine*. See www.tjitzedejong.com.

[82] Robert Scaer, *The Body Bears the Burden*, Haworth Medical Press, 2001.

[83] Peter Levine's self-help book *Healing Trauma*, Sounds True, 2005, includes a CD that leads you through his process of Somatic Experiencing. Bradford Keeney's book *Shaking Medicine*, Destiny Books, 2007, includes a CD of ecstatic drumming. I also find Gabrielle Roth's music excellent for this process.

[84] Karl Dawson and Sasha Allenby, *Matrix Reimprinting*, Hay House, 2010.

[85] You can also watch a live example of bipolar disorder being resolved on the DVDs on Meta-Medicine and EFT, available from Karl Dawson's website – www.eftcoursesuk.com.

[86] Two good books about this are: Sandra Ingerman, *Soul Retrieval*, HarperOne, 2006, and Alberto Villoldo, *Mending the Past and Healing the Future with Soul Retrieval*, Hay House, 2006.

[87] L.G. Russek and G. E. Schwarz, 'Perceptions of parental caring predict health status in midlife: a 35-year follow-up of the Harvard Mastery of Stress Study', *Psychosomatic Medicine*, 1997, vol. 59 (2), pp. 144–149. See also Dean Ornish, *Love and Survival*, HarperPerennial, 1999, pp. 32–35.

[88] The rare exceptions I have seen to this are where someone has a burning desire to make a difference in the world and the illness helps get them 'back on track' towards their higher purpose.

[89] There is a lot of evidence that we are affected by experiences

within the womb and at birth later in life, and many therapies work specifically with this, such as rebirthing, Matrix Birth Reimprinting and the TARA Approach (see Resources for Health and Well-being, p. 325). See also the endnote below.

[90] For example, see Sue Gerhardt, *Love Matters*, Routledge, 2004, for an excellent overview of how stress affects children and relationships – from pregnancy onwards.

[91] Heard in a PBS lecture (2007) by Christiane Northrup on PBS television when I was in the USA.

[92] See Dawson Church, *The Genie in Your Genes*, Elite Books, 2007, pp. 58–61 for a summary of these studies by Dr Gail Ironson. For example, Gail Ironson et al., 'The Ironson-Woods Spirituality/Religiosity Index is associated with long survival, health behaviors, less distress and low cortisol in people with HIV/AIDS', *Annals of Behavioral Medicine*, 2002, vol. 24, issue 1, p. 34.

[93] See my earlier books *Wild Love*, Piatkus, 2006, and *Life is a Gift*, Piatkus, 2007, for more about 'Does God need therapy?' and seeing life as a gift rather than a trial or accident.

[94] These techniques are based upon Psych-K, a form of kinesiology and energy psychology developed by Rob Williams – see website www.Psych-k.com.

[95] Paul MacLean, *The Triune Brain in Evolution*, Plenum Press, 1990.

[96] See Joe Dispenza, *Evolve Your Brain*, Health Communications, 2007, for more about the neurochemistry of habits and growth.

[97] Darren Weissman, *The Power of Infinite Love and Gratitude*, Hay House, 2007, p. 38.

[98] From Lazaris, channelled by Jach Pursel – www.lazaris.com.

[99] Joe Dispenza, *Evolve Your Brain*, Health Communications, p. 376.

[100] Candace Pert, *Molecules of Emotion*, Simon & Schuster, 1998, p. 265.

[101] The teachings of Abraham confirm this. See Chapter 7 – and website www.abraham-hicks.com.

[102] Leonard Laskow, *Healing With Love*, iUniverse, 1992/2008.

[103] Norman Cousins, *Anatomy of an Illness*, Bantam, 1981.

[104] For example, Larry Dossey, *Healing Beyond the Body*, Time Warner, 2002, pp. 146–147.

[105] Interview on BBC's *Woman's Hour*. Also see Ellen MacArthur, *Taking on the World*, Penguin, 2002.

[106] For example, see Theodore Roszak et al. (eds), *Ecopsychology*, Sierra Club, 1995, and David Abrams, *The Spell of the Sensuous*, Vintage, 1997. There are countless books about the healing power of nature, including: T. C. McLuhan, *Cathedrals of the Spirit*, HarperPerennial, 1996; Connie Goldman and Richard Mahler, *Tending the Earth, Mending the Spirit*, Hazelden, 2000; and Donald Norfolk, *The Soul Garden*, Overlook Press, 2002.

[107] See Jeanne Achterberg, *Imagery in Healing*, Shambala, 1985, p. 104.

[108] Reported in Joe Dispenza, *Evolve Your Brain*, Health Communications, 2007, pp. 441–442. The study was conducted at the Department of Neurology at Bellevue Hospital, New York in the 1970s.

[109] For example, Norman Doidge, *The Brain That Changes Itself*, Penguin, 2007.

[110] Nora Weeks, *The Medical Discoveries of Edward Bach Physician*, C. W. Daniel, 1973.

[111] Excerpt from workshop in Los Angeles on 7 March 2000. Website: www.abraham-hicks.com.

[112] Hale Dwoskin, *The Sedona Method*, Element, 2005.

[113] See my earlier book *Stepping into the Magic*, Piatkus, 1993. Also books by Serge Kahili King, such as *Urban Shaman*, Simon & Schuster, 1990.

[114] Reported in David Hamilton, *How Your Mind Can Heal Your Body*, Hay House, 2008, p. 6 – study at University of Utah, 2006: T. W. Smith, C. Berg et al., 'Marital conflict behavior and coronary artery calcification', paper presented at American Psychosomatic Society, Denver, 3 March 2006.

[115] See Dean Ornish, *Love and Survival*, HarperCollins, 1998, for a good compilation of these and other research studies.

[116] Susan Forward, *Emotional Blackmail*, Harper, 1998.

[117] A useful guide to healthy divorce is Debbie Ford, *Spiritual Divorce*, HarperCollins, 2002.

[118] For example, see Joe Vitale and Ihaleakala Hew Len, *Zero Limits*, Wiley, 2008.

[119] To learn healthy patterns of communication – beyond fear, blame, guilt and demands – Non-Violent Communication is an excellent starting point. Workshops in NVC are readily available, or you can read books such as *Non Violent Communication* by Marshall Rosenberg (PuddleDancer, 2003).

[120] See Byron Katie, *Who Would You Be Without Your Story*, Hay House, 2008. For further information about Byron Katie and The Work, see www.thework.com.

[121] Excerpt from workshop held in Atlanta, Georgia on 4 November 2000 – www.abraham-hicks.com.

[122] See Gary Craig, *The EFT Manual*, Energy Psychology Press, 2002.

[123] See Esther and Jerry Hicks, *Ask and it Is Given*, Hay House, 2008. Other books by Esther and Jerry Hicks may also be of interest or www.abraham-hicks.com.

[124] Abraham calls this the benefit of 'contrast'. I explore this further in my books *Wild Love*, Piatkus, 2006, and *Life Is a Gift*, Piatkus, 2007.

[125] For further information about power animals and animal messengers, see Steven Farmer, *Animal Spirit Guides*, Hay House, 2007; Andrea Wansbury, *Birds: Divine Messengers*, Findhorn Press, 2006; and the classic from the Native American tradition by Jamie Sams and David Carson, *Medicine Cards*, Bear & Co, 1988.

[126] Workshop with Lewis Mehl-Madrona in Cumbria, England, 2009.

[127] For example, see Jim Robbins, *A Symphony in the Brain*, Grove Press, 2008.

[128] This is based upon the Emotional Scale in the teachings of Abraham and used by permission.

[129] Joe Dispenza, *Evolve Your Brain*, Health Communications, p. 446.

[130] For further information about creating our own reality, see my earlier books such as *Living Magically*, Piatkus, 2006, *Wild Love*, Piatkus, 2006, and *Life Is a Gift*, Piatkus, 2007 – or books by Louise L. Hay, Esther and Jerry Hicks, Sanaya

Roman, Jane Roberts, Neale Donald Walsch and countless other metaphysical authors. Many 'new scientists' have also come to this conclusion, such as Amit Goswami and Fred Alan Wolf (new physics) and Candace Pert and Bruce Lipton (new biology).

[131] One of a series of well-known studies on cancer, for example S. Greer, T. Morris, K. Pettingale, 'Psychological response to breast cancer: effect on outcome', *Lancet*, 13 October 1979, vol. 314, issue 8146, pp. 785–787. You can find a compilation of this and other research studies on the website: www.healingcancernaturally.com.

[132] Bernie Siegel, *Love, Medicine & Miracles*, Arrow, 1988.

[133] Louise L. Hay, *You Can Heal Your Life*, Hay House, 1984, p. 127.

[134] Louise L. Hay, *Heal Your Body A–Z*, Hay House, 1998, pp. v–vii.

[135] Louise L. Hay, *You Can Heal Your Life*, Hay House, 1984.

[136] See www.EFTuniverse.com for original article.

[137] Nancy Mellon, *Body Eloquence*, Energy Psychology Press, 2008, pp. 48–49.

[138] Darren Weissman, *Awakening to the Secret Code of Your Mind*, Hay House, 2010.

[139] Donna Eden, *Energy Medicine*, Tarcher/Putnam, 1998, p. 29.

[140] Barbara Ann Brennan, *Hands of Light*, Bantam, 1988, p. 89.

[141] James Reston, 'Now, Let Me Tell You About My Appendectomy in Peking', *New York Times*, 26 July 1971.

[142] Cyndi Dale, *The Subtle Body*, Sounds True, 2009, p. 160; also see pp. 177–181. Researchers such as Dr Robert Becker and Dr Hiroshi Motoyama became well known for their scientific studies on the subtle energy body. The website www.compassionateacupuncture.com lists 111 scientific studies on the health benefits of acupuncture.

[143] These were all reported in Gary Craig's EFT newsletters (www.emofree.com) before he retired. Original articles are now available at www.EFTuniverse.com.

[144] For more about energy psychology, see Chapter 4 of my earlier book, *Wild Love*, Piatkus, 2006.

[145] From chapter by Bernie Siegel in Dawson Church and Alan Sherr (eds), *The Heart of the Healer*, Elite Books, 2004, p. 205.

[146] See Donna Eden, *Energy Medicine*, Tarcher/Putnam, 1998, p. 251.

[147] Barbara Ann Brennan, *Light Emerging*, Bantam, 1993, p. 177.

[148] William Nolen, *Healing: A Doctor in Search of a Miracle*, Random House, 1974.

[149] K. B. Thomas, 'General practice consultations: Is there any point in being positive?', *British Medical Journal*, 1987, vol. 294, pp. 1200–2.

[150] Daniel Moerman, *Meaning, Medicine and the 'Placebo Effect'*, Cambridge University Press, 2002.

[151] Daniel Moerman, *Meaning, Medicine and the 'Placebo Effect'*, Cambridge University Press, 2002; also Michael T. Murray, *What the Drug Companies Won't Tell You and Your Doctor Doesn't Know*, Simon & Schuster, 2009, pp. 27–32; David Hamilton, *How Your Mind Can Heal Your Body*, Hay House, 2008, pp. 19–42; Zelda Di Blasi, 'The crack in the biomedical box', *Psychologist*, February 2003, vol. 16, no. 2, pp. 72-75.

[152] A. J. M. De Craen, P. J. Roos, A. L. de Vries, J. Kleijnen, 'Effect of colour of drugs: systemic review of perceived effect of drugs and of their effectiveness', *British Medical Journal*, 1996, vol. 313, pp. 1624–1626.

[153] T. Luparello et al., 'The interaction of psychologic stimuli and pharmacologic agents on airway reactivity in asthmatic subjects', *Psychosomatic Medicine*, 1970, vol. 32, pp. 509–513. A. J. Barsky et al., 'Nonspecific medication side effects and the nocebo phenomenon', *Journal of American Medical Association*, 2002, vol. 287, pp. 622–627. 'The nocebo response', Harvard Mental Health Letter, March 2005.

[154] S. I. Cohen, 'Psychosomatic death: Voodoo death in a modern perspective', *Integrative Psychiatry*, 1985, vol. 3, pp. 46–51.

[155] For example, see Jane Roberts, *The Individual and the Nature of Mass Events*, Amber-Allen, 1981/1995, Chapter 2.

[156] Daniel Block, *The Revolution of Naturopathic Medicine*, Collective Co-op Publishing, 2003.

[157] Jon Kabat-Zinn, *Full Catastrophe Living*, Piatkus, 2001.

[158] Grace Gawler, *Women of Silence*, Hill of Content, 1994.

[159] Barbara Hoberman Levine, *Your Body Believes Every Word You Say*, Words Work Press, 2000.

[160] There are many techniques for distant healing, but she used Theta Healing – see Resources for Health and Well-being, p. 326.

[161] Adam, *Dreamhealer*, Sphere, 2007.

[162] Randolph C. Byrd, 'Positive Therapeutic Effects of Intercessory Prayer in a Coronary Care Unit Population', *Southern Medical Journal*, 1988, vol. 81, no. 7, pp. 826–829.

[163] An excellent source of information for EFT practitioners is Pamela Bruner and John Bullough (eds), *EFT and Beyond*, Energy Publications, 2009.

[164] See books by Jon Kabat-Zinn such as *Full Catastrophe Living*, Piatkus, 2001 and *Coming to our Senses*, Piatkus, 2005; also Saki Santorelli, *Heal Thy Self: Lessons on Mindfulness in Medicine*, Three Rivers Press, 1999.

[165] Richard Bartlett, *The Physics of Miracles*, Simon & Schuster, 2009.

[166] Friedrich Nietzsche, *Thus Spoke Zarathustra*, Penguin Classics, 2003.

[167] *Ithaka* by Constantine Cavafy, in C. P. Cavafy, *Collected Poems*, edited by George Savidis, Princeton University Press, 1992.

[168] John Harrison, *Love Your Disease*, Angus & Robertson, 1984.

[169] Janice Dolley and Ursula Burton – in press.

[170] For example, Bert Hellinger, *To the Heart of the Matter*, Carl-Auer-Systeme Verlag, 2003 – brief therapies using family constellations that include many examples of working with illness, suicide and 'accidents'.

[171] I heard this story from therapist Dietrich Klinghardt at a workshop on family constellations in 2001.

[172] Rupert Sheldrake, *The Presence of the Past*, HarperCollins, 1988.

[173] Rupert Sheldrake, *A New Science of Life*, Paladin, 1983. Revised edition published in 2009.

[174] Valerie V. Hunt, *Infinite Mind*, Malibu, 1989/1996, p. 141. For more about how energy can be left in an environment,

see Karen Kingston, *Creating Sacred Space with Feng Shui*, Piatkus, 1996.

[175] See www.hellinger.co.uk for a list of workshops and practitioners of Family Constellations. I have also produced a self-help CD, *Healing Your Family Tree*.

[176] Study conducted by holistic physician Gabriel Cousens and other researchers. The entertaining and informative DVD about this study is *Simply Raw*, 2009 – see www.rawfor30days.com. Also see Gabriel Cousens, *There Is a Cure for Diabetes*, North Atlantic Books, 2008.

[177] Joe Dispenza, *Evolve Your Brain*, Health Communications, 2007, p. 280.

[178] Study at Yale University, reported in Joe Dispenza, *Evolve Your Brain*, Health Communications, 2007, p. 274: G. E. Schwarz, D. A. Weinberger, J. A. Singer, 'Cardiovascular differentiation of happiness, sadness, anger and fear following imagery and exercise', *Psychosomatic Medicine*, August 1981, vol. 43, no. 4, pp. 343–364.

[179] See www.abraham-hicks.com and books by Esther and Jerry Hicks.

[180] This emerged from personal conversations with Bruce Lipton, author of *The Biology of Belief*, Hay House, 2008.

[181] Michael Werner and Thomas Stöckli, *Life From Light*, Clairview, 2007.

[182] Andreas Moritz, *Cancer Is Not a Disease*, Cygnus Books, 2009, p. 29.

[183] Darren Weissman, *The Power of Infinite Love and Gratitude*, Hay House, 2007.

[184] Donna Eden, *Energy Medicine*, Tarcher/Putnam, 1998, p. 254.

[185] A useful guide to eating intuitively is Susie Miller and Karen Knowler, *Feel-good Food: A Guide to Intuitive Eating*, Women's Press, 2000.

[186] From CD by Christiane Northrup, *The Power of Joy*, Hay House, 2008.

Recommended Reading

This is just a small selection of recent, classic or favourite books from my own library that give a fresh, inspiring approach to health and healing, or help us step into a conscious universe – plus a few recommended DVDs.

My Top Ten Recommendations

✧ Rudolph Ballentine, *Radical Healing* (Harmony Books, 1999). A thick, thoughtful and informative guide to holistic healthcare by a medical doctor. Covers homoeopathy, herbs, nutrition, exercise, detox, breath, chakras, miasms etc. – with a great chapter on healing as transformation.

✧ Barbara Brennan, *Hands of Light* (Bantam, 1988). By a former NASA scientist who turned to energy healing and channelling. A classic handbook on healing and the human energy field, which still seems ahead of its time.

✧ Dawson Church, *The Genie in Your Genes* (Elite Books, 2007). An exciting look at how our beliefs and emotions shape our biology, the science behind why EFT and other forms of energy medicine work, and how science and spirituality are moving closer together.

❖ Joe Dispenza, *Evolve Your Brain* (Health Communications, 2007). Joe Dispenza healed himself of severe spinal injuries using the power of his mind. This book explores how the neural pathways in the brain can support health or dis-ease, why we tend to repeat the same patterns and why change is so difficult.

❖ Donna Eden, *Energy Medicine* (Tarcher/Putnam, 1998). A practical guidebook to helping yourself and others using energy medicine – by a delightful and innovative healer who 'sees' energy fields. Clearly written and packed with fascinating information and self-help tools.

❖ Amit Goswami, *The Quantum Doctor* (Hampton Roads, 2004). An integrative approach to medicine, which shows that allopathic medicine does have a role – albeit limited – within new paradigm medicine. By a quantum physicist with a longstanding interest in healing, who sees consciousness as the basis of health.

❖ Louise L. Hay, *You Can Heal Your Life* (Hay House, 1984). A pioneer of the new metaphysics, Louise L. Hay noticed that specific illnesses were linked with specific negative beliefs. She had her own healing journey through vaginal cancer, following childhood abuse. One of the perennial classics on positive thinking and health.

❖ Bruce Lipton, *The Biology of Belief* (Hay House, 2008). If you are going to read just one book on this list, make it this one. Top molecular biologist Bruce Lipton's ebullient and readable account of how psychology controls biology should create a healthcare revolution.

❖ Candace B. Pert, *Molecules of Emotion* (Simon & Schuster, 1998). A scientific yet personal account of the biomolecular basis for how the mind impacts on the body by a pioneering neuroscientist who discovered the biochemical correlates of emotion, which led her towards spirituality. Rapidly became a classic.

✧ Norman Shealy and Dawson Church, *Soul Medicine* (Elite Books, 2006). Why the cutting edge of medicine lies in what used to be regarded as 'soft medicine' – such as energy healing, prayer, acupressure – rather than hi-tech approaches. Looks at what creates a healer, the history of medicine, etc. Very readable.

John Abramson, *Overdosed America: The Broken Promise of American Medicine* (HarperPerennial, 2005). A doctor reveals the shocking ways in which drug companies misrepresent evidence and mislead doctors, and how 'medical care' can compromise health.

Jeanne Achterberg, *Lightning at the Gate: A Visionary Journey of Healing* (Shambhala, 2002). A personal and moving account of the author's healing journey through ocular melanoma, after being a pioneer of imagery and ritual in healing.

Adam, *Dreamhealer: A True Story of Miracle Healings* (Sphere, 2007). First of a series of Dreamhealer books by the Canadian teenager known only as Adam. Adam – now training in medicine – discovered he had an amazing power to see energy and heal others, along with the ability to channel information about the emergent new paradigm.

Marc Ian Barasch, *The Healing Path: A Soul Approach to Illness* (Penguin/Arkana, 1995). How illness can become a catalyst for profound personal change – a truly soulful journey. The author looks at the 'disease-prone personality', and describes his personal journey through thyroid cancer.

Marc Ian Barasch and Caryle Hirshberg, *Remarkable Recovery: What Extraordinary Healings Tell Us About Getting Well* (Headline Books, 1995). An easy-to-read account of people who have recovered from supposedly terminal illness – and what they can teach us.

Richard Bartlett, *Matrix Energetics: The Science and Art of Transformation* (Beyond Words, 2007). At the cutting edge of conscious medicine, chiropractor and naturopath Richard Bartlett describes his method of helping people shift into different probable realities – creating everyday miracles in health and healing. Entertaining and mind-blowing stuff!

Richard Bartlett, *The Physics of Miracles: Tapping into the Field of Consciousness* (Simon & Schuster, 2009). This follow-up book to *Matrix Energetics* focuses more on the science behind miraculous healing. Fascinating and thought-provoking.

Brandon Bays, *The Journey™: An Extraordinary Guide for Healing Yourself and Setting Yourself Free* (Thorsons, 1999). Brandon Bays famously healed herself of a football-sized growth in her abdomen in six weeks, using self-help techniques that led to The Journey workshops.

Robert O. Becker and Gary Selden, *The Body Electric: Electromagnetism and the Foundation of Life* (William Morrow, 1985). One of the first books that pointed towards the scientific basis for the new medicine, and challenged the old mechanistic model of the body. How our bioelectric selves connect us to the oneness, and how this can help in healing.

Harriet Beinfield and Efrem Korngold, *Between Heaven and Earth: A Guide to Chinese Medicine* (Ballantine, 1991). Readable and fairly comprehensive guide to the theory and practice of Chinese medicine.

Herbert Benson with Marg Stark, *Timeless Healing: The Power and Biology of Belief* (Fireside, 1997). An excellent book on the power and biology of belief and spirituality by the doctor who also wrote *The Relaxation Response* (Avon Books, 2000).

Carmen Renee Berry, *Is Your Body Trying to Tell You Something? How Massage and Body Work Can Help You Understand Why You Feel the Way You Do* (PageMill, 1993/1997). Lots of good psychology, some science and a body-centred approach to disease as a helpful message about unresolved issues – and the use of touch and bodywork to heal old wounds.

Beata Bishop, *A Time To Heal: Teaching the Whole Body to Beat Incurable Cancer* (Arkana, 1996). The story of how the author healed herself of malignant melanoma using the Gerson nutritional therapy. I suggest you read it with an eye on her emotional-vibrational journey – and perhaps question how much of her healing was due to the dietary regime.

Jill Bolte Taylor, *My Stroke of Insight: A Brain Scientist's Personal Journey* (Hodder & Stoughton, 2009). A neuroscientist's remarkable first-person account of having a stroke – and recovering. Fascinating account of how the right hemisphere holds our experience of oneness and joy, and how to tap into that *without* having a left-hemisphere stroke!

Gregg Braden, *The Divine Matrix: Bridging Time, Space, Miracles and Belief* (Hay House, 2007). A quantum-based approach to the new reality we are moving towards, in which we consciously create our own reality, and know that we are an integral part of All That Is. Includes some great stuff on health.

Barbara Ann Brennan, *Light Emerging: The Journey of Personal Healing* (Bantam, 1993). Her follow-up book to *Hands of Light* (Bantam, 1988) – packed with information and insights, including lots about healthy/unhealthy relationships.

Martin Brofman, *Anything Can Be Healed* (Findhorn, 2003). The author healed himself of 'terminal cancer' in 1975 by radically changing his life from the inside out. A practical book integrating Western psychology and Eastern spirituality to offer an approach to health that focuses on the chakras.

Eve Bruce, *Shaman MD: A Plastic Surgeon's Remarkable Journey into the World of Shapeshifting* (Destiny, 2002). A plastic surgeon ventures into the world of shamanism and shapeshifting, bringing back gifts and lessons for Western medicine and society. Autobiographical and thought-provoking.

Bruce Burger, *Esoteric Anatomy: The Body as Consciousness* (North Atlantic Books, 1998). Offers energy-balancing tools from Polarity Therapy – synthesising Ayurveda, naturopathy, osteopathy, craniosacral therapy, hermetics and quantum physics, and seeing the body as a field of conscious energy.

Jonathan Chamberlain, *The Cancer Recovery Guide: 15 Alternative and Complementary Strategies for Restoring Health* (Clairview, 2008). One of the very few books about cancer that has the 'feel-good factor'. The author's wife died of cancer – or rather, from medical treatment for cancer – before he discovered how many people had healed cancer using gentle approaches.

Doc Childre and Howard Martin, *The HeartMath Solution: The Institute of Heartmath's Revolutionary Program for Engaging the Power of the Heart's Intelligence* (Piatkus, 1999). Combines scientific research with emotional wisdom to look at how the heart/love controls the body, from the prestigious Institute of HeartMath. Very readable and practical.

Deepak Chopra, *Perfect Health: The Complete Mind Body Guide* (Bantam, 1990). Focuses on the ancient art of Ayurvedic medicine, and how it relates to the new medicine. Discover your dosha type, and how to come into balance for perfect health.

Deepak Chopra, *Quantum Healing: Exploring the Frontiers of Mind/Body Medicine* (Bantam, 1989). A classic on then-new frontiers of mind-body medicine. Like all his books, a wonderful combination of stories, science, fresh thinking and spiritual wisdom.

Dawson Church, Alan Sherr (eds), *The Heart of the Healer* (Elite Books, 2004). A lovely and inspiring compilation of chapters from leading voices within new paradigm medicine. For healers or those in search of healing.

Nancy Connor and Bradford Keeney (eds), *Shamans of the World: Extraordinary First-person Accounts of Healing, Mysteries, and Miracles* (Sounds True, 2008). Edited book by traditional healers; great insights into shamanism.

Gary Craig, *The EFT Manual* (Energy Psychology Press, 2002). This is the official guide to EFT by its creator. It leads you through the step-by-step process of EFT, and illustrates the use of EFT for emotional and physical issues.

Cyndi Dale, *The Subtle Body: An Encyclopedia of Your Subtle Anatomy* (Sounds True, 2009). An amazing body of work on the new energetic science of healing, and the nature of human energetic anatomy. Full colour illustrations.

Alan Davidson, *Body Brilliance: Mastering Your Five Vital Intelligences* (Elite Books, 2006). A lovely book by a massage therapist on working through the body to awaken our five 'vital intelligences'. Lots of illustrations.

Karl Dawson and Sasha Allenby, *Matrix Reimprinting Using EFT: Rewrite Your Past, Transform Your Future* (Hay House, 2010). I love Matrix Reimprinting – a major development of EFT – and wrote the Foreword to this book. It offers detailed instructions on how to practise Matrix Reimprinting, and also an excellent guide to new paradigm thinking about health.

Norman Doidge, *The Brain That Changes Itself: Stories of Personal Triumph from the Frontiers of Brain Science* (Penguin, 2007). A highly readable account of the new brain science, focusing on the incredible neuroplasticity of the brain. Packed with riveting case histories.

Larry Dossey, *Healing Words: The Power of Prayer and the Practice of Medicine* (HarperCollins, 1993). Looks at the power of prayer in healing, exploring the scientific research as well as the spiritual implications.

Larry Dossey, *Healing Beyond the Body: Medicine and the Infinite Reach of the Mind* (Time Warner, 2002). An absorbing collection of essays on consciousness, spirituality and medicine.

Larry Dossey, *Healing Breakthroughs: How Your Attitudes and Beliefs Can Affect Your Health* (Piatkus, 1993). Packed with fascinating case studies about how the mind impacts on health and healing. Science has moved on, but the stories are just as relevant today.

Larry Dossey, *Reinventing Medicine: Beyond Mind-Body to a New Era of Healing* (Element, 1999). A visionary look at the future of medicine, once it takes on board the 'non-local mind', by one of the pioneers of new paradigm medicine.

Donna Eden, *Energy Medicine for Women: Aligning Your Body's Energies to Boost Your Health and Vitality* (Piatkus, 2009). Wonderful energy medicine techniques for women's health problems – from PMT and infertility to menopause and weight issues.

Masaru Emoto, *Messages from Water, Vols 1 and 2* (HADO Kyoikusha Co, 2001). The remarkable images of crystallising water from different sources, or exposed to different words, music and prayers.

David Feinstein, Donna Eden and Gary Craig, *The Healing Power of EFT and Energy Psychology: Revolutionary Tools for Dramatic Personal Change* (Piatkus, 2006). A practical guide to the theory and practice of energy psychology, for those who are new to this amazing field.

Richard Flook with Rob van Overbruggen, *Why Am I Sick? What's Really Wrong and How You Can Solve it Using Meta-Medicine®*(MPG Books, 2009). Based on the theory of Meta-Medicine®, which links specific forms of emotional trauma with specific diseases.

Ursula Franke, *The River Never Looks Back: Historical and Practical Foundations of Bert Hellinger's Family Constellations* (Carl-Auer-Systeme Verlag, 2003). One of the best introductions to Bert Hellinger's pioneering work with the family soul, using family constellations.

Peter H. Fraser and Peter Massey, *Decoding the Human Body-Field: The New Science of Information as Medicine* (Healing Arts Press, 2008). A book about the development of the Nutri-Energetics System (NES), a healing system that feeds pure information into the biofield. Combines personal story and science with an introduction to NES.

Norman Friedman, *The Hidden Domain: Home of the Quantum Wave Function, Nature's Creative Source* (Woodbridge Group, 1997). A rare scientist who combines the new physics with the channelled material of Seth/Jane Roberts – building bridges between quantum physics, psychology and spirituality. Not easy reading unless you have some science background.

Grace Gawler, *Women of Silence: The Emotional Healing of Breast Cancer* (Hill of Content, 1994). An excellent book about the emotional roots of cancer and how to heal it.

Michael Gearin-Tosh, *Living Proof: A Medical Mutiny* (Scribner, 2003). The author's personal account of dealing with cancer (myeloma) using diet, visualisation and supplements – and being alive and well, eight years on.

Richard Gerber, *Vibrational Medicine: The Number 1 Handbook of Subtle Energy Therapies* (Bear & Co, 2001). A comprehensive textbook on the science of subtle-energy medicine by a medical doctor.

Richard Gerber, *Vibrational Medicine for the 21st Century: A Complete Guide to Energy Healing and Spiritual Transformation* (Piatkus, 2000). A more accessible guide than the above, with chapters on homoeopathy, acupuncture, flower essences, colour healing, hands-on healing, etc.

Sue Gerhardt, *Why Love Matters: How Affection Shapes a Baby's Brain* (Routledge, 2004). A psychotherapist takes a fascinating look at how early relationships shape neural pathways in the brain, affecting how we later deal with stress – often paving the way for poor relationships and health problems.

Richard Gordon, *Quantum Touch: The Power to Heal* (North Atlantic Books, 1999/2006). Quantum Touch is an easy-to-learn hands-on healing technique that can get remarkable results. It focuses and amplifies the flow of Source energy (chi) so that you create a higher vibrational energy field to which the client then resonates.

Amit Goswami, *The Self-Aware Universe: How Consciousness Creates the Material World* (Tarcher/Putnam, 1993). A theoretical physicist explains why the paradoxes of quantum physics can only be resolved if we assume that consciousness *creates* physical reality. Instead of seeing matter as primary, we must see consciousness as primary.

Brian Greene, *The Elegant Universe: Superstrings, Hidden Dimensions, and the Quest for the Ultimate Theory* (Vintage, 2000). For those who love modern science – an absorbing journey through superstring theory, black holes, higher dimensions, quantum geometry and much more.

David R. Hamilton, *How Your Mind Can Heal Your Body* (Hay House, 2008). The author used to work in the pharmaceutical industry, and was fascinated by the power of the placebo. Packed with research on the mind-body connection.

Leon Hammer, *Dragon Rises, Red Bird Flies: Psychology and Chinese Medicine* (Eastland Press, 2005). An excellent textbook on the psychology which underlies disease, based upon five element theory in Chinese medicine.

John Harrison, *Love Your Disease: It's Keeping You Healthy* (Angus & Robertson, 1984). An insightful look at how the mind creates disease, why we might subconsciously 'want' to be ill, and how to heal ourselves.

Joyce Whiteley Hawkes, *Cell-Level Healing: The Bridge from Soul to Cell* (Beyond Words, 2006). A cell biologist who became a healer after a near-death experience writes beautifully in this little book about the bridge between our cells, our psychology and higher dimensions of reality. Full of practical tools.

Bert Hellinger, *To The Heart of the Matter: Brief Therapies* (Carl-Auer-Systeme Verlag, 2003). Fascinating scripts that illustrate family constellation work in brief therapy. Many of the examples deal with physical disease.

Cecil Helman, *Suburban Shaman: Tales from Medicine's Frontline* (Hammersmith, 2006). One of my doctor friends gives this to his trainees. It stops far short of conscious medicine, but is a stepping stone into a broader view of health, from a family doctor in London who is also an anthropologist and storyteller.

Bill Henderson, *Cancer-Free: Your Guide to Gentle, Non-toxic Healing* (Booklocker, 2008). A practical guide to gentle, non-toxic healing approaches to cancer (which also outlines the problems with conventional treatment). It underplays the emotional factors, but does acknowledge that cancer is usually triggered by stress.

Esther and Jerry Hicks, *Money and the Law of Attraction: Learning to Attract Wealth, Health, and Happiness* (Hay House, 2008). This might seem an odd book title to include here, but this book by Abraham has two large sections on health and the body. It also provides an overview of seeing the world as vibrational and understanding how we create our reality.

Valerie V. Hunt, *Infinite Mind: Science of the Human Vibrations of Consciousness* (Malibu, 1989/1996). A fascinating account of the research into the human energy field, from the woman who pioneered scientific measurement of the aura in the 1970s.

Susan Jamieson, *Medical to Mystical* (Findhorn, 2010). A British medical doctor who practises holistic medicine in Hong Kong writes in a practical and accessible way about our true nature as 'beings of light'. Looks at chakras and meridians, and offers energy exercises.

Anodea Judith, *Wheels of Life: A User's Guide to the Chakra System* (Llewellyn, 2002). A classic handbook on health and the chakra system, by one of the world's foremost experts on chakras.

Jon Kabat-Zinn, *Coming to Our Senses: Healing Ourselves and the World Through Mindfulness* (Piatkus, 2005). A fat book about being more present in our lives, and the practice of mindfulness meditation, by a long-time pioneer of mind-body medicine and founder of the famous Stress Reduction Clinic in Massachusetts. (Also see *Full Catastrophe Living*, Piatkus, 2001.)

Laura Alden Kamm, *Intuitive Wellness: Using Your Body's Inner Wisdom to Heal* (Simon & Schuster, 2007). A gentle and insightful book about using your body's winner wisdom to heal. The author became a medical intuitive after a near-death experience.

Ted Kaptchuk, *Chinese Medicine: The Web That Has No Weaver* (Rider, 1983). One of the first books I ever read on Chinese medicine: a classic introduction to its theory and practice.

Bradford Keeney, *Shaking Medicine: The Healing Power of Ecstatic Movement* (Destiny Books, 2007). Looks at the 'oldest and newest' form of healing – ecstatic shaking – in cultures across the world. This has clear links to the discharge response in trauma.

Deborah King, *Truth Heals: What You Hide Can Hurt You* (Hay House, 2009). The author had a journey through childhood sexual abuse and cancer before waking up, facing the truth – and healing. A healing journey through the chakras.

Joan C. King, *Cellular Wisdom: The Code of Authentic Living* (Celestial Arts, 2004). Another integrative book about the emotional brain, by a doctor-turned-life-coach who applies recent research about our psychophysiology to everyday life.

Leonard Laskow, *Healing with Love: A Breakthrough Mind/Body Medical Program for Healing Yourself and Others* (iUniverse, 1992/2008). This lovely book introduces holoenergetic healing, which recognises both the roots and secondary gain of illness and dis-ease.

Ervin Laszlo, *Science and the Akashic Field: An Integral Theory of Everything* (Inner Traditions, 2004/2007). An impressive *tour de force* that integrates modern science and ancient mysticism – for those who love ideas and philosophy.

G. Frank Lawlis, *Transpersonal Medicine: A New Approach to Healing Body-Mind-Spirit* (Shambala, 1996). Chapters by pioneers of the new medicine such as Larry Dossey, Dean

Ornish, Jeanne Achterberg and Carl Simonton on topics such as ritual and imagery.

Susan Lawrence, *Creating a Healing Society: The Impact of Human Emotional Pain and Trauma on Society and the World* (Elite Books, 2006). How emotional trauma is passed down and across the generations, and its impact on society, personal relationships and health. Lots of case histories.

Darian Leader and David Corfield, *Why Do People Get Ill?* (Penguin, 2007). A popularised look at the research on mind-body medicine. Full of good stuff, though it doesn't really tackle mind-body dualism.

Karen Leffler and Heather Cumming, *John of God: Healing Through Love* (Beyond Words, 2007). An account of John of God, the renowned Brazilian healer who turns his body over to 'spirit doctors' for three days each week, making no charge for his often miraculous healings. Includes photos of surgery.

Peter A. Levine, *Waking the Tiger: The Innate Capacity to Transform Overwhelming Experiences* (North Atlantic Books, 1997). The first book to suggest that the undischarged freeze response to trauma is the basis of PTSD, and much emotional and physical dis-ease.

Peter A. Levine, *Healing Trauma: A Pioneering Program for Restoring the Wisdom of Your Body* (Sounds True, 2005). A simpler account of his classic *Waking the Tiger* book (see above) with accompanying CD. Designed for self-help.

Eleanor Limmer, *The Body Language of Illness* (Freedom Press, 1995/2004). Excellent book by a spiritual therapist who looks at the emotional conflicts that underlie any dis-ease, and how to listen to the messages from our body – including the secondary gain of illness. Lots of research and interesting case studies.

Cassandra Lorius, *Homoeopathy for the Soul: Ways to Emotional Healing* (Thorsons, 2001). A very readable book about constitutional treatment in homoeopathy, and how this stimulates emotional healing and spiritual growth.

Paul Martin, *The Sickening Mind: Brain, Behaviour, Immunity and Disease* (Harper Perennial, 2005). How our thoughts and behaviour impact upon our health – scientific but easy to read. Takes us beyond the usual mind-body dualism, but doesn't venture into spirituality (and curiously suggests that rejecting dualism means rejecting the idea of life after death).

Lynne McTaggart, *What Doctors Won't Tell You: The Truth About the Dangers of Modern Medicine* (Thorsons, 1996). A well-researched exposé about the dangers of conventional medicine, including diagnostic tests, vaccination, drugs and surgery.

Lynne McTaggart, *The Field: The Quest for the Secret Force of the Universe* (HarperCollins, 2001). A readable and much-quoted exploration of what the zero point energy field means for our understanding of reality – largely through telling the stories of cutting-edge scientists. See also her book, *The Intention Experiment*, (HarperCollins, 2008) which has lots of implications for health.

Lewis Mehl-Madrona, *Coyote Medicine: The Power of Story in Healing* (Fireside, 1997). A doctor trained in Western medicine explores his Native American roots, after seeing the damage which modern medicine could do – and witnesses some miracles from shamanic healing and narrative medicine that open him to a wider reality.

Lewis Mehl-Madrona, *Narrative Medicine: The Use of History and Story in the Healing Process* (Bear & Co, 2007). A doctor-shaman explores how stories can be crucial in the process of healing. Includes talking to diabetes, asthma, cancer and other diseases.

Nancy Mellon with Ashley Ramsden, *Body Eloquence: The Power of Myth and Story to Awaken the Body's Energies* (Energy Psychology Press, 2008). A lovely book that combines storytelling with traditional Chinese medicine to explore how the body speaks to us through disease – and how to heal.

Emmett E. Miller, *Deep Healing: The Essence of Mind/Body Medicine* (Hay House, 1997). Practical guidebook to self-healing – using affirmations, imagery, emotional healing, etc. – by a medical doctor and pioneer of mind–body medicine.

Arnold Mindell, *The Quantum Mind and Healing: How to Listen and Respond to Your Body's Symptoms* (Hampton Roads, 2004). A Jungian psychotherapist explores where psychology meets quantum physics, to access our self-healing potential.

Stephanie Mines, *We Are All In Shock: How Overwhelming Experiences Shatter You . . . And What You Can Do About It* (New Page Books, 2003). A neuropsychologist looks at the huge impact of shock and trauma on our bodymind. It also introduces the TARA approach, a gentle touch-based approach that awakens the strange flows as a way of resolving shock.

Andreas Moritz, *Cancer Is Not a Disease: It's a Survival Mechanism* (Cygnus Books, 2009). One of the few books on cancer that takes a positive approach, by a well-known naturopath. Moritz sees cancer as a survival mechanism for the body following toxic overload, and shows how healing the root causes can lead us to be healthier than ever.

Michael T. Murray, *What the Drug Companies Won't Tell You and Your Doctor Doesn't Know* (Simon & Schuster, 2009). A naturopath takes a well-researched look at the risks of conventional medicine, and natural alternatives that support health and well-being.

Caroline Myss, *Anatomy of the Spirit: The Seven Stages of Power and Healing* (Bantam, 1997). First solo book on health by the well-known medical intuitive. Synthesises spirituality with energy medicine to offer a model for the self-healing journey.

Caroline Myss, *Why People Don't Heal and How They Can* (Bantam, 1998). A chakra-based model for understanding illness and the healing journey. Shows how our fixed stories about life or dis-ease, and our attachment to our 'wounds', can block healing.

Bradley Nelson, *The Emotion Code: How to Release Your Trapped Emotions for Abundant Health, Love and Happiness* (Wellness

Unmasked, 2007). How to use magnets to release 'trapped emotions', which can create illness or block healing. Everything you need to know is in the book, so you can practise right away. All you need is a magnet!

William Nolen, *Healing: A Doctor in Search of a Miracle* (Random House, 1974). A surgeon goes in search of the truth about faith healing and psychic surgery, and hears about or witnesses some miracles.

Patrick Obissier, *Biogeneaology: Decoding the Psychic Roots of Illness: Freedom from the Ancestral Origins of Disease* (Healing Arts Press, 2003). A fascinating look at how unresolved conflicts can be passed down the generations, by a French psychotherapist. As with Bert Hellinger's pioneering work, the 'family soul' can add another dimension to our understanding of health.

Dean Ornish, *The Spectrum: A Scientifically Proven Program to Feel Better, Live Longer, Lose Weight, and Gain Health* (Ballantine, 2007). Dean Ornish was the first doctor to prove that heart disease can be reversed by changing lifestyle and psychological habits. He also wrote *Love and Survival* (1999).

James L. Oschman, *Energy Medicine: The Scientific Basis* (Harcourt, 2000). A somewhat heavy textbook on the science behind energy medicine – for health professionals who like to integrate left and right brain!

Rob van Overbruggen, *Healing Psyche: The Patterns in Psychological Cancer Treatment* (BookSurge, 2006). A look at the power of the mind in healing cancer, and the psychological patterns in those who develop cancer, by the medical pioneer of Complementary Psychological Cancer Treatment. A research dissertation, with lots of useful ideas and tools.

Christine Page, *Frontiers of Health: How to Heal the Whole Person* (Random House, 1992/2000). A doctor looks at healing from a psycho-energetic and mystical viewpoint, much of it exploring the chakras. Looks at the underlying emotional conflicts and blockages behind many common disorders. Very readable and insightful.

Joseph Chilton Pearce, *The Biology of Transcendence: A Blueprint of the Human Spirit* (Park Street Press, 2004). Fascinating look at how spirituality is hard-wired into our physiology, and how we're biologically designed to evolve consciously.

Candace B. Pert, *Everything You Need to Know to Feel Go(o)d* (Hay House, 2006). An entertaining and honest exploration of how being 'hard-wired for bliss' links with our spiritual journey, by the biologist who discovered 'molecules of emotion'.

Dean Radin, *The Conscious Universe: The Scientific Truth of Psychic Phenomena* (HarperCollins, 1997). A rigorous look at the impressive scientific research on parapsychology, and what this tells us about reality – which also has big implications for health and healing.

Rachel Naomi Remen, *Kitchen Table Wisdom: Stories That Heal* (Riverhead Books, 1997). Heartwarming stories that restore what traditional medicine is often lacking: heart and soul. By a doctor whose own journey through illness awakened her to a deeper understanding of health, wholeness and spirituality.

Jane Roberts, *The Way Toward Health* (Amber-Allen, 1997). The final Seth book, published long after Jane Roberts's death in 1984, and channelled during her prolonged final illness. It addresses many aspects of health, healing and disease – including why medicine often perpetuates illness.

Ron Roth with Peter Occhiogrosso, *Prayer and the Five Stages of Healing* (Hay House, 1999). A good book for Christians – or those with a religious background – who are interested in prayer as a healing path.

John Ruskan, *Emotional Clearing: An East/West Guide to Releasing Negative Feelings and Awakening Unconditional Happiness* (Rider, 1998). Excellent self-help approach to processing our emotions – based on the assumption that we create our own reality – which helps us move beyond blame, defensiveness, addictions and dependency.

Saki Santorelli, *Heal Thy Self: Lessons on Mindfulness in Medicine* (Three Rivers Press, 1999). A beautifully written and thought-provoking look at the dynamics of the healing relationship and the need for presence, heart and authenticity in healing by the director of the well-known Stress Reduction Clinic in Massachusetts.

Robert M. Sapolsky, *Why Zebras Don't Get Ulcers* (First Owl, 2004). An acclaimed 'popular science' book about the impact of stress on our physiology and health. Entertaining and informative.

Swami Saradananda, *The Power of Breath* (Duncan Baird, 2009). A practical guide to healthy breathing with breathing exercises for common emotional and physical health problems.

John E. Sarno, *The Divided Mind: The Epidemic of Mindbody Disorders* (Duckworth Overlook, 2008). By the pioneering author of *Healing Back Pain* (Warner Books, 1991) this book explores how inner conflict creates dis-ease in the body – with practical advice on how to tackle many common disorders, from tinnitus and IBS to hypertension.

Robert Scaer, *The Body Bears the Burden: Trauma, Dissociation, and Disease* (Haworth Medical Press, 2001). Fascinating account by an MD of the theory that undischarged trauma is the root cause of most disease. It assumes familiarity with medical terminology, though I'm told the second edition is more layperson-friendly.

Marilyn Schiltz and Tina Amorok with Marc Micozzi, *Consciousness and Healing: Integral Approaches to Mind-Body Medicine* (Elsevier, 2005). Sixty-plus essays from top names in new paradigm medicine, including Deepak Chopra, Larry Dossey, Jon Kabat-Zinn, Dean Ornish and Candace Pert.

Deb Shapiro, *Your Body Speaks Your Mind: Decoding the Emotional, Psychological, and Spiritual Messages That Underlie Illness* (Piatkus, 1996/2006). An excellent self-help book that looks at how various parts of the bodymind system express what is going on in our lives – with chapters on digestion, eyes/ears, skin, etc. – and how our thoughts/feelings affect our biochemistry.

Norman Shealy and Caroline Myss, *The Creation of Health: The Emotional, Psychological, and Spiritual Responses That Promote Health and Healing* (Stillpoint, 1988). Packed with case studies, this marked a creative collaboration between a pioneering doctor and medical intuitive. It shows the emotional and spiritual issues which underlie dis-ease. Offers an 'energy analysis' of many case histories.

Rupert Sheldrake, *The Presence of the Past: Morphic Resonance and the Habits of Nature* (HarperCollins, 1988). The seminal book by this pioneering biologist which introduced his theory of morphic fields. The full implications for health have yet to be explored.

Bernie S. Siegel, *Love, Medicine & Miracles: Lessons Learned about Self-Healing from a Surgeon's Experience with Exceptional Patients* (Arrow, 1988). One of the classics on mind-body medicine. A doctor looks at the healing power of love and the will to live.

José Silva and Robert B. Stone, *You the Healer: The World-Famous Silva Method on How to Heal Yourself and Others* (H. J. Kramer, 1989). A book on the well-known Silva Mind Control method – which helps you shift your consciousness into alpha, then heal yourself and others.

David Simon, *Free to Love, Free to Heal: Heal Your Body by Healing Your Emotions* (Chopra Center Press, 2009). The medical director of the Chopra Center writes about how to heal your body by healing your emotional issues. Practical and intelligent guide to releasing negative beliefs and emotional pain, which can lead to health problems.

Claire Sylvia with William Novak, *A Change of Heart* (Little, Brown & Co, 1997). The remarkable autobiography of a woman who had a heart and lung transplant. A gripping and thought-provoking read.

Michael Talbot, *The Holographic Universe* (HarperCollins, 2006). Is the universe a hologram constructed by our brains? Where do paranormal phenomena fit in? Understandable science and great stories.

Russell Targ and Jane Katra, *Miracles of Mind: Exploring Nonlocal Consciousness and Spiritual Healing* (New World Library, 1999). The physicist and renowned expert on 'remote viewing' explores his own rapid journey from metastatic liver cancer to health, with the help of healer and co-author Jane Katra. It also looks at Targ's pioneering research on consciousness.

William Tiller, *Science and Human Transformation: Subtle Energies, Intentionality and Consciousness* (Pavior, 1997). How subtle energies and intention affect the material world, by a Stanford professor. The physics and mathematics are heavy going at times, but the vision is broad and spectacular, and some of the research studies are fascinating.

Karol K. Truman, *Feelings Buried Alive Never Die* (Olympus, 2003). How our negative thoughts and suppressed feelings turn into emotional and physical dis-ease – along with a 'Script' process for healing. Rather religious in tone, but a good self-help book. Includes helpful 'dream dictionary' of illness.

John Veltheim, *The BodyTalk System: The Missing Link to Optimum Health* (PaRama, 1999). Another healing approach which has emerged in recent years – based upon using kinesiology to ask the body what needs to be reconnected in order to heal.

George Vithoulkas, *The Science of Homoeopathy* (Grove Press, 1980). An old classic about the laws and principles of cure in homoeopathy, and how homoeopathy is used in practice.

Michael Wayne, *Quantum Integral Medicine: Towards a New Science of Healing and Human Potential* (iThink Books, 2005). Looks at our healing potential from a quantum reality viewpoint. By an acupuncturist who combines quantum physics, creativity research and the science of consciousness to look at emergent properties, and how this relates to the 'new medicine'.

Darren Weissman, *The Power of Infinite Love and Gratitude: An Evolutionary Journey to Awakening Your Spirit* (Hay House, 2007). Full of love and wisdom, this offers another new approach that is having remarkable success in healing dis-ease – though to practise the Lifeline Technique, you have to send for the excellent training DVDs or attend a workshop. (As this book went to press, his second book was published, *Awakening to the Secret Code of Your Mind* (Hay House, 2010) which includes much more about how to practise the Lifeline Technique.)

Robyn Elizabeth Welch, *Conversations with the Body* (Hodder & Stoughton, 2002). The personal story of a medical intuitive and energy healer who has conversations with body parts and can 'see' within the body.

Stella Weller, *The Breath Book: 20 Ways to Breathe Away Stress, Anxiety, and Fatigue* (HarperCollins, 1999). A simple and practical guide to breathing – and why it is so crucial – with exercises for stress, fatigue, anxiety, voice and childbirth.

Michael Werner and Thomas Stöckli, *Life from Light: Is it Possible to Live Without Food?* (Clairview, 2007). A scientist who has not eaten any food for several years looks at the huge implications of this for how we see physical reality and the body.

Hank Wesselman and Jill Kuykendall, *Spirit Medicine: Healing in the Sacred Realms* (Hay House, 2004). Lovely little book on a shamanic approach to healing, especially the Huna wisdom. Includes CD of drumming/rattling for inner journeys.

And just a few recommended DVDs:

The Living Matrix: A Film on the New Science of Healing – One of the best DVDs so far on new paradigm medicine, including interviews with top experts such as Bruce Lipton, Lynne McTaggart, James Oschman, Rupert Sheldrake, Eric Pearl, Marilyn Schlitz and Peter Fraser – with case studies from those who have experienced unconventional healing, including Arielle Essex. See www.livingmatrixshop.com.

EFT for the Prevention and Treatment of Serious Diseases – DVD set by Karl Dawson, EFT Master and founder of Matrix Reimprinting. See www.matrixreimprinting.com. (See also the book, *Matrix Reimprinting*.)

A Vibrational Approach to Health and Illness – DVD set by Carol Look, EFT Master. See www.attractingabundance.com.

The New Biology by Bruce Lipton – or *The Biology of Perception, The Psychology of Change*. See www.brucelipton.com.

Resources for Health and Well-being

Here are some recommended resources within conscious medicine. It is a vast and growing field, so this can only be a limited selection. Many healing practitioners (especially in energy psychology) offer telephone or Skype consultations, so that you do not have to travel.

ENERGY PSYCHOLOGY

Here are some of the most popular forms of energy psychology:

Be Set Free Fast (BSFF) – easy-to-learn tool based on re-programming the subconscious using cue words – see www.besetfreefast.com

Deep State Repatterning (Tania Prince) – recent development by an EFT Master in the north of England – see www.eft-courses.co.uk

EFT – see Chapters 1 and 9 – www.EFTuniverse.com and www.EFTmastersworldwide.com for courses in EFT, and www.eft-workshops.net. Also see www.eft-alive.com for articles and resource materials. For EFT practitioners worldwide, see www.theAMT.com or www.aamet.org

Emo-Trance – see Chapter 2 – www.emotrance.com or www.passionforhealth.com

Matrix Reimprinting (Karl Dawson and Sasha Allenby) – see Chapter 4 – a powerful recent development of EFT – www.eftcoursesuk.com or www.matrixreimprintingcourse.com

Psych-K – see Chapter 4 – popular form of energy psychology that uses kinesiology to access the subconscious and change beliefs. See www.psych-k.com

TAT (Tapas Fleming) – see Chapter 1 – Tapas Acupressure Technique, another popular form of energy psychology. See www.tatlife.com

Theta Healing (Vianna Stibal) – technique that uses theta brainwaves to access intuition, tapping into unconditional love for healing – www.thetahealing.com

Yuen Method – recent development of Chinese energetic medicine; non-touch technique – see www.yuenmethod.com

ZPoint (Grant Connolly) – similar approach to Be Set Free Fast (above) – see www.zpointforpeace.com

For other energy psychology practitioners and courses, see www.theAMT.com or www.aamet.org

There are two UK practitioners I can recommend from personal experience:

Kay Gire (EFT therapist – Blackburn, England). Phone sessions available – www.nirvana-life.com

Ted Wilmont (EFT/Matrix Reimprinting therapist – London, England). Phone sessions available – www.eft4life.co.uk

ENERGY-BASED HEALING

Acupuncture – see Chapters 1 and 9 – www.acupuncture.org.uk or www.acupuncture.com

Barbara Brennan School of Healing – Energy healing based in the 'new science', with practitioners worldwide, self-help CDs etc. See www.barbarabrennan.com

Brofman Foundation for Advancement of Healing (Martin Brofman) – see Chapter 1 – www.healer.ch

Cranio-sacral therapy – see Foreword –www.craniosacral.co.uk, www.craniosacraltherapy.org or www.upledger.com

Eden Energy Medicine (Donna Eden) – see Chapters 1 and 10 – www.innersource.net

Holoenergetic Healing (Leonard Laskow) – see Chapter 5 – www.laskow.net

Homoeopathy – see Foreword – www.homeopathy-soh.org, www.a-r-h.org or www.homeopathic.org for practitioners

Tjitze de Jong (energetic cellular healing, Forres, Scotland) – see Chapters 1, 4 and 11 – www.tjitzedejong.com

Matrix Energetics (Richard Bartlett) – see Chapters 1 and 10 – www.matrixenergetics.com

Matthew Manning, healer (Suffolk, England) – see Chapter 2 – www.matthewmanning.com

Reconnective Healing (Eric Pearl) – energy healing which reconnects our etheric DNA – www.thereconnection.com

Shiatsu (healing massage or acupressure) – www.shiatsu.org

TARA Approach (Stephanie Mines) – see Chapters 4 and 9 – www.tara-approach.org

Zero Balancing – visit the website www.zerobalancing.com or www.zerobalancinguk.org

KINESIOLOGY-BASED HEALING

The Body Code/Emotion Code (Bradley Nelson) – see Chapter 10 – www.drbradleynelson.com

BodyTalk – see Chapters 4 and 10 – www.bodytalksystem.com or www.bodytalkuk.co.uk

The Lifeline Technique (Darren Weissman) – see Chapters 4 and 10 – www.infiniteloveandgratitude.com

Also see Psych-K (under energy psychology).

BODYWORK, DANCE AND BREATHING

Five Rhythms work – moving to your centre through dance – www.gabrielleroth.com

Hakomi – body-centred psychotherapy – see www.hakomi.co.uk or www.hakomi.com

Holotropic Breathwork – see Chapter 3 on breathing – www.holotropic.com

Yoga – see www.yoga.co.uk or www.bwy.org.uk (for UK) or www.yoga-centers-directory.net (international) – although yoga classes are widely available in most towns

FLOWER AND VIBRATIONAL ESSENCES

For workshops, training courses and practitioners worldwide, see www.bfvea.org

To buy essences online, see www.healthlines.co.uk

My favourite essence ranges are: Australian Bush Flower Essences, Californian (FES) Essences, Alaskan Essences, Wild Earth Animal Essences, Pacific Essences, Indigo Essences, Bailey Essences and Lightbringer Essences – which all have their own websites – as well as my own Lakeland Essences.

OTHER RESOURCES

Arielle Essex – NLP Master, life coach and author of *Compassionate Coaching* (see Chapter 6) – www.arielle-essex. co.uk

Bruce Lipton (new biology) – see Chapter 3 – www.brucelipton.com

Byron Katie and The Work – see Chapter 6 – profound questions for shifting beliefs that are causing pain – www.thework.com

Caduceus – magazine on alternative health, sacred healing and the environment – www.caduceus.info

Hellinger Family Constellations – see Chapter 11 – www.hellinger.co.uk

Institute of HeartMath – see Chapters 2, 3 and 7 – www.heartmath.com

Kindred Spirit – mind-body-spirit magazine that lists UK workshops, courses, practitioners and other resources – see www.kindredspirit.co.uk

Meta-Medicine – see Chapter 4 – diagnostic tool that can point towards which traumas underlie disease. See www.metamedicine.org.uk or www.metamedicine.info

NLP (neurolinguistic programming) – a set of tools and techniques to re-programme your mind, emotions and behaviour – www.anlp.org or www.nlpacademy.co.uk

Nutri-Energetics System, or NES – healing tool that scans the body then prescribes bottled 'infoceuticals' to correct the energy system – see www.nutrienergetics.com

Stress Reduction Clinic, Centre for Mindfulness in Medicine, Healthcare and Society, Massachusetts – see Chapter 10. Courses worldwide, books and CDs for self-help, professional resources for health professionals and educators – www.unmassmed.edu/cfm

CONSCIOUS MEDICINE CIRCLE

Those in the original Conscious Medicine Circle who offer private consultations or workshops in Cumbria and the English Lake District:

Sue Birkett, creative writing and energy work for health – email suebirkett@dialstart.net

Angie Jackson, homoeopathy and flower essences – www.healthlines.co.uk

Mary Parr, quantum shiatsu – www.Shiatsukendal.co.uk

Peter Thompson, acupuncture and Zero Balancing – www.souldeephealing.com

FEEL-GOOD MOVIES

Some of my own favourites: *A Hard Day's Night, A River Runs Through It, Babe, Billy Elliot, Breakfast at Tiffany's, Bridget Jones's Diary, Chariots of Fire, Chocolat, Close Encounters of The Third Kind, Educating Rita, ET, Field of Dreams, Finding Nemo, Four Weddings and a Funeral, The Full Monty, Groundhog Day, Harry Potter and the Philosopher's Stone, It's a Wonderful*

Life, *It's Complicated*, *Julie and Julia*, *Love Actually*, *Mamma Mia!*, *Mary Poppins*, *Michael Jackson's This Is It*, *Miracle on 34th Street* (original 1947 version), *Moonstruck*, *Notting Hill*, *On Golden Pond*, *The Philadelphia Story*, *Pretty Woman*, *Roman Holiday*, *Shirley Valentine*, *Shrek*, *Singin' in the Rain*, *Sleepless in Seattle*, *The Snowman*, *Some Like It Hot*, *The Sound of Music*, *Toy Story*, *Truly*, *Madly*, *Deeply*, *Under the Tuscan Sun*, *Walk the Line*, *Whale Rider*, *When Harry Met Sally*, *White Christmas*, *The Wizard of Oz*.

GILL EDWARDS

For further information about workshops and personal consultations with Gill Edwards, books, self-help CDs, Lakeland Essences, etc., please contact our office.

Living Magically
Fisherbeck Mill
Old Lake Road
Ambleside
Cumbria LA22 0DH
Tel: (015394) 31943
Email: LivMagic@aol.com
Or see our website: www.livingmagically.co.uk

CDs:
Overcoming Inner Blockages
Changing Your Beliefs
Healing Your Inner Child
Healing or Releasing a Relationship
Soul Retrieval
Discovering Your Life's Work
Owning Your Shadow
Inner Peace
The Morning CD
The 2012 CD
Healing Your Family Tree

Your Future Self
Journey into Past Lives
Healing Dis-ease
The Magic of Health (double CD)
Creating Prosperity (double CD)
Attracting a Soulmate (double CD)
Wish Upon a Star (double CD for children)
Living in the 4th Dimension (4 CDs)

Index

Please note that page references to non-textual matter will be in *italic* print

Abraham, spiritual teachings of 153, 156–7, 167, 173, 177
Abram, David 117
acceptance 125, 126
Achterberg, Jeanne 118
acu-points 214
acupuncture 10, 203, 204
Adam (teenage healer) 241
addictions 82
adrenal glands, exhaustion 83
adrenalin 49, 94
Advanced Psych-K 215
affirmations 95, 96
Age of Awakening/Consciousness 17
ageing and stress 68–9, 80
agoraphobia 79
ailments *see* illnesses
Alice's Adventures in Wonderland (Carroll) 2, 3, 8
Allenby, Sasha 84–5
allergies 11, 74–5, 188
aloneness 117
alpha brainwaves xvi, 166
'alters' (split personalities) 3
amygdala 48, 91, 101–2
anaemia 188
analgesia 204
animals 49–50, 78, 79, 116–17
ankle injury 188
ankylosing spondylitis 114
anorexia 253
antibiotics xv, 15, 75
approval-seeking 95, 111, 112
arthritis 188
arthroscopic knee surgery 4
asthma 10, 188
astigmatism 187
attached entities 262
attraction, law of 30, 173–4, 176, 178
aura 183, 201, 202
auto-immune disorders 188, 227
auto-pilot, acting on 49
Ayurvedic medicine 216

Bach, Donna 9
Bach, Edward/Bach Flower Remedies 121–2
back pain 185–6, 188
  see also spinal problems
bacteria 37, 39, 53
balance, creating 227–9
Ballentine, Rudolph 16
Bartlett, Richard 7, 8, 246
beliefs
  changing 97–100
  conflicting 113
  negative 67, 76, 93, 94, 95, 129
  from past 92–7
  sick or healthy 237–8
  healing 'sick' beliefs 238–9
  see also thoughts
Benor, Dan 192
biochemical stimuli 63, 65
biofield 183, 201, 202
biological conflict-shock 72
Biology of Belief, The (Lipton) 66–7
bipolar disorder 84, 85, 86
Black, Sylvia 7
black sheep of families 92
bladder disorders 73, 189
bladder meridian 215
blame 144, 177, 179–80
bliss 109, 110–12, 155, 259
Block, Daniel 235
blood disorders 188
blood pressure difficulties 190
body language 177, 192–4, 225
body side 187
bodymind 65, 176, 181, 233, 248
Bohm, David 29
Bolte-Taylor, Jill 33, 35
bone-pointing, Aboriginal tradition 236
bowel conditions 184, 188, 189, 190, 206
brain 62, 73, 120
  alpha brainwaves xvi, 166
  frontal lobes 106–10, 121
  and HPA axis 49, 102, 264
  and imagery 118–20

and stress response 48–9
triune 101–3
whole brain posture 99–100
brain hemispheres 9, 32–4, 35, 42, 55
brainstem 101
brainwaves xvi, 166
breast, symbol of 225
breast cancer 67, 164, 188
diagnosis of author, journey of
xiii–xx, 39, 122, 145, 146, 179, 195,
236–7, 284
see also life-threatening illness
breathing, focus on 56–7
Brennan, Barbara 201, 230
Breuer, Josef 78
Brofman, Martin 5–6
bronchitis 76
bronchoconstrictors 233
bronchodilators 233, 234
brow chakra 222–3
Buddhism 29
burnout 83–4

Callahan, Roger 204, 205
Campbell, Joseph 110, 285
cancer
breast *see* breast cancer
chemotherapy treatment xviii
diagnosis, effects 73, 236
EFT for 206, 207
Hodgkin's disease 190
loss or separation prior to onset of
72
ovarian 207, 256
pancreatic 240–1
psychology xiv
underlying meaning 188
see also life-threatening illness
Cancer Is Not a Disease (Moritz) 267
'cancer personality' xiv
carpal tunnel syndrome 188, 197
Carroll, Lewis 2, 3, 8
Cartesian–Newtonian world view 21, 24
cataracts 187
Catholicism 21
cats, as spiritual teachers 116
causation of disease 263
Cavafy (Greek poet) 249–50
cell membrane 62, 63
cells, recycling 68–9
cerebellum 101
chakras 184, 202–4
balancing 224–5
language of 216–26
meanings 217–24
change, benefits of 108–9, 169
chemotherapy xviii
Chi 28
childhood trauma 76, 79, 85, 88–92, 159
Chinese medicine 10, 35, 76, 156

choices, inspired 242–3
cholesterol treatment 14
chronic diseases 78–9
stress 83, 91, 102, 103
chronic fatigue syndrome 58, 188,
195–6
Church, Dawson 19, 44
clairvoyance 26
clinical psychologist, author as xiv, xvi,
87, 130, 156
clockwork universe 21, 29
coeliac disease 87
cold sores 188
colon disorders 73
common cold virus 39, 188
computed tomography (CT) scans 73
concussion 189
conditional love 123, 143
congenital disorders 68
conjunctivitis 189
conscious medicine xix, xxii–xxiii
conventional medicine contrasted 182,
243–5
Conscious Medicine Circle xx–xxi, xxii,
9, 23, 235, 240
conscious universe 27–30, 134, 155
consciousness
and DNA 63–5
and energy *see* energy-consciousness
states of 46–7
waves and particles 31, 46–8
constipation 184, 189
conventional medicine xix, 16, 75, 186
conscious medicine contrasted 182,
243–5
making inspired choices 242–3
problems/limitations 12–15, 17,
19–20, 38, 75
view of disease 128
Copernicus 27
corticosteroids 94
cortisol 49, 83, 91, 92
cough 189
Cousins, Norman 114
Craig, Gary 205, 244
cranial osteopathy xv
creation of disease xix–xx, 179
creativity 110
Crohn's disease 189
cross-crawling 100
crown chakra 223–4
crystals 54, 55
cystitis 189

Dale, Cyndi 216
daydreaming 120
death wishes 255–63
separation of death as illusion 258–9
dementia 189
depression 76, 264

Descartes, René 21, 22, 286
desires 172–3
detached retina 73
detoxification 268
DHEA (anti-ageing hormone) 110
diabetes 3, 11, 20, 189, 263, 264
diagnosis of illness
  effect on course of condition 234–7
  responses 193, 249
  as a verb 39–40
  see also under life-threatening illnesses
diagnostic labels, limitations 20
dialogue with body 194–8
diarrhoea 184, 189
dietary factors 263, 264, 268
dis-ease 4, 67, 75, 216, 252–4
  finding trigger for 76–7
  gifts of 279–82
diseases see illnesses; life-threatening illness
Dispenza, Joe 6, 72, 107, 169
dissociative identity disorder (DID) 3, 4
distant healing 30, 64, 240–2
Divine Intelligence (Source) 29, 31, 32,
    105, 157
divorce 140–1
dizziness 189
DNA 61–2, 63–5
doctors, effect on healing 232
Dossey, Larry 1, 118
drama triangle 130–3, 252
  moving beyond 133–5
dream dictionary 183–7, 187, 191, 202
drug treatment, dangers/limitations 13,
    14, 16, 20, 75, 234
drug trials 13, 26
dummy pills 233

ear problems 73, 187, 189, 191
ear-rolls 100
eating disorders 55, 253
ECHO (Energetic Conscious Hologram)
    86
ecopsychology 117
eczema 189
Eden, Donna 6, 201, 216, 229, 268
EFT (Emotional Freedom Technique)
    9–10, 74, 112, 156, 244
  exercises 208–12
  self-help 207–8
  successes 205–7
ego 47, 157, 169, 170, 181
ego gap 174–5
Einstein, Albert 63, 70, 105, 128, 278
ELF (extremely low-frequency) 202
Emotional Freedom Technique (EFT) see
    EFT (Emotional Freedom Technique)
emotional intelligence 35, 171
emotional ladder 167–70, *168*, 181
  climbing 170–2, 180
emotional set point 167

Emotional Stress Release (ESR) 108
emotions 33, 202, 216, 232
  as guidance 155–8
  link with meridians and tapping points
    213–14
  molecules of 65
  negative 53, 156, 171–2, 181
  and thoughts 157, 167, 169
Emoto, Masaru 54
Emo-Trance 40
endogenous depression 76
endorphins 14, 78
enemy, making peace with 127–9
Energetic Conscious Hologram (ECHO)
    86
energy fields 63, 64, 183, 201, 262
energy healing 230
Energy Medicine (Eden) 6, 216, 229
energy psychology 9–12, 75, 84, 186,
    214, 248
energy-consciousness 8–9, 29, 62, 69, 85,
    154, 244
enlightenment 105
epigenetics 62–3, 64, 265
epilepsy 189
ESR (Emotional Stress Release) 108
Essex, Arielle 128–9, 249
evolving 278–9
exercise 264
exercises
  breathing meditation 56–7
  chakras, balancing 224–5
  Emotional Freedom Technique
    208–12
  finding dis-ease trigger 76–7
  fire ceremony 277–8
  frontal lobes, waking up 108–10
  future self, becoming 282–3
  heart coherence 36
  Ho'oponopono (tool for healing
    relationships) 141–2
  living from the heart 66
  lizard voices, spotting 165
  meeting disease/inner healer 198–9
  muscle-testing 97–100
  power animals 161–2
  relaxation 59–60
  shock, healing 84–5
  telling new story 270–1
  turnarounds 147–50
  twelve steps towards wellness
    273–6
extraordinary meridians 226
extremely low-frequency (ELF) 202
eye problems 73, 186–7, 189

fake operations 4
family and friends, influence 239–40
family constellations 260–3
family soul 259–60, 269

fear 138, 163
Feelings Buried Alive Never Die (Truman)
    191
fibroids 73–4
fibromyalgia 84
fight-or-flight response 49, 80, 91, 95,
    132, 178, 226
  and freeze response 77, 78
  in relationships 135, 136, 137–8, 139,
    140, 143
  and sympathetic shock 82
  triune brain 101, 102
  see also stress
figure of 8s 100
fire ceremony exercise 277–8
flow 46, 47, 48
flower essences 117, 121–2
focussed intention 230
FOG (Fear, Obligation and Guilt) 138
foot disorders 189
forebrain 101, 106
Forward, Susan 138
fractures 194
Francis of Assisi 256
free will 258
freedom 113, 123
  and love 285–7
freeze response 77–9, 87, 132, 138, 170
  see also fight-or-flight response
Freud, Sigmund 78
friendly universe 105–6, 123, 126–7
frontal lobes of brain 106–8, 121
  exercises 108–10
fungal infections 189
future self 276–7
  becoming 282–3

Galbraith, John Kenneth 12
gall bladder meridian 42
gallstones 41–2, 189
gamut point 228
Gawler, Grace 236
genetic disorders 67, 68
German New Medicine 73
Getting In the Gap (Dyer) 55
'ghost in the machine,' person as 21, 22
gifts
  illnesses as 196, 279–82
  problems as 152
Glaser, Ronald 53–4
Glaxo 14
Glendinning, Chellis 117
Goswami, Amit 16, 29, 30
grief 76
Groesbeck, Gary 9
guilt 144, 177, 179
  death wishes 257–8

Hamer, Dirk 72
Hamer, Geerd 72, 73

hands-on healing 203, 230
hand washing 37
happiness 110, 113, 115, 123
Hard Time 45
hatha yoga 56, 203
Hawaiian shamanism 126
Hawkins, Ronnie 240–1
Hay, Louise L. 182, 183, 184, 191
headache/migraine 163, 189
Heal Your Body (Hay) 191
healer, role 230, 231–2
healing 4, 74, 203, 230
  distant 30, 64, 240–2
  and evolving 278–9
  and hope 180–1
  self-healing 1–2, 6
  of shock 84–5
  surrogate 64, 241
  traditional methods *see* shamans
    (traditional healers)
  world 283–5
Healing: A Doctor In Search of a Miracle
    (Nolen) 230
healing crisis 73
healing miracles 5–8, 65, 129, 183, 246–7
  and conscious universe 26, 28, 30
health
  as default mode 166, 181
  and happiness 110
  love, benefits of 135–6
  and particle response 53–5, 154
  as vibrational 177–8
healthcare
  costs 13
  future of 15–18
  preventive 199
  whether materialism scientific base for
    24–5
  see also conventional medicine
hearing problems 73, 187, 189
heart chakra 219–21, 225
heart coherence/heart-centredness 34, 35,
    36, 64, 158
heart problems 190
'heart-brain' 35
Hellinger, Bert 259, 260, 261, 262
Helman, Cecil 39
hepatitis 194–5, 205
heretics 26, 61
hero's journey 285
herpes 190
Hicks, Esther 157
higher purpose 121–3
higher self 157, 176, 181, 276, 278
  voice of 160–1, 164, 169
Hillman, James 117
hindbrain 101
Hinduism 29
Hodgkin's disease 190
holiday mindset 44–5

holistic medicine 266
Holmes and Rahe Stress Scale 57
homeopathy xv, 14
homo spiritus 18, 285
Ho'oponopono (tool for healing
  relationships) 141–2
hope, and healing 180–1
Hospital With No Medicine (China)
  28–9
HPA axis, brain 49, 102, 264
Human Genome Project 61
Huna wisdom 126, 141–2
Hunt, Valerie 201–2, 261–2
Huntington's chorea 190
hypertension 190
hypotension 190
hypothalamus 226

iatrogenic (treatment-caused) disease 12
ideas 109
illnesses
  and attitude of doctors 232
  chronic *see* chronic diseases
  common patterns 188–91
  life-threatening *see* life-threatening
    illness
  meaning of 184–7, 188–91
  meeting disease/inner healer 198–9
  secondary gain 250–5
imagery 118–20
imagination 109
immune system 35, 39, 53, 54
immunoglobulin (IgA) 54, 115
incontinence 190
infectious diseases 14, 53, 189
infertility 41, 128, 129, 205, 254
Infinite Mind (Hunt) 201–2
inflammation 190
inflammatory bowel disease (IBD) 188
influenza 190
injury 190
Inner Child chakra 219
insight 242
inspiration 243
Institute of HeartMath, Colorado 34, 35,
  54, 64, 158
integrative medicine 245–6
intestinal disorders *see* bowel conditions
invisible energy forms 8, 9, 21, 70
irritable bowel syndrome (IBS) 190,
  206
Ithaca, journey to 250, 262, 285

Jarstad, Marit 194–5
Jeans, Sir James 27
jerking of body, shaking medicine 80
Jesus Christ 5, 232
joyful activities 109
judging 158
junk food 264

K-27s (tapping point) 214–15
Kabat-Zinn, Jon 236
Karate Chop point 209, 211
Katie, Byron 147
kidney disorders 190
Kiecolt-Glaser, Janice 53–4
kinesiology 256
kinesiology (muscle testing) 10, 96–7
  exercises 97–100, 224, 225
Klein, Louis 235
knee problems 4, 190
Kuhn, Thomas 26

large intestine meridian 215
laryngitis 190
Laskow, Leonard 113
laughter 114–15
left brain 32, 33, 34, 42, 62
  and meditation 55
Levenson, Lester 125–6
Levine, Barbara 236
Levine, Peter 79, 80
life-script 270
life-threatening illness
  battling with 126, 127, 128, 129, 178,
    180
  cancer diagnosis triggering secondary
    tumours 73
  chemotherapy treatment, cancer xviii
  and emotional ladder 177, 178
  as friend and teacher xviii, 123–4, 128,
    129, 146, 178, 179–80
  healing miracles 5–8, 26, 28, 30, 65,
    129, 183
  imagery work 119
  loss or separation prior to onset of
    cancer 72
  psychology of cancer xiv
  relationships, importance 145–6
  subconscious causes 256
  un-creating xix
  see also breast cancer; cancer
ligaments, disorders affecting 190
limbic brain 101
Lipton, Bruce xiii, 61, 62, 66–7
liver disease 190, 194–5
liver meridian 215, 225
Living Magically (Edwards) 217–18
lizard brain 101, 102, 164
lizard voices 159–60, 165, 169, 171, 177,
  181
loneliness 117
long-sightedness 186
love 34–5, 45, 65
  and freedom 285–7
  and health 135–6
  self-love 35, 113, 267
  unconditional *see* unconditional love
lumpectomy treatment, breast cancer
  xviii

lung disorders 73, 76, 190
lupus 190

MacArthur, Ellen 117
'magic bullet,' myth of 13
Manning, Matthew 26
marriage difficulties xvi–xvii, 54, 57, 186
 see also personal relationships
material universe 8, 21–2, 23–5, 235, 286
Matrix Energetics (quantum healing
 system) 7
Matrix Reimprinting 84, 86, 87
McCraty, Rollin 54
ME see chronic fatigue syndrome
meditation, healing power of 55–7, 110
Meditation for Beginners (Kornfield) 55
Mehl-Madrona, Lewis 23, 163
mem-brain (cell membrane) 62, 63
meridians 42, 76, 184, 202–4
 link with emotions and tapping points
 212–16, *213–14*
 strange flows 226–7
 tapping 204–8
Meta-Medicine 73
mid-brain 101
migraine 163, 190
mind-body medicine, as bridge 42–3
mind-body split 21, 24
mind-body unity 4, 17
mindfulness techniques 244
Mines, Stephanie 82, 83, 229
miracles, healing 5–8, 26, 28, 30, 65, 129,
 183, 246–7
mirror neurons 111
Mitchell, William 22
molecules of emotion 65
Moritz, Andreas 267
morphic fields 261
Moss, Richard 6
Mother Teresa 178
motivation 243
multiple personality 3, 4
multiple sclerosis 190
muscle-testing 10, 96–7, 256
 exercises 97–100, 224, 225
myasthenia gravis 235
myopia 186
Myss, Caroline 31–2, 269–70
mysticism 29, 31, 33

National Health Service (NHS) 13
Native American viewpoint 22–3, 40
nature, healing power of 115–18
neck pain 190
neocortex 101, 102
neural net 175
neural pathways 167, 175
neurochemistry 105, 111, 139, 169, 172
neuroplasticity, brain 120
New England Journal of Medicine 4

Newton, Isaac 21, 22, 24, 29, 30, 286
Nietzsche, Friedrich 248
Nightingale, Florence 83–4
nocebo response 233–4
Nolen, William 230
Northrup, Christiane 92, 273
nosebleeds 183
nutritional medicine 266

organic diet 268
Ornish, Dean 118
orthodox medicine see conventional
 medicine
osteoarthritis of knee 4
osteoporosis 193
'out-of-body' experience 78
ovarian cancer 207, 256
over-caring/self-sacrifice 34, 35

pain
 acceptance of 125, 126
 acupuncture for 204
 back 185–6, 188
 meaning of 191
 neck 190
pancreatic cancer 240–1
panic attacks 79
paradigm shifts 26, 37, 47, 155
 new physics 27, 41, 154
parapsychology 25
parasympathetic shock 82–3, 85
particle response 46–7, 48–53, 71, 108, 127
 common signs 51–2, 56, 72
 continuum of 48, 155
 getting stuck in 79, 83
 and health 53–5, 154
 inherited thinking patterns 92
 loneliness 117
 love and freedom 113
 see also stress
particles, and waves 30–2, 46–8, 155
Pasteur, Louis 38
Patch Adams (film) 115
penicillin 38
perceptions 94, 158
Persecutor role, drama triangle 130, 131,
 131, 132, 133, 252
personal growth 110
personal relationships 124, 125–51
 being your own best friend 150–1
 conventional 139
 stress in 136–9
 toxic 138
 turnarounds 147–50
 withdrawal from 83
 see also marriage difficulties
Pert, Candace 65, 70, 110
phantom limb pain 206
pharmaceutical industries, profits of
 13

phobias 205
phoenix voices 169
physical activity 264
physical factors 263–9
placebo response 233
positive thinking 166, 180, 181
possession 262
post-traumatic stress disorder (PTSD) 78
power animals 161–2, 163
practitioner, choice of 243–5
prayer 241
prefrontal cortex 62
pregnant mothers, effects of stress 91
premenstrual syndrome 191
prescription drugs 13, 14
prostate problems 191
Protestantism 21
psychic circuits 226
Psych-K (muscle testing technique) 10, 11, 215
psychoanalysis 78
psychological reversal 248
psychoneuroimmunology (PNI) 39, 53
psychosomatic network 65

Qi Gong techniques 28
Quantum Doctor, The (Goswami) 16
quantum physics xvi, xxii, 8, 27, 28, 29
  poetry analogy 30–1
quantum self 31

reality, surface and deep 46
Reformation 21
relationships see personal relationships
relaxation 59–60, 74
religion 21, 40
  belief in loving or judgemental God 92–3
  Catholicism and guilt 257
  scientists and doctors as new priests 11–12, 23–4
reptilian brain 101
Rescuer role, drama triangle 130, 131–2, 252
resistance 126, 248, 249
responsibility, and blame 179–80
restless legs syndrome 206
Reston, James 204
right brain 32–3, 34, 35
  energy as right-brain concept 42
Rilke, Rainer Maria 104
Roberts, Jane xvi
root chakra 217–18
Roszak, Theodore 117
Rumi (poet) 285

sacral chakra 218
Sawyer, Sue 10
Scaer, Bob 80, 83

secondary gain of illness 250–5
  common forms 251–2
Sedona Method, The 125–6
self-healing 1–2, 6
self-love 35, 113, 267
self-responsibility 179–80
separation feelings 83
Seth ('energy personality') xvi
Shadow self 112, 130
shaking therapy 79–80, 81
sham operations 4
shamanic ceremonies 5
shamanism (traditional healing) 22–3, 29, 87, 126, 158, 194, 262
Shapiro, Deb 191
Shealy, Norman 12, 19, 32, 118
Sheldrake, Rupert 261
shell shock 78
shingles 191
shock, and stress 82–4
short-sightedness 186
Siegel, Bernie 118, 178, 255
Silva Mind Control xvi
Simonton, Carl 118
sinus problems 191
skin disorders 73, 75, 185, 189
Soft Time 45
solar plexus chakra 219
solitude 117
soul loss 87–8, 262
Source 29, 31, 32, 105, 157
spinal problems 191
spiritual awakening 17, 110
spleen disorders 197
split personality 3, 4
statins 14
statistics 129
Stibal, Vianna 191
stomach meridian 204–5
strange flows 226–7, 228
stress response 32, 134, 154, 176, 244
  and ageing 68–9
  chronic stress 83, 91, 102, 103, 139, 265
  creating stress for ourselves 57–9
  and DNA/genes 65, 67
  and drama triangle 131, 133
  and illness 154, 264
  and lizard voices 165–6
  and negativity 65, 67, 156
  and particle response 46–7, 48–53
  physical signs 51–2, 56, 72
  psychological signs 52
  recognition of stress 45
  in relationships 136–9
  and shock 82–4
  and subconscious 158
  and thoughts 50, 51, 58, 166, 268
  see also fight-or-flight response; particle response

stroke 191
Structure of Scientific Revolutions, The (Kuhn) 26
subconscious 49, 65, 70–1, 107
  clash with conscious mind 158, 159
  death wishes 256
  and past experience 86, 88, 90, 95–6, 159
Subjective Units of Distress (SUDS) 208, 210
Subtle Body, The (Dale) 216
suicidal thoughts 170, 258, 260
'superbugs' 15
surgical operations 4–5, 37, 79
surrender 126
surrogate healing 64, 241
survival instinct 258
Sway Test 98
Sylvia, Claire 37–8
sympathetic shock 82, 83

talk therapy 74, 81, 244
talking to body 194–8
Tapas Acupressure Technique (TAT) 10, 11
tapping, in EFT 9, 10
TARA Approach 229
telepathy 26, 27
theta brainwaves 166
Theta Healing: Disease and Disorder (Stibal) 191
Thought Field Therapy (TFT) 205
thoughts 54, 55, 63
  and emotions 157, 167, 169
  as energy fields 63–4
  new 175–7
  and stress response 50, 51, 58, 166, 268
  and vibrations 165–7
  see also beliefs
three selves philosophy (Shamanism) 158
throat, sore 191
throat chakra 221–2
thyroid disorders 73, 191
tinnitus 191
Tjitze de Jong (healer) 7, 80, 256
TMJ of jaw 191
toxins 264
traditional Chinese medicine (TCM) 10, 35, 76, 156
transplant patients, experiences 37–8
trauma
  childhood 76, 79, 85, 88–92, 159
  EFT use 10

and freeze response 78
  healing 74
  post-traumatic stress disorder 78
  as trigger event for disease 72, 73, 74–6
  undischarged 79–80, 94, 154
triple warmer 226, 227
triune brain 101–3
Truman, Karol K. 191
turnarounds 147–50
twelve steps towards wellness (exercise) 273–6
twin experiments 61

ulcers 191
unconditional love 113, 126, 129, 134, 143, 146, 159
  and freedom 123–4

vaccination myths/dangers 14–15
varicose veins 191
vibrational frequencies 25, 63, 111, 166, 176, 180
victim mentality 269–70
Victim role, drama triangle 130, 132–3, 252
viruses 53
visualisation 118–20
voice loss 190
voice management 163–5

warts 68
water 54, 55
wave response 105, 106, 108, 113–14, 116, 154, 230
  and love 286–7
  relationships in 142–3
  unconditional love 123, 124, 126
waves, and particles 30–2, 46–8, 155
We Are All In Shock (Mines) 82, 229
Weissman, Darren 104, 196, 267–8
Werner, Michael 266
whole brain posture 99–100, 256
wholefood diet 268
Why People Don't Heal and How They Can (Myss) 269
Wild Love workshops 144
world healing 283–5
world view 3

yoga 56, 203
Your Body Believes Every Word You Say (Levine) 236
Your Body Speaks Your Mind (Shapiro) 191